SHOW ME

Also available from ASQC Quality Press

Show Me: Storyboard Workbook and Template
Harry I. Forsha

The Pursuit of Quality Through Personal Change
Harry I. Forsha

Reinventing Communication: A Guide to Using Visual Language for Planning, Problem Solving, and Reengineering
Larry Raymond

Process Reengineering: The Key to Achieving Breakthrough Success
Lon Roberts

Team Fitness: A How-To Manual for Building a Winning Work Team
Meg Hartzler and Jane E. Henry, Ph.D.

Mapping Work Processes
Dianne Galloway

To request a complimentary catalog of publications, call 800-248-1946.

SHOW ME

The Complete Guide to Storyboarding and Problem Solving

Harry I. Forsha

ASQC Quality Press
Milwaukee, Wisconsin

Show Me: The Complete Guide to Storyboarding and Problem Solving
Harry I. Forsha
Library of Congress Cataloging-in-Publication Data
Forsha, Harry I., 1946–
Show me: the complete guide to storyboarding and problem solving / Harry I. Forsha.
p. cm.
Includes bibliographical references and index.
ISBN 0-87389-255-0
1. Group problem solving—Handbooks, manuals, etc. 2. Service industries—Management—Handbooks, man uals, etc. I. Title.
HD30.29.F68 1995
658.4'036—dc20 94-24724
CIP

10 9 8 7 6 5 4 3 2

ISBN 0-87389-255-0

Acquisitions Editor: Susan Westergard
Project Editor: Kelley Cardinal
Production Editor: Annette Wall
Marketing Administrator: Mark Olson
Set in Utopia and Gill Sans by Precision Graphic Services, Inc.
Cover design by Montgomery Media, Inc.
Printed and bound by BookCrafters, Inc.

ASQC Mission: To facilitate continuous improvement and increase customer satisfaction by identifying, communicating, and promoting the use of quality principles, concepts, and technologies; and thereby be recognized throughout the world as the leading authority on, and champion for, quality.

For a free copy of the ASQC Quality Press Publications Catalog, including ASQC membership information, call 800-248-1946.

Printed in the United States of America

Printed on acid-free recycled paper

ASQC
Quality Press
611 East Wisconsin Avenue
Milwaukee, Wisconsin 53202

To my father

The easiest way to cope with change
is to help create it.

—Anonymous

CONTENTS

FIGURE LIST

PREFACE

This book began with the idea that storyboarding, while rooted in an ancient tradition of storytelling, is underutilized. Why? Perhaps because it takes practice; perhaps because it tends to force whole-brained thinking; or perhaps because there is no universal language and discipline of storyboarding. Everybody does it differently.

Out of this thinking came a purpose: to define, describe, and explain the practical use of storyboards. I am not talking about the kind of storyboards used in advertising and industry, or the kind used for presentations, but all kinds. The storyboard is a powerful tool. In fact, it is a metatool that uses other tools. The storyboard works; it gives people a comprehensive way to communicate with one another; and it is fun.

A storyboard is used because it provides an organized framework in which to put thoughts, plans, and activities. Storyboards are recognized by people worldwide. As the globe shrinks ever smaller in terms of communication, it becomes even more important to transcend language barriers. I'm not sure how all this will sort out, but visual communication through storyboards can help. The benefits include clear thinking, improved organizational relationships, better solutions, the satisfaction that comes from routinely and effectively solving problems and capitalizing on opportunities, and, of course, fun.

A discussion of teams is inserted into this storyboard book, because, whether you realize it or not, you are always on at least one team and probably many more. The way people select (or get drafted into), nurture, and grow their teams can make the difference between success and failure. It is not my objective to duplicate the many fine works that already exist on the subject of teams, but rather to make clear how storyboarding and teamwork interrelate.

What are the risks? Essentially none. The title is a difficult taskmaster. Yet "Show me!" is a phrase that continually raises its head when someone is trying to introduce change. Decision makers want to see and understand the reasons for proposed actions, and the facts that justify those actions. Due to time pressures and the many presentations heard daily on a variety of subjects, it is vital that presentations be brief, factual, clear, and interesting. If these requirements are not met, chances of success are slim.

The purpose of this book is to present the storyboard as a tool to get things done. Individuals, by themselves or as a part of an organization, can use storyboards to accomplish their objectives.

This book can never be truly complete. Yet a sincere effort has been made to expose you to all aspects of storyboarding, including the creative and the scientific aspects. Thus, the vision is that this book can provide a framework in which to put new developments. In order to make the material as clear as possible, the book is organized around three concepts.

1. The book discusses storyboarding with frequent use of real-world examples to clarify the presentation.
2. The workbook is a storyboard. It tells the story by doing the work. The idea of initial, basic, and feasible comes from matrix algebra, but applies very well to the storyboard. The workbook is designed for practical use, and to come as close as possible to a fill-in-the-blanks approach.
3. The tool pages provided in Appendix C are organized alphabetically by tool name. The idea here is to separate the discussion of tools from the discussion of the storyboard. In that way, skilled readers are not delayed by a discussion of material already known, while any novices can make ready reference to the tool discussed.

At its best, storyboarding is a tool for getting things done.

ACKNOWLEDGMENTS

This is my favorite part of the book, because it is in this section that I can publicly express my heartfelt appreciation to all those who have helped me in its preparation.

To Judy Schalick, who is a continual source of inspiration;

To Kent Starrett and Bob Scanlon of Southern Pacific Transportation, for their assistance with the implementation aspects of storyboards;

To Harry A. Betker, one of the first to rediscover and apply storyboards for an industrial problem-solving application, for use of his landmark materials, and for his assistance in understanding the progress of this technology;

To Arne, George, and Norman Flolo, and all my friends at Flolo Corporation, who performed reality checks on much of this material and actually put it to use;

To my editors, Susan Westergard, whose idea this book was in the first place, and whose encouragement and insight are irreplaceable; to Kelley Cardinal and Annette Wall, whose attention to detail has made a big difference in the quality of the book; and to Shannon Eglinton, for insight, creativity, and the spirit of teamwork in making the workbook the best possible product;

And most of all to my wife, Diane, my daughter, Elizabeth, and my son, Chris, for being patient when Dad was "somewhere else."

Chapter One

BACKGROUND AND INTRODUCTION

It would be an understatement to say I've been doing a lot of thinking about storyboards lately. Yet it always amazes me how much information is laying in wait just under the surface. Researching a book is like opening a series of doors; behind each is something to explore. Some doors lead into closets, which have shelves and boxes to examine. Other doors lead into large rooms with many other doors. That is why I like writing. It gives me a reason to open certain doors that I otherwise might have left closed.

The world of information has many rooms. You have probably been spending most of your time in only one room—the one of words—when there are many other rooms to see. One key concept that I hope to communicate in this book is that most people become stifled and sometimes discouraged. They have been steered away from the excitement and creativity that are natural parts of their normal selves. They've been that way for so long that it looks normal to them.

Some have rebelled. Thomas Edison, for instance, is renowned for a creativity so strong that he had to be removed from public school and taught by his mother. But for every Edison, there are who knows how many potential Edisons who have not rebelled and who suffer in silence.

I would like to share with you the excitement that I have shared with those in many businesses during the past few years; that is, learning about their problems, solving their challenges, and exploring their uses of storyboards. Even more than that, though, I would like to encourage, incite, and stimulate you to create visions, explore options, remove barriers, and push limits.

The storyboard is a metatool. In other words, it is a tool that uses other tools. It has many forms. But then, a storyboard is many things.

NO RULES

This book describes tools, techniques, and approaches that are in actual use. The benefit of the material presented is that it can provide ideas and a frame of reference. The danger is in thinking that there is one right way or one wrong way to attack a problem or opportunity. Use what works for you, and keep the rest in mind because it worked for somebody else, and you may need it later. So please keep the first (and only) rule in mind as you approach the subject of storyboards: *There are no rules.*

OBJECTIVE STATEMENT—WHY AM I HERE?

A fairy tale begins with the phrase "Once upon a time." A business story begins the same way. I have found it increasingly useful to ask myself at the beginning of each effort "Why am I here doing this?" It is not too soon, even at the beginning of an effort, to consider how results will be measured.

> The objective is to present storyboard concepts in a concise, easy-to-understand fashion, by using words, numbers, and pictures. Upon using this book, or any portion of it, you should be able to apply the subject matter without further instruction. Results will be measured by the actual comments received from readers, the number of books in use, and the number of organizations adopting this book as a practical guide.

STORYBOARD DEFINED

The word *storyboard* appears in dictionaries.[1] It is here that storyboards are specifically associated with advertising and filmmaking. Now that the storyboard is firmly entrenched in the quality improvement world, being used by organizations of all types, the industry-specific language must be stripped away and the definition must be generalized to something like the following: *A series of panels showing, in order of occurrence, important changes.*

That's really stripped! Perhaps you can look a little further, by breaking the word down into its parts—*story* and *board.*

According to the dictionaries, a story can either be the truth, as in "What's the story?" or a lie, as in "That was some story he fabricated!" Using the dictionaries as a guide, try to create a definition that will apply to all possible uses of the story, focusing on its function.

> *Story—The events in the history of a person or thing that taken together are of sufficient interest and significance to serve as likely subject matter for an account.*[2]

This definition hits at the heart of important issues that have, to some extent, become barriers to the broad use of storyboards.

A storyboard, to be effective, must tell a story. It must be *interesting* and *significant.*

So far, so good. Look at the example in Figure 1.1.

Southern Pacific Transportation, in its team leader training manual, points out that the quality improvement story should show "a clear picture of the logical process used."[3] Here, then, is an additional characteristic: *A storyboard must have clarity.*

What can you gain from information you don't understand? I'll vote for clarity. Add that to the definition.

> *Storyboard—A series of panels showing* clearly, *in* order *of occurrence,* important *(significant) changes that taken together are* interesting.

If all that is true, why is it that of all the important issues to choose from, I can most readily quote the recent life history of Bill the Cat? Read on.

THREE DIMENSIONS

The ancient history of storyboards is entirely visual. It consisted of sequential pictures showing significant events. Cave paintings, for instance, could be thought of as storyboards. In the Wei Dynasty of China, carvings and paintings were arranged in sequential panels.[4] Many centuries later, the ceiling of the Sistine chapel was organized like a storyboard (see Figure 1.2).

The recent history of the storyboard is also primarily visual, beginning in the early twentieth century with the popularization of movies. Then with talkies, television, and the growth of the advertising industry, words were added. In all three areas, the storyboard is used routinely to plan and develop the stories told in a movie, television show, or commercial.

It was only in the 1950s, with its translation into the world of quality improvement, that the storyboard became a numerical tool. In other words, the quality improvement community, while adding the numerical dimension to the storyboard, minimized the visual aspect, although perhaps not deliberately.

I say, put the pictures back. Frank Gladstone, director of animation training for Disney/MGM Studios, has suggested that organizations might go so far as to add an artist to every corporate board of directors. It shouldn't be hard to find an artist who agrees with that point of view.

FIGURE 1.1. *Traditional training method versus paradigm discovery learning.*

Traditional Training Method

Day 1

Cognitive material . . .
Includes course outline and critical content information.

Day 2

Positive video model . . .
Provides orientation to "real life;" an overview of essential steps.

Day 3

Instructional lecture . . .
For in-depth understanding of cognitive material.

Day 4

Assessment of trainees . . .
Reveals information retention.

Day 5

Trainee feedback . . .
Accolades for the course and the leader's instructional skills.

Day 6

Certificates of completion . . .
"Suitable for framing."

FIGURE 1.1. *(continued)*

Used with the permission of Paradigm Communications, of Tampa, Florida.

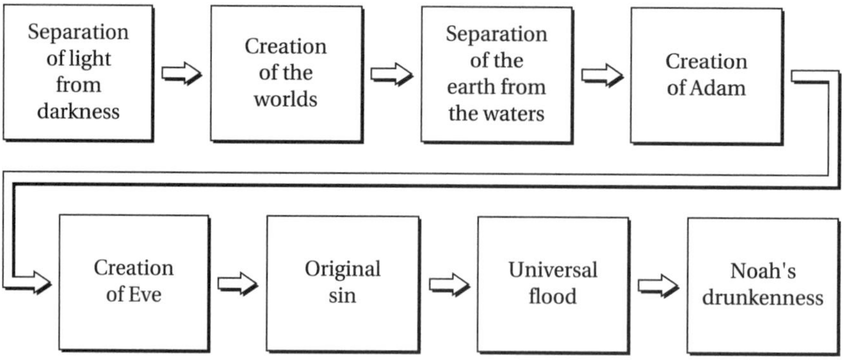

FIGURE 1.2. *Sistine chapel ceiling as a storyboard.*

When you consider that one of the benefits of having teams is the value of adding people with different points of view, Gladstone's idea sounds pretty good.

Considering the long visual history of the storyboard, return to the definition.

> . . . *a series of panels showing clearly,* using pictures, numbers, and words, *important (significant) changes, in order of appearance, that taken together are interesting.*

Wait a minute! Where's the story? The story has been taken out of the storyboard. Put it back!

> *STORYBOARD—A series of panels showing clearly, using pictures, numbers, and words, important changes, in order of occurrence, that taken together* tell an interesting story.

This is the definition that will be used as a starting point for the discussion of storyboards.

Can you tell a story with only one panel? Yes, but you've got to be good. Figure 1.3 shows one of my favorites.

Why would anybody look at your storyboard if it doesn't tell an interesting story? Need this story be confined to the results of one of the many structured problem-solving paradigms? No! Need this story be limited to problems at all? No!

The storyboard can be used to tell any story you want, as amply demonstrated by the only portion of the Sunday paper to be dignified with complete color. Does the story have to be humorless? No! Must it be funny? No!

"It's hopeless. I'll never be able to catch my tail."

FIGURE 1.3. *Single-panel storyboard.*
From the *Wall Street Journal.* Permission, Cartoon Features, Syndicate.

A storyboard doesn't *have* to be anything at all, except

- A (panel or) series of panels
- Showing clearly
- Using pictures, numbers, and words
- Important changes
- In order of occurrence
- That tell an interesting story

What could that include? Before you continue, you may wish to take a moment to consider the possibilities.

TYPES OF STORYBOARD

The storyboard appears in many forms. In my effort to be comprehensive, I will summarize all the forms of which I am aware.

THE ORIGINAL

In this century, the storyboard was originally a rough draft of a story line used as a planning tool for a commercial or cartoon. This type of storyboard is a working document. Because its function is temporary in nature, little effort is devoted to cleanup or polish. It doesn't have to be pretty, just functional. This is the type of storyboard that served as an early model for the quality improvement community.

THE FINISHED STORYBOARD

GTE, Florida Power and Light (FPL), Alcoa, and others included storyboards as a key part of their quality programs. Since storyboards were an official method of communication within and outside the organizations, serious efforts were made to present the information in a visually appealing way. In its ultimate extension, this form resulted in professionally produced, full-color storyboards that would fit right in with the graphic work in a fine book or magazine (see Figure 1.4).

THE STORYBOOK

Not far behind the storyboard idea came the storybook. Many teams found it impractical or uneconomical to produce the storyboard as described in the previous section. First, you need a *big* posterboard. Then, at a minimum, you need drafting tools and a steady hand.

One simple solution to the problem was to produce the storyboard in booklet form. Since most of the original work is on standard $8\frac{1}{2}" \times 11"$ paper stock or lined notebook paper, it is a simple matter to organize the information into booklet form. This still fits the definition of storyboard, if the word *page* is substituted for the word *panel.* This technique also allows for a cover page, which can be embellished graphically to provide visual interest (see Figure 1.5).

With the increasing popularity of computer graphics programs, it is now possible to make high-quality, single-page graphic presentations, which could be used both as an element on a storyboard and as a page in a storybook. In order to preserve the distinction between the two presentation methods, the booklet form will be referred to as a storybook and anything designed for on-the-wall presentation will be referred to as a storyboard. Unless otherwise stated, the discussions in this book apply to both.

Even without computer graphics, however, a picture and words used together can make a powerful team. Figure 1.6 is one of my favorite examples.

A finely produced version of this particular graph appears in the Carter Center in Atlanta, Georgia. It was the unpolished version, no doubt, that was the working document.

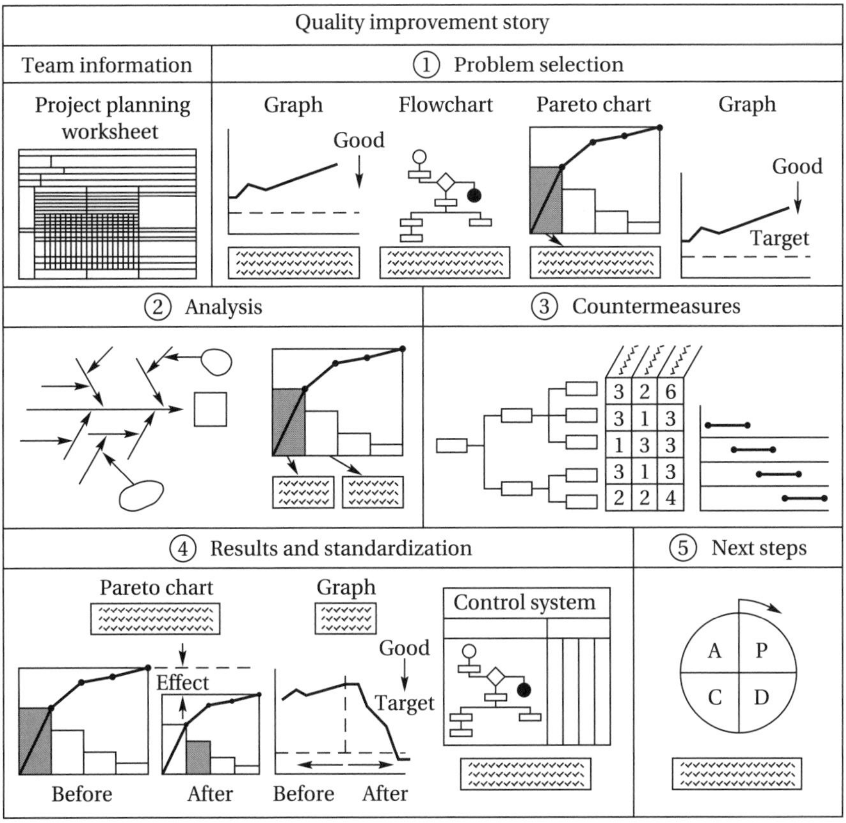

FIGURE 1.4. *FPL storyboard plate.*

Note: Adapted from the concept of the QC story, originally named by Mr. Nogawa, president of Komatsu, for the purpose of reporting improvement activities. Professor Ikezawa and others expanded the procedure to include its use as a guide for solving a problem.

NOTECARDS

Another method of developing a storyboard, which combines creativity and problem-solving techniques with the storyboard concept, is the use of notecards or self-adhesive flags. When this technique is used, participants generate ideas on notecards, with one idea per card. Then they place the notecards on the wall or other convenient surface. Team members can then rearrange the ideas according to their closeness, order, or other organizing concepts. This provides an opportunity to compare ideas, to generate new ideas, to look at the issue from many points of view, and to visualize the progress of a project. Sometimes called an *affinity diagram,* this process can be a good way to get started.

When this technique is used, it may never be produced for final consumption. It stays simple. It is possible to take a project to completion

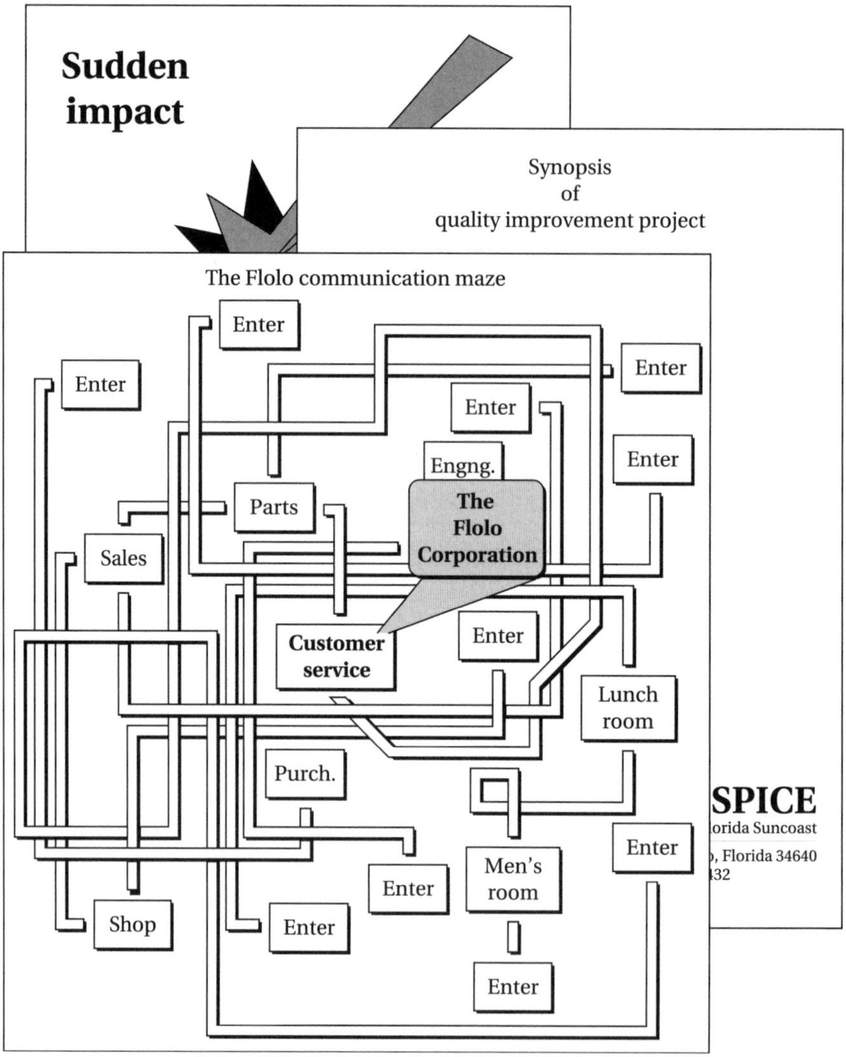

FIGURE 1.5. *Storyboard covers.*

without ever expending one whit of effort on visual appeal. There are arguments on both sides of this issue. On the one hand, the quick-and-dirty approach gets the job done fast and with a minimum of effort. On the other hand, clear language, crisp graphics, and well-prepared numerical tables significantly enhance your ability to tell your story to others. It is in the telling, not the problem solving, that most people fall short.

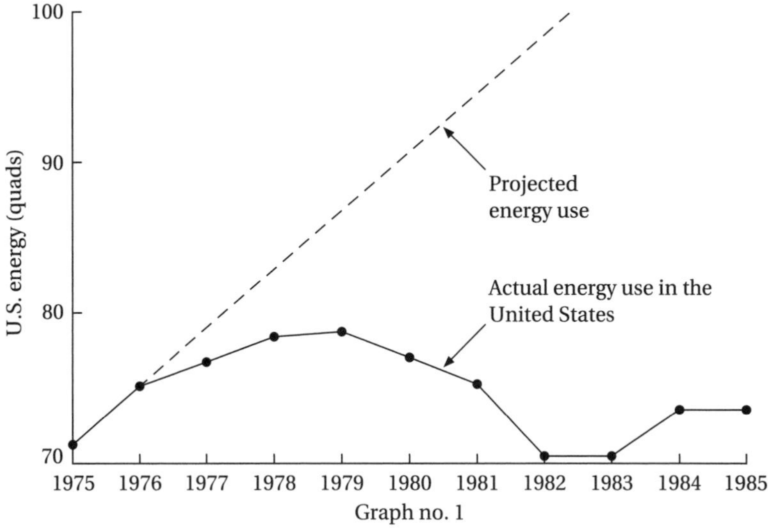

21 May 1986
To Lorraine

I have examined the information Steve obtained, & have extracted a few pertinent quotes that you may use. Also, I have prepared a couple of simple graphs, which you can improve. Since I don't recall exactly what you already have, there may be some overlap. Call me if you have any questions.

"U.S. energy use in 1985 was about 30% below the business-as-usual projection from 1975. About 60% of this saving was from improved energy efficiency, caused by higher energy prices, promotion of conservation, and the beneficial impact of mandatory legislation passed during the Carter administration." See graph #1.

"Our new laws de-regulating oil and natural gas prices, encouraging people to save energy, and requiring more efficient automobiles have helped to reduce energy use far below what historical trends would have suggested. In fact, if today's economy still operated at the wasteful level of 1973, we would be importing four times as much oil and spending an extra $150 billion per year for energy."

"New cars are now 67% more efficient than the average car on the road in 1973. Mandatory efficiency standards have so far been met by U.S. automobile manufacturers." See graph #2.

Jimmy

FIGURE 1.6. *Jimmy Carter's original draft on energy use.*

The exception that proves the rule exists is in the form of a person called Tinker. Now, Tinker tells stories. Not just any old stories, but fantastic stories. Some of them are even true. But he is such a good storyteller that I don't care whether the story is true or false. I always want to hear the whole thing. Now, that's good storytelling, and that is one of the objectives in creating a storyboard. You would like the viewer to see the whole thing. So it had better be interesting.

EXPANDING THE SCOPE

The definition of storyboard allows room for an infinite range of forms. For example, the use of easel pads, which are taped sequentially on the walls of a room, has become a popular and effective technique. Sometimes, these walls are left as is for the duration of the project, with modifications made as needed.

The Disney organization is widely known to use storyboards for planning everything from rides to restaurants. Storyboard concepts are useful in generating business plans, particularly in helping executives visualize a business process all the way from the initial idea through to the results.

Storyboards are still in use in the film, television, and advertising industries. The same principles of good communication apply to small issues and big ones.

TYPICAL STORYBOARD USES

- Stimulating creative thinking
- Planning a project
- Collecting ideas
- Exploring an organization
- Communicating a concept
- Illustrating a briefing
- Understanding the big picture

Why not use a storyboard to plan an important speech or even a critical conversation? Why not tell your life story in seven panels? (Some psychologists use a similar approach in getting to know a patient.) Why not plan to exploit an exciting opportunity? (Disney does, why not you?)

On a personal level, people often behave according to an image of themselves, rather than the reality of their situation. This is referred to as a basic operating fantasy. If you were a cartoon character, who would you be? Use Figure 1.7 as a guide.

Even simple drawings can help to make a point. See the example in Figure 1.8.

Please insert the cartoon that best describes you in the space provided. Go ahead: cut it out and tape it in. Use cartoons or pictures from magazines to amplify your story. Or learn to draw. Even stick figures can make a strong visual impression. Then come back in a few years and see if the portrait has changed.

FIGURE 1.7. *Portrait of yourself as a cartoon character.*

FIGURE 1.8. *The picture of success.*

If visual images can be used, why not use sound, or even smell, to amplify a storyboard presentation? In industrial applications, vibration is monitored by the ear as well as electronic devices.

SUMMARY

The definition of the storyboard, coupled with the examples provided here, is part of the platform on which to build. There are two other planks on the platform—teams and problem-solving techniques. Chapters 2 and 3 will deal with these issues in turn.

As an example, I have already started my own storyboard, with the selection of an area of interest—storyboards. So let me sketch out a cover for my book, which I can also use as a first panel for my storyboard (see Figure 1.9). A lot of time won't be wasted on fancy production, because this is a rough (and maybe final) draft. Throughout the book, I will show some of the techniques actually used to create the book itself.

SHOW ME

The Complete Guide to Storyboarding and Problem Solving

Harry I. Forsha

FIGURE 1.9. *First panel of a storyboard.*

Chapter Two

THE IMPORTANCE OF TEAMS

If the first plank of the storyboarding platform is the storyboard itself, then the second plank is the use of teams. The area of teams (selection, growth, development, and performance) is a separate area of study, richly rewarding and deserving of time and effort. Rather than attempt to deal with teams in detail, I would like to point out the basics that affect the storyboarding effort.

KEY REASONS FOR CREATING A TEAM

- I don't have everything I need.
- I can benefit from another point of view.
- Others would like to be included in the process.

Most tasks are easier with the support of others.

As demonstrated on the flowchart in Figure 2.1, some projects can be done without outside assistance. In fact, a person with a can-do attitude and an interest in continuous improvement can accomplish a lot just with things under his or her direct control. On the other hand, organizations are made up of intricate, formal, and informal networks of individuals, each one interacting with the other in ways that are not always obvious. Therefore, it would be dangerous to assume that actions taken to improve your own work have no effect on others.

There is another side to teamwork often overlooked by highly motivated individuals. Have you ever considered inviting someone at work to be on a team because *they* wanted to be included? Since your activities may affect others in ways you may not be aware of, it is very reasonable to include others' ideas in your improvements. This kills two birds with one stone. It avoids a sense of isolation, which can exist even in small organizations, and it makes other people feel needed and useful.

PREREQUISITES FOR TEAM CREATION

Stated simply, teams are created because they work. A team is greater than the sum of its parts when people build on each other's ideas and

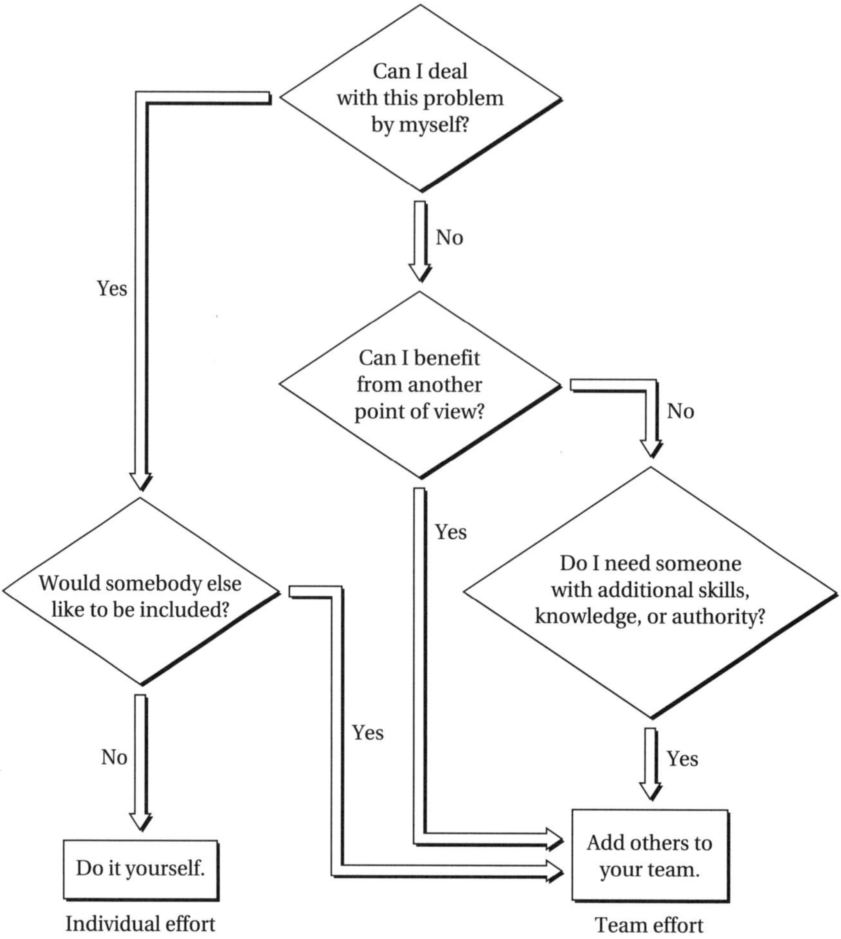

FIGURE 2.1. *Decision flow for team selection.*

support one another in their efforts. Since everyone has a blind spot, people with different points of view help you see the whole picture, by exposing biases you may have as an individual. Finally, any challenge can be accomplished with the right blend of skills, knowledge, and authority. If you choose your team well, you will find the right blend.

WAYS OF LOOKING AT A TEAM

There are all kinds of teams, and they are called together for many different purposes. Naturally, you don't want to spend more to develop the team than you will gain from its existence. Yet there are a few simple concepts that may be helpful to any team.

TEAM TRAINING

Team training, whether done in house or purchased from a training organization, helps potential team members understand behaviors that will be helpful to them as team members. While useful, this training is only a beginning.

Your interactions with others are frequently guided by early life experiences, which may have been strongly negative. Complicating the situation is the fact that schools frequently discourage cooperation in favor of competition. This may be done either deliberately or accidentally, but it is nevertheless done. As a result, it will be beneficial, as Deming suggests, to train and retrain.[1] Or, perhaps, more to the point, train, and then train in greater depth.

The road to personal discovery is long and sometimes hard. It can run the gamut from casual reading, to team member or team leader training, to in-depth personal counselling.

Quality improvement consulting organizations cited in this chapter, such as Qualtec and Joiner Associates, have trained thousands of people in team skills. Leading corporations, such as Florida Power and Light and Alcoa, have trained not only their own employees, but also passed knowledge onto their business partners and suppliers.[2] Still other training organizations provide team problem solving in an outdoor setting to get teams to work together effectively.

The point here is that you should never suffer from lack of team training information. It is readily available at all levels.

Regardless of your level of training and expertise, there is benefit gained from keeping a good team together. When you have finished the task at hand, consider what other issues the team could attack. By staying together after the first project is complete, the team takes advantage of the learning curve that every team must go through to finally work together as a unit. When a team does stay together, defining its own issues, it is referred to as a *self-directed work team.*

THE INFORMAL TEAM

Some issues may not warrant the time and expense of a formal team. This is where your network of friends and business associates comes in handy. You may get enough information or assistance to resolve an issue just by asking. If you don't know anyone who could be of assistance, maybe one of your associates does. Try asking them.

In this way, you can frequently muster the resources you need without expending time and energy on a formal team. People frequently want to help, but are reluctant to provide their opinion until they have been asked. So ask.

THE FORMAL TEAM

Formal teams are appropriate for issues that have sufficient cost of poor quality or other justification to be worth the cost of the team. Cost of the team includes the expense of meetings, plus the expense of outside time spent on the project by team members and support staff. Cost is only one reason why you don't want to put a team on a trivial issue. The other reason is that it will violate team members' value of common sense, producing negative attitudes toward the whole process. Assuming that the task at hand requires a team, how do you get started?

GETTING ORGANIZED

The first step is the recruitment process. You will want to have variety on your team. There are some excellent tools for understanding behavior styles. Meyers-Briggs or Ned Herrmann[3] represent two paradigms in use today. If this is a highly visible project, you may wish to learn more about them. For many projects, however, common sense and mutual respect will be sufficient for team selection.

You will want to have sufficient authority among members of the team to cover the subject area. You don't want to get to the end of a project only to find that you can't implement an improvement because additional approvals are required. This does not mean that all the key executives must attend every meeting. It may mean, however, that you keep them posted on developments, and make them welcome at team meetings, particularly if you get into an area requiring their input. The same approach may be appropriate for experts on an issue. Some organizations, anticipating that bringing people into the team late in a story is the normal case, have provided a special place to document those additions (see Figure 2.2).

There are some practical considerations and specific functions on the team. These will help the team's organization.

TEAM SIZE

Teams can be of any size; however, the risks and benefits of various sized teams must be considered. If the team is too small, you sacrifice diversity, and may run the risk of not having enough coverage to deal with the whole issue. If the team consists of more than 10–15 people, you risk inhibited input, uneven participation, chaos, and discouragement. Yet you may gain in the diversity and coverage.

A good balance is to keep the team at 10 or fewer members. Many experts recommend teams of five to eight persons for best results.

Team members

(The people with critical process knowledge)

Team members	Department/position
______________________	______________________
______________________	______________________
______________________	______________________
______________________	______________________
______________________	______________________
______________________	______________________
______________________	______________________
______________________	______________________
______________________	______________________
______________________	______________________

Team members added later

______________________	______________________
Name	Date added
______________________	
Department or position	
______________________	______________________
Name	Date added
______________________	
Department or position	
______________________	______________________
Name	Date added
______________________	
Department or position	

Page ________ Date ________

FIGURE 2.2. *West Paces Hospital team page.*
Used with permission of West Paces Medical Center.

TEAM GROWTH AND FUNCTION

Just because you have formed a team is no reason to assume that its members will behave as a team. Team participants must go through a phase of learning about each other and how to work together. This takes time. It may be shortened by explaining what will happen. Joiner,[4] QualTeam,[5] and Forsha[6] all offer paradigms for team growth. To me, the easiest way to look at this is that the team must go through the stages of change together, as it explores the issue before it. Team members must be sensitive to both verbal and nonverbal communication in order to avoid hidden problems that will be discovered later in the process and at increased cost. People are frequently so used to avoiding issues, in the interest of keeping peace in the family, that it is difficult to bring them into the open. It takes patience and practice to get the issues to the surface. Once visible, problems can sometimes be solved with astonishing speed.

SPECIFIC ROLES

On large teams, there is more opportunity to have separate functions without sacrificing the benefits of individual participation. On small teams, however, you may need to combine roles, or use them only as needed.

TEAM LEADER

This is one role that can't be sacrificed. Somebody's got to be in charge. If the issue is your idea, then you're the leader until somebody takes it away from you. Take responsibility and go with it. There are many reasons for this approach.

- You lead by example. If this project is your brainchild, then you will be the best standard-bearer. "Every successful idea has a champion."[7]
- Team leadership is a great place to demonstrate your personal leadership qualities. This gives your company officers a chance to see skills that you may not have the opportunity to demonstrate in your regular job.
- Mobilizing others around an issue that you feel is important is an excellent expression of the empowerment that so many people are talking about.

The responsibilities of the team leader include planning the team's activities, setting the agenda, acting as a contact point between the team and the rest of the organization, and keeping team records. As is true of so many job descriptions, the unwritten last task is anything else it takes to get the job done.

FACILITATOR OR QUALITY ADVISOR[8]

Facilitator can mean many things to many people. In the context of storyboarding, the facilitator is the expert on quality tools, the storyboarding process, and the team process. In other words, the resident expert. Many large organizations have staff members who are specially trained to fulfill this function. For the small company, the team leader may often be the one who fills these shoes as well.

OBSERVER

This role can be particularly important during the first few team meetings, and then again if the team reaches an impasse. In one company, the personnel manager acted as a professional observer. He made a study of not knowing anything about the issues, but providing insight on the dynamics of individual and group relationships. This practice allowed him to fill a very important function for the whole company.

In the same way, an observer is assigned to focus on the dynamics of the group. Figure 2.3 shows a check sheet method for observing behavior in the group.

Observer training is provided in many programs so that each team member can be aware of key types of behavior. Using a simple check sheet, any team member can quickly and simply check his or her behavior or the interactions in the group without getting distracted from the issue at hand.

SCRIBE

Somebody must take notes at meetings. Otherwise it is easy to forget important information and miss future assignments and deadlines. In large groups, this could be a permanent assignment. In some organizations, a secretary may be brought in to fulfill this role.

In a small organization or group, the leader may also be the scribe. The negative side of this is that it can slow down the action, and it can distract the leader from critical conversation. On the other hand, it can be effective if reviewing the team notes helps the leader focus on the meeting minutes and stay aware of critical points.

TEAM MEETINGS

Your organization may set a pace and an expectation level for your project in terms of tangible outputs (deliverables) and time. Here are a few of the most useful ideas.

1. I used to say, "Never have a meeting without an agenda." But that is not entirely true. Instead, consider your objective for the

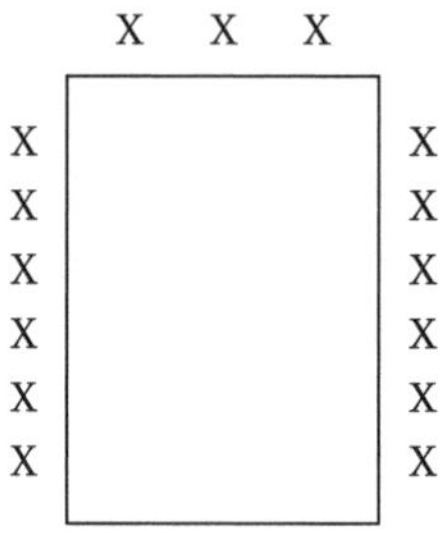

Instructions

1. Place a check mark beside a team member each time he or she participates.
2. Draw arrows between participants indicating direction and frequency of dialog.
3. Use abbreviations to note particular behaviors which the team wishes to encourage or discourage.
4. Give nonjudgmental feedback to the team.

FIGURE 2.3. *Check sheet for team behaviors.*

meeting, and give other participants fair warning. If you're going to have a creative meeting, you may not want an agenda.

2. The value of inputs and interactions begins to decline after the first full hour of a meeting. If a meeting is well organized, it can last longer and still be a good use of time.
3. If you don't know your schedule in the early going, schedule the next meeting in two to four weeks. From a practical standpoint, it is difficult for people to accomplish much, in addition to their regular work, in less than two weeks. Also, it will probably be at least a day or two before the meeting summary is distributed with individual assignments, making a one-week cycle impractical. On the other hand, if you get more than one month in between meetings, the sense of continuity begins to disappear, and interest may be lost by team members.
4. The key exception to (3) may occur when you are actually implementing a project, in which case the data-collecting activities will drive the meeting schedule.

MAINTAINING FOCUS

The best tool for maintaining focus is the storyboard itself. In support of the storyboard, and running a close second, is the meeting summary. This tool accomplishes several tasks.

1. The team meeting summary assures communication with all team members, especially those who may have missed a meeting.
2. It summarizes the accomplishments, discussion, and action plans.
3. It provides official notice of the next meeting, and sets the agenda for the next meeting. (A reminder may still be necessary.)
4. A summary says thanks. (Opportunities to say something positive are often overlooked.)
5. A summary provides copies for other interested parties, so that they may be aware of team activities.
6. The meeting summary helps keep on track.

Figure 2.4 shows a simple format for a meeting summary.

To: (List all team members alphabetically)
From: (Team leader)
Date: (Use meeting date for clarity)
Subject: Meeting summary: Inventory control team (Team nickname)

Paragraph One: Brief description of the flow of the meeting, summarizing key points and activities.

Action items
(Due by next meeting)

Action item	Due date	Responsibility
Action item	Due date	Responsibility

The next meeting will be held on (day of week), January 14, 1994, at (time) in Conference Room 104.

Thank you all for your contributions. (Change the wording each time. Everybody knows if you have a word processor. If you don't change the wording, you may seem insincere.)

cc: (All nonteam members who are interested or should be notified.)

FIGURE 2.4. *Example of meeting summary.*

Word processing is extremely helpful in this area, because it is necessary only to change dates and some text. Action item lists only require the removal of old items and the addition of new ones.

TEAM NICKNAME

Many companies encourage the use of nicknames or mascots for teams. This is not just for fun. It also helps maintain focus. If you feel the urge to name your team, please do and be creative. Sometimes a company joke reveals an opportunity for improvement. This may also provide a great name for a team. One good example with some humor in it is The Drips (water conservation). Another is the Mid-Knights. (Is there any doubt which shift this team worked?) This nickname can provide visual interest for a storyboard or storybook.

BITE-SIZE ACTIVITIES

Everybody has some need for a sense of accomplishment. In a group, this need must balance the fact that large projects take a long time to complete. If you are not sure how much to schedule for one meeting, begin by taking the problem-solving steps one at a time. This gives you a chance to celebrate results after each meeting, rather than just once at the end of the project.

RULES OF CONDUCT

There are a few simple guidelines for successful meetings, particularly when you are working on sticky issues. I have seen many lists, but can't improve much on the following:

- Be prompt. Show up on time.
- Listen constructively.
- Act with mutual respect.
- Suspend judgment. Keep an open mind.
- Criticize ideas, not people.
- Ask questions.
- Take personal responsibility for results.

Figure 2.5 is an example of convenient back-to-front filing of storyboard materials. It always shows the current step on the top of the heap.

SUMMARY

- Create a team, if you can benefit from one.
- Consider an informal team for minor issues.

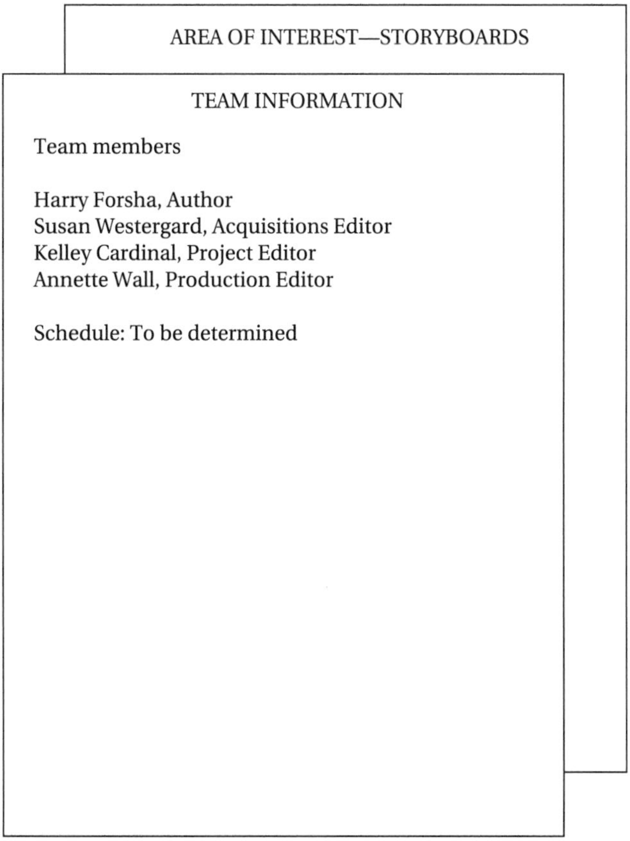

FIGURE 2.5. *Reality check for this book.*

- Provide the training and background necessary to get the team off to a good start. A dysfunctional team is useless or worse.
- Never have a meeting without sufficient notice.
- Cover all the special functions of leader, facilitator, observer, and scribe, even if they must be overlapped with regular team member assignments.
- Stay on track.
- Celebrate progress.

Chapter Three

PROBLEM SOLVING

INTRODUCTION

It is impossible to talk about storyboards without saying something about problem-solving methods. After all, the storyboard is a way to communicate or show how a problem was identified and solved.

In the story of the three little pigs, the author did not digress to discuss his method for writing the story. If he had stopped to do that, the story may not have stood the test of time. But you must digress from the flow of this story to discuss your method, so that successful problem-solving techniques can be incorporated into future storyboards, enhancing their clarity. What is essential is that the story must make sense. It must flow conceptually from beginning to end, and it must be logically complete, with one panel leading to the next, regardless of which storyboard method is used.

If you are working with an organization that endorses a particular problem-solving method, and trains its people in that method, you will certainly want to continue to use it. On the other hand, there are benefits to each approach, and you can use it to enrich your present process. You may also find the comparison chart in Appendix B helpful in relating other problem-solving approaches to the one you know best.

PROBLEMS, OPPORTUNITIES, AND ISSUES

These three words are interchangeable in function, but what they communicate is a different story. (The pun is only slightly intended.)

PROBLEMS

Don't you hate to always have problems, problems, problems? The boss says, "Don't bring me problems, bring me solutions." Who wants to be a problem employee?

Problems are a fact of life. But by the same token, not all things worth improving are problems. Some are simply deserving of improvement. Many organizations engage in quality improvement, not because they are problem companies, but because they are already well run and want to be better.

For want of a better name, a body of investigation, understanding, and literature has grown around the general topic of problem solving. Since that is where the information is, I will use the term *problem* more often than it deserves. For the purposes of this discussion, I would like to consider two other words as equally valid for generating storyboards—*opportunities* and *issues.*

OPPORTUNITIES

The word *opportunity* has more positive connotations than the word *problem. Opportunity* conjures up images of the chance of a lifetime or the pursuit of something you might enjoy. It is an old saw in sales training that with every problem comes an opportunity. For instance, you could work on improving your shop scheduling, not because it was viewed as a problem, but because it showed the greatest promise for saving time and money, as compared to other opportunities.

The major pitfall with the word *opportunity* is its potential use as a substitute word when what is really meant is *problem.* As long as *opportunity* is not used as a euphemism for *problem,* opportunities are fertile ground for storyboards.

ISSUES

In my search for a neutral term, I found the word *issue.* Use of this term may help to develop a better understanding of whatever you are dealing with. An issue is simply a point of question. This definition makes no value judgment and, while bland, is neutral. An issue may not require problem-solving techniques. It may simply need to be negotiated among interested parties.

The techniques in this book may be applied to problem solving, opportunity realizing, or issue resolving. Each situation is unique, and may be approached from any of the three perspectives. It is important to know where you are starting from, so that you don't become confused in your objectives. In deference to the body of literature already existing, and in support of common language, I will continue to use problem solving as the term of choice. The three points of departure are contrasted as follows:

- **Problem:** Any question or matter involving doubt, uncertainty, or difficulty. At least some of the doubt, uncertainty, or difficulty should be removed by identifying the key facts, by increasing awareness, and by communicating.
- **Issue:** A point in question or a matter that is in dispute. Even after improving awareness and communication, some dispute may remain. The process of change, individually or with a group, can assist in removing disputes, leading to the establishment of a goal.

- **Opportunity:** A situation or condition favorable to attainment of a goal. Now, you are ready to accomplish something.

Note: You can start anywhere, but it is important to know where you are when you start.

PROBLEM-SOLVING TECHNIQUES VERSUS STORYBOARDS

When I was first learning quality improvement techniques, I became confused because of the apparent conflict between a seven-step, problem-solving method and a different seven-step storyboard process. In this book, I would like to draw a clear distinction between problem-solving techniques and storyboarding. In order to get off to a good start, the storyboard has been defined. The cover page, or title, has also been created, and the team information, which also goes at the beginning of the story, has been started. Taking that as a beginning, storyboarding is the art and practice of creating a storyboard, or of telling a story.

Problem solving is an organized procedure for addressing problems, opportunities, or issues. It is possible to approach an issue haphazardly or with serendipity. As the stakes rise, however, you should frequently rely on an organized method to reduce the risk of failure.

If someone—either yourself or your customers and associates—will benefit from the activities or results of a problem-solving activity, then you can use a storyboard to communicate the story. There is, however, no necessary link between the two. A beneficial link, perhaps, but not a necessary one.

For instance, you may solve a personal problem using the quality tools described later in this book, including a problem-solving method. You may *not* choose to tell others about your problem or your solution.

Another example comes from the world of planning. Many companies do strategic planning. They may or may not use storyboards to accomplish this planning. They sometimes communicate the results in their annual reports. Storyboards can be used to facilitate the planning process.

PROBLEM-SOLVING METHODS

THE SEVEN-STEP METHOD

The seven-step method, as popularized by Florida Power and Light (FPL), consists of the following stages.[1] I was first introduced to the FPL method in 1986, when the company was working on the Deming Award. Although the method has changed somewhat over time, the steps have stayed essentially the same (see Figure 3.1). Take particular note of FPL's use of a visual icon to depict each stage.

The FPL method was spun off to Qualtec, which provides training in this method. FPL was responsible for passing this technology on to many organizations. As a result, this technique is in wide use.

Reason for improvement
To identify a theme and the reasons (indicator) for working on it.

Current situation
To select a problem and set a target for improvement.

Analysis
To identify and verify the root causes(s) of the problem.

Countermeasures
To plan and implement countermeasures that will correct the root causes of the problem.

Results
To confirm that the problem and its root causes have been decreased and the target for the improvement has been met.

Standardization
To prevent the problem and its root causes from recurring.

Future plans
To plan what is to be done about any remaining problems and to evaluate the team's effectiveness.

Used with permission of Qualtec Quality Services.

FIGURE 3.1. *The FPL method.*

THE FIVE-STEP METHOD

The five-step method, as practiced by Southern Pacific Transportation (SPT), is a distillation of the FPL method (see Figure 3.2).[2] This is no surprise, because some of the people who developed the paradigm for FPL later went on to develop it for SPT.

A COMPARISON OF METHODS

In order to build a strong foundation, it will be useful to look at the FPL and SPT methods side by side (see Figure 3.3). Then, pieces from other methods will be added in order to build a complete picture.

There are three differences in these methods. The first two steps in the FPL model are combined into one step in the SPT model. If you look deeper into the documentation, however, the apparent differences disappear.

1. Problem selection
2. Analysis
3. Countermeasures
4. Results and standardization
5. Next steps

FIGURE 3.2. *The SPT method.*

FPL	**SPT**
Reason for improvement	Problem selection
Current situation	
Analysis	Analysis
Countermeasures	Countermeasures
Results	Results/standardization
Standardization	
Future plans	Next steps

FIGURE 3.3. *Comparison of the FPL and SPT problem-solving methods.*

Both state that the "need for improvement was demonstrated using data," and that "the indicator correctly represented the problem area."

The second apparent difference between the two methods is that results and standardization are combined into one step in the SPT model. I interpret this to be a difference in name only, not in process. Clearly, there must be positive results before any decision can be made to standardize them.

Third, if you can accept that the terms *future plans* and *next steps* have a similar meaning, then you are looking at essentially the same model. Now, look at a third model, that of Technicomp, a training organization. It will be compared to the first two methods.

TECHNICOMP

Technicomp also endorses a five-step method, but it is slightly different from the others.[3] The major difference revolves around its approach to practical workplace problem solving (see Figure 3.4).

While starting with problem identification, as the other methods do, Technicomp guides users to isolate and contain the problem. This approach can be a two-edged sword.

FPL	SPT	Technicomp
Reason for improvement	Problem selection	Identify and define problem
Current situation		Isolate and contain problem
Analysis	Analysis	Collect and analyze data
Countermeasures	Countermeasures	Correct or reduce problem
Results	Results/ standardization	Monitor and document change
Standardization		
Future plans	Next steps	

FIGURE 3.4. *Comparison of the FPL, SPT, and Technicomp problem-solving methods.*

Isolate and contain is frequently taken to mean to isolate the external customer from the problem, containing it by bottling it up in the organization, and not allowing it to escape. In concept, at least if not universally, this effort can be counterproductive if it does not extend beyond protecting the customer.

Isolation and containment may not be problem solving at all, especially if it is problem shifting. You run the risk of spending time and effort only to shift the problem to a different place. Then, you have to go on to solve the real problem anyway, so why delay?

On the other hand, if by isolation and containment you are talking about narrowing and defining the scope of the problem, by use of solid problem-solving skills and good information, then the Technicomp approach is consistent with other problem-solving techniques. An example of the positive use of the phrase *isolate and contain* occurs where a serious product defect is discovered, and a recall is used to contain the problem and its potential consequences.

COMPARISON OF THE THREE APPROACHES

There is still something bothering me about the structured problem-solving approaches. Something seems to be missing. Perhaps it is the fact that people really do fire one for range. Maybe not deliberately, but that may frequently be the way it works out.[4] Maybe a simple process is actually gone through twice; once to define the problem, and then a second time to solve it. An examination of some work described as "creative problem solving" illustrates the concept.

CREATIVE PROBLEM SOLVING

VanGundy, who works in the area of creativity and problem solving, takes a somewhat different approach.[5] While it does not conflict with the more common quality problem-solving methods, it provides a different insight into the way people really operate.

VanGundy breaks the process of problem solving into a series of focused tasks, as do the other methods. He, however, names the tasks according to what might be called psychological functions, rather than work functions. VanGundy's creative problem-solving method includes the following:

1. Objective finding
2. Fact finding
3. Problem finding
4. Idea finding

5. Solution finding
6. Acceptance finding

There is no direct link between these stages and the steps in the other models. For instance, you may begin with objective finding. That sounds almost like reason for improvement. So, fact finding must begin almost immediately, but will continue throughout the problem-solving process. Idea finding could also occur at the beginning, as you consider what you are actually working on; and again when you are considering possible solutions.

There are two things I like about the VanGundy model. First, it helps me to know exactly what it is I'm trying to do. Serious conflicts can occur in a team if one person is trying to generate ideas while another is looking for facts.

The second key point in VanGundy's method is the concept of divergent and convergent thinking. In each step of his method, divergent thinking is used to generate as many ideas as possible, hoping to assure that all the ideas relating to the subject have been revealed. Then, convergent thinking is used to select the best ideas.

I like to paraphrase the concepts of divergent thinking and convergent thinking by calling them creative thinking and critical thinking, respectively. My rationale for this is that creativity tools, like brainstorming, are usually designed to generate ideas, or make unusual connections, with the idea of thinking of something new or different. Convergent thinking, on the other hand, is frequently accomplished by applying the skills of critical analysis, by picking the ideas apart, and by weeding out the ones that don't pass muster.

I add to this list the concept of reflective thinking, which is my description of the periods of time when people are not actively engaged in a problem, but are thinking about it subconsciously. Many of the best ideas come at this time. Therefore, it is important to acknowledge its presence to assure that time is allowed for reflective thinking.

This divergent-convergent thinking could be compared to breathing. You breathe in, expanding your lungs (divergent), pause for a brief moment (reflective), then breathe out (convergent), and pause again. This analogy can be useful in checking your use of natural thought processes in problem solving.

THE PROCESS OF CHANGE

In both individuals and groups, you cannot escape the process of change. When you engage in problem-solving activities, somebody and something will have to change. As a result, you must be continuously aware of where you are in the process and where you are going.

The wishbone diagram in Figure 3.5 can be used to understand hang-ups in the problem-solving process, which can run deeper than the problem itself. Sometimes the key factor in problem resolution is personal acceptance of change.[6]

APPENDIX B

Appendix B contains a spreadsheet comparing problem-solving methods, so that you may see their similarities and differences firsthand. In general, all the models fall into one of the three types discussed in this chapter.

AN INTEGRATIVE APPROACH

With dozens of methods to choose from, how do you approach a problem, opportunity, or issue? What is considered normal? My suggestion is a synthesis of the creative problem-solving world and, for want of another term, the scientific or linear problem-solving world. This method should respect both the benefits of freewheeling thinking and organization; that is, both left- and right-brained thinking. Not everybody will solve a problem in the same way. No two people will have exactly the same ideas. So why shouldn't there be a place for everybody in the problem-solving model? I believe that the model presented here takes advantage of the significant work that has been done, while applying directly

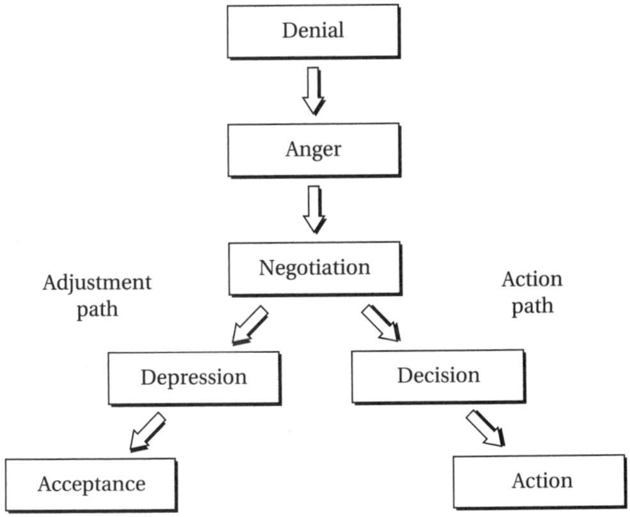

FIGURE 3.5. *Wishbone diagram.*
Note: Adapted from Noel M. Tichy and Mary Anne Devanna, *The Transformational Leader* (New York: John Wiley & Sons, 1990), p. 68.

to the way people actually function at work and in life. The integrative approach includes the following:

1. Identify the problem. Find the reason for improvement.
2. Understand the problem and the current situation.
3. Analyze the problem.
4. Generate potential actions.
5. Evaluate and select actions.
6. Implement actions.
7. Appraise or evaluate.

The result, I hope, will be a solid problem-solving method that takes advantage of all the learnings that have gone before, and that will be broken up into meaningful step names. Then, you can communicate with other people worldwide, through storyboards, regardless of the problem-solving method they have learned. Each step will be discussed in a chapter of its own.

STEP 1. IDENTIFY THE PROBLEM. FIND THE REASON FOR IMPROVEMENT.

This step should not be confused with the problem definition or the objective statement. You can get started on a problem in one of two ways: (1) It is either on your personal agenda; or (2) It is on your organization's agenda. If there is some methodical way of prioritizing opportunities for improvement, then that should be reported here. Otherwise, you may simply begin by stating that the problem exists. The Kepner-Tregoe method begins with a "deviation statement," which makes sense, if you have good information with which to begin.[7] But frequently, you do not.

It is hard to do much better than to simply ask the question "Why?" at the beginning of any activity. If the answer is satisfactory, continue.

STEP 2. UNDERSTAND THE PROBLEM AND THE CURRENT SITUATION.

Gather data and look at it from all points of view. The purpose of this segment is to describe the situation in a sufficient number of ways to assure that you truly understand the problem, issue, or opportunity.

If data gathering is important later in the process, then it is critical here. Preliminary data must be gathered to verify that there really is a problem, to assist in understanding the problem, and to develop a measurement system that can be used throughout the problem-solving process. The measurement process itself is frequently refined in the early stages of problem solving, causing the establishment of a new baseline against which to measure results. Eitington dignifies data gathering at this point as a separate step.[8]

STEP 3. ANALYZE THE PROBLEM.

Borrowing from VanGundy, I would suggest that more creativity can be put into the problem-solving process. This would assure that you both expand your thinking, considering all the possibilities, and contract your thinking, focusing on the best possibilities.

Aside from the alternative name of *situation analysis,* the majority of methods have this step in the process in common. The end result of this step should be a clear definition of the problem, as expressed by clear objectives, and supplemented by a measurement method.

STEP 4. GENERATE POTENTIAL ACTIONS.

Return to the breathing in and breathing out. You've decided by this point what the problem is. Now it's time to think about possible actions. So you are ready to do another cycle of divergent or creative thinking. You want to look at all the possible actions.

STEP 5. EVALUATE AND SELECT ACTIONS.

Now you are ready for convergent thinking. You are evaluating options, comparing the chances of success, or maybe even doing a trial implementation on one or more of the better alternatives.

STEP 6. IMPLEMENT ACTIONS.

There is substantial agreement that action should be taken. Results should also be monitored and documented.

STEP 7. APPRAISE OR EVALUATE.

If results were successful, this step will usually generate a change in procedure, which should be documented in the form of a procedure revision. The increasing attention to ISO 9000 standards has had a beneficial effect in raising the visibility of the need for documentation. Even temporary changes should be documented, because they are frequently not so temporary as originally planned, and they end up being the way things are done.

Two key items in this step are the importance of reviewing the process as well as the results. One phrase typically heard among Juran devotees is "lessons learned." I like that. Another useful way to end a process is with future plans.

EVERYBODY STARTS SOMEWHERE

One of the interesting facets of problem solving is that problem solvers never start with a clean slate. They are always somewhere down the road before they suspect that they made a wrong turn. You are not just buying a computer system, you are converting from an old system, with both strengths and weaknesses, to a new system, with different strengths and weaknesses. You are halfway into one implementation when the situation changes, and you are forced to initiate another. An important part of your process is to know where you are when you start and what your objective happens to be. Although you will be frequently entering the problem-solving process at the assessment of some other process,[9] it is useful to realize that you may be anywhere. Your first task is to find out where you really are.

SUMMARY

A story is told of a seeker who asked a holy man, "Which way to God is the right way?"

The holy man responded, "All ways to God are the right way."

In this chapter, several problem-solving methods were presented. There is no right or wrong. It is up to you to use good judgment and awareness as guides and to think of the method as a way to get to a solution.

If you are working on a problem in your organization, you will benefit by using the technique that the company endorses. If you are communicating outside your organization, then you should be most concerned with the logical flow of your presentation. The integrative approach suggested in this chapter should help.

Chapter Four

QUALITY IMPROVEMENT TOOLS

TOOLS DEFINED

Tool—Something that serves as a means to an end.

Talk about vague! Unfortunately, that is the only definition that covers the breadth and depth of the so-called quality tools.

Since I want you to try what this book is suggesting, do some expansive thinking first. Then narrow down the territory. How many ways can you look at quality tools? Here are some ideas.

- The basic seven quality tools
- The seven new tools quality tools
- Other business tools that could be applied to continuous improvement
- Any helpful technique
- Any combination of tools
- Any tool or combination of tools applied anytime and anywhere

CREATIVE EXPANSION

I suggest that as a starting point, you consider the use of any tool or technique that is available or that comes to mind. In other words, start by opening all the doors or by breathing in. You will suspend judgment, for the time being, and allow yourself to consider all the possibilities. This process is typically called brainstorming or idea generation.

An attempt to be all-inclusive would set an impossible target, because I cannot know all the uses of every tool at all places. As a result, I am using this book. I encourage you to do the same, as a place to put ideas and as a way to organize your reality. I hope that as time goes on, a revision based upon new information will be possible. In the meantime, you have a place to put your newly discovered tools and combinations.

USE OF THE TOOL PAGES

In this chapter, you will consider common, practical tools and combinations that have been effective in actual use. In designing this book, I have provided a separate place for tools, designated as tool pages, in Appendix C. Each tool page is a simple, step-by-step description of the tool and how to use it. There is a place in each discussion to add your own suggestions on applications, and I encourage you to mark it up to your heart's content. Add your own tool pages, and cross-reference them in the spaces provided. Use this book as a tool and let it be a means to an end for you.

This book is designed to be used by both experienced professionals and beginners. For those professionals who are experienced in the use of quality tools, hopefully, there will be at least one tool that you have not used already, or some combination of tools that is new and different. For the beginners, each tool page is designed to be used as needed.

THE BASIC QUALITY TOOLS

I am focusing on the four tools shown in Figure 4.1 because they are essential to understanding most problems. Without understanding the problem, you have little hope of solving it. Since the original basic seven

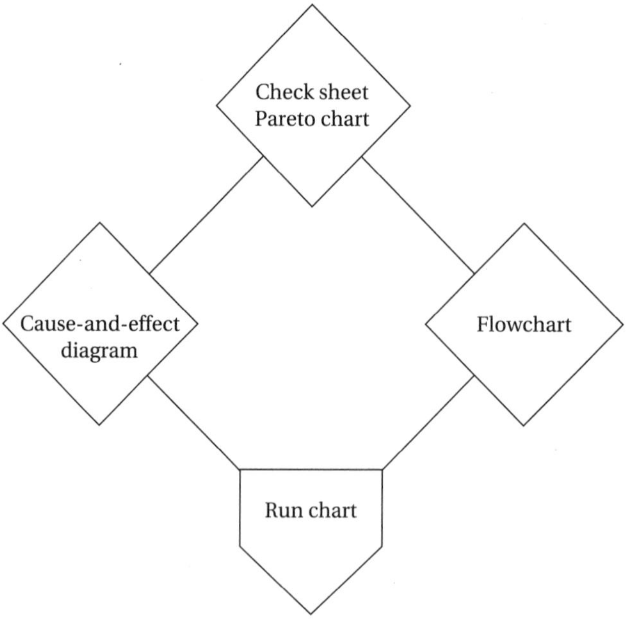

FIGURE 4.1. *The basic necessities.*

tools have expanded over the past several years, they will be discussed in the tool pages.

If you accept that you are already monitoring the key result area, or that the proposed effect of your action will be obvious, the flowchart, check sheet/Pareto chart, and cause-and-effect diagram offer a great start. In training potential storyboarders, however, it is useful to insist that the key result or key indicator be tracked using a run chart.

Although I'm not a baseball fan, this sport offers the best analogy I can propose.

- The run is how your successes are counted.
- If you want to score, you've got to cover all the bases.
- Each base is played differently.
- Regardless of which field you play on, the bases are always the same.

In this analogy, each base has a specific purpose. The flowchart helps to understand the system with which you are working. It helps you organize your thinking, and paves the way for understanding underlying causes of problems. (Read that as variation if you wish.)

The check sheet enables you to count the number of occurrences by problem area. You may even want to use the flowchart itself to count where the problem areas are. The Pareto chart helps to prioritize problem areas or causes by putting them in order. It allows you to compare their relative contributions to the situation.

The cause-and-effect diagram helps you to consider all the possible contributing causes. It will help you sort out the key culprits.

The run chart enables you to stay in touch with your key indicator. Hopefully, this is the link to the larger system, whether it is a total quality management system, a business operating system, or a customer satisfaction system. The run chart tracks key results; it tells you if you're hitting a home run or not. The run chart is the scoreboard.

It has often been said, "Sometimes you win, sometimes you lose, and sometimes you get rained out." The cloud diagram is like the cloud over the field of play (see Figure 4.2). You can indicate where the clouds are on any of your bases, or on other tools when they are used. The cloud diagram helps you analyze the problem, but even more, it helps you communicate with others by showing clearly which area is a concern (see Figure 4.3).

This cloud pattern is used to draw attention to a particular place, whether on the flowchart, on a spreadsheet, or in a written page of information. I like it because it encloses the area of concern, leaving no doubt as to the content.

FIGURE 4.2. *The mighty cloud.*

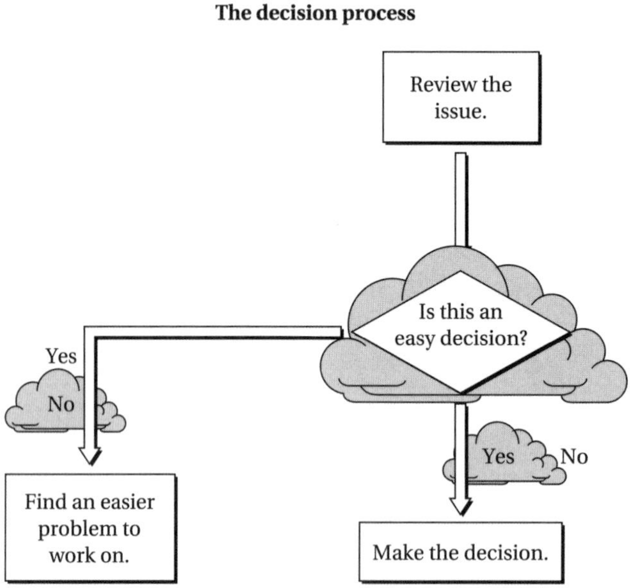

FIGURE 4.3. *Cloud pattern highlights process problems.*

THE RUN CHART

The run chart is a variant of the control chart. There is at least one phrase in the quality lexicon which is so old that nobody will claim it. *What gets measured, gets done.*

One of the first things you need to address in any kind of problem or opportunity is one key indicator that you can measure. This is so you can determine if you have made any progress, and so you can set an achievable objective. You can only do this if you know from where you are starting.

Now comes the first experience with variation. I'm walking around the halls one day, and I see that the telephone switchboard is backed up and the switchboard operator is going crazy. I do some quick calculations and find that calls are coming in at the rate of one per minute. That's a problem, because it exceeds the operator's capacity.

Being a hotshot executive, I mount my white horse and swing into action—only to find later that I happened to observe the operator on an exceptional occasion. The purpose of this little story is to draw attention to the importance of understanding variation, and, therefore, of establishing a baseline from which to measure.

A run chart, in its simplest form, is simply a recording of a measurement repeated over time. In the case of the switchboard operator, it may look like Figure 4.4.

Of particular interest in tracking results is the measurement interval. When the number of calls handled in a day is measured, the curve may be relatively smooth, as in Figure 4.4. What happens in real life, however, is that a switchboard changes by the minute. If the calls are measured in 15-minute intervals, a totally different picture is drawn, as in Figure 4.5.

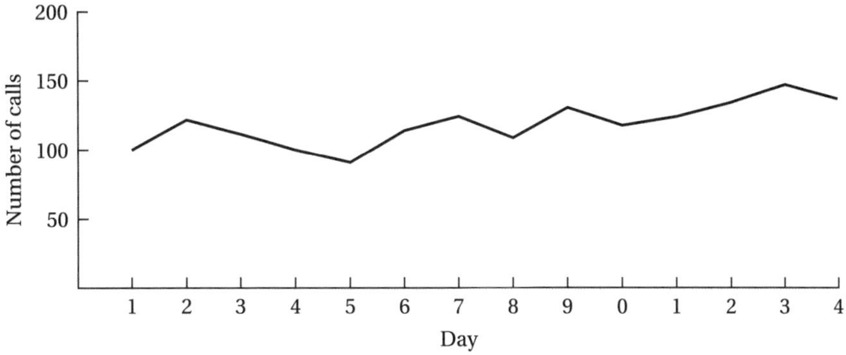

FIGURE 4.4. *Run chart of incoming calls.*

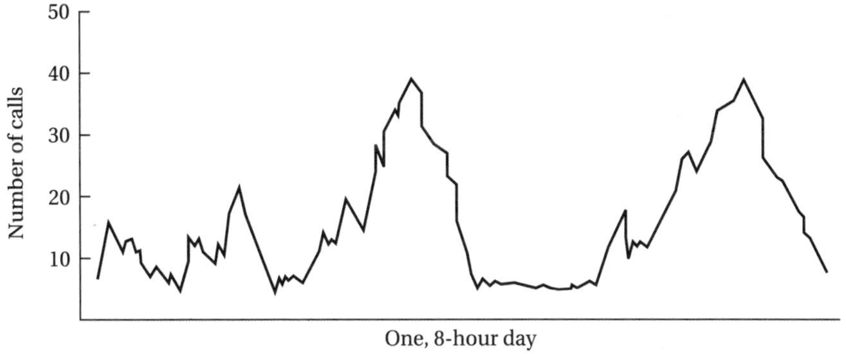

FIGURE 4.5. *Incoming calls in 15-minute periods.*

If the measurements do not confirm that a problem exists, take a moment to be certain that the right interval is being measured.

Once the average number of calls and the typical variation around that average have been established, then there is a baseline for comparison. In the case of telephone activity, it will be necessary to track data for more than one month, because there is cyclicity based upon time of the month. This will also mean that results will have to be measured for a similar period to determine their comparison to the baseline.

THE FLOWCHART

Steven Covey's admonition, "First seek to understand" applies as well to problem solving as it does to interpersonal communications.[1] Arguably the best tool for understanding a process is the flowchart. The flowchart can be used in many ways, but it is a good idea to begin with a flowchart of what *is*. Just identifying what *is* can sometimes be quite an undertaking.

Begin with a simple process, one that became the focus of some very interesting conversations. It is the process of decision making among senior managers, illustrated in Figure 4.6. (I leave it to you to determine whether this is a real or fictitious company.) This concept is shown more graphically, and with some humor, in Figure 4.7.

Sometimes a point can be made better with a little bit of humor. The flowchart can be used to compare the underground process and the official process.

The result of the process, as demonstrated by the flowcharts, is that only easy decisions got made. The flow of thinking prioritized problems

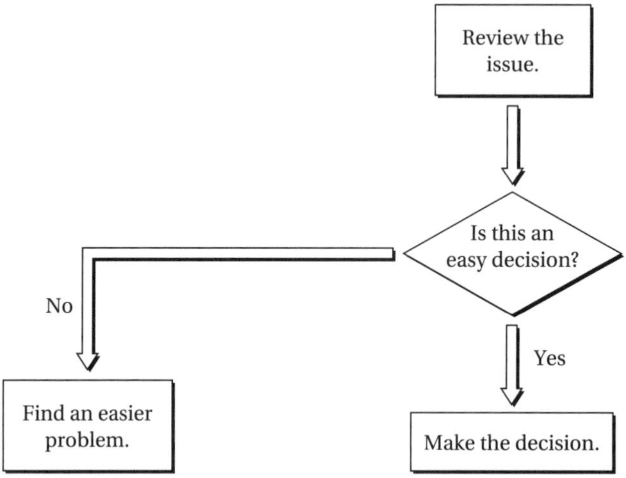

FIGURE 4.6. *The decision process.*

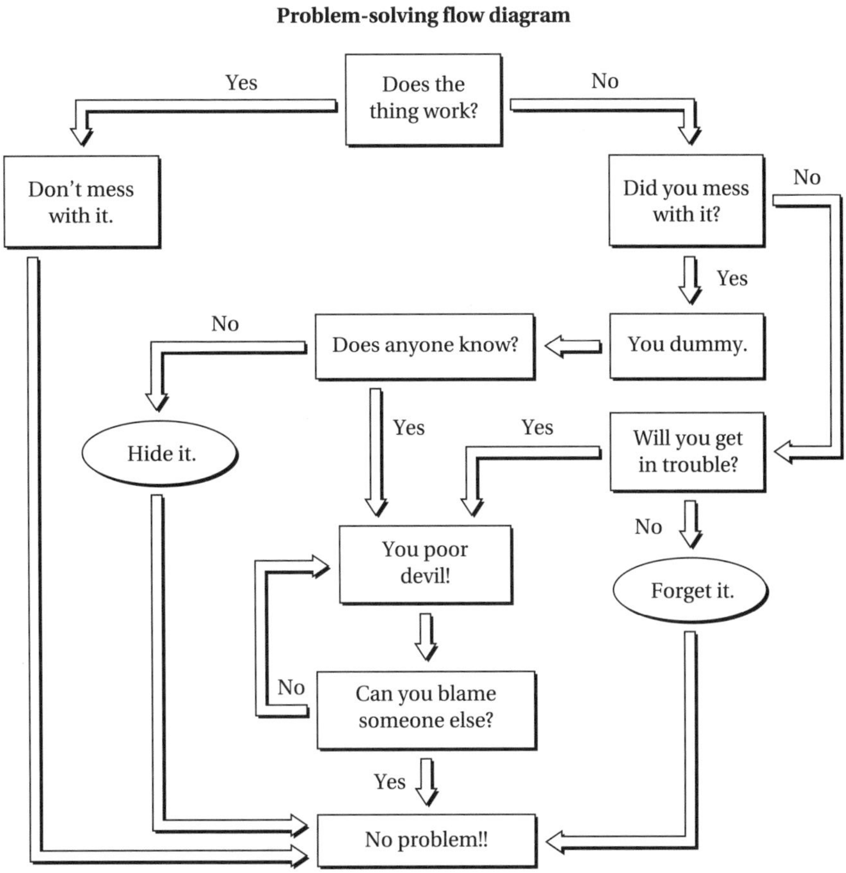

FIGURE 4.7. *The underground version.*

by ease of solution. The system produced exactly what it was designed to produce—easy decisions.

Now, assume that the resolution of difficult issues became a source of pride to this organization. Consider the effects upon decision flow with the changed set of values (see Figure 4.8). In this case, all the boxes and diamonds are the same, only the procedure has changed. The process is improved by eliminating unnecessary or counterproductive steps. That's one way to use a flowchart.

Now look at a different kind of flowchart, shown in Figure 4.9. In this case, the movement of a process across organizational boundaries is tracked. The flowchart is used like a road map. It shows how a process moves around the organization.

This type of flowchart makes it very easy for workers to see where they fit into the process. You will notice that no box or diamond is

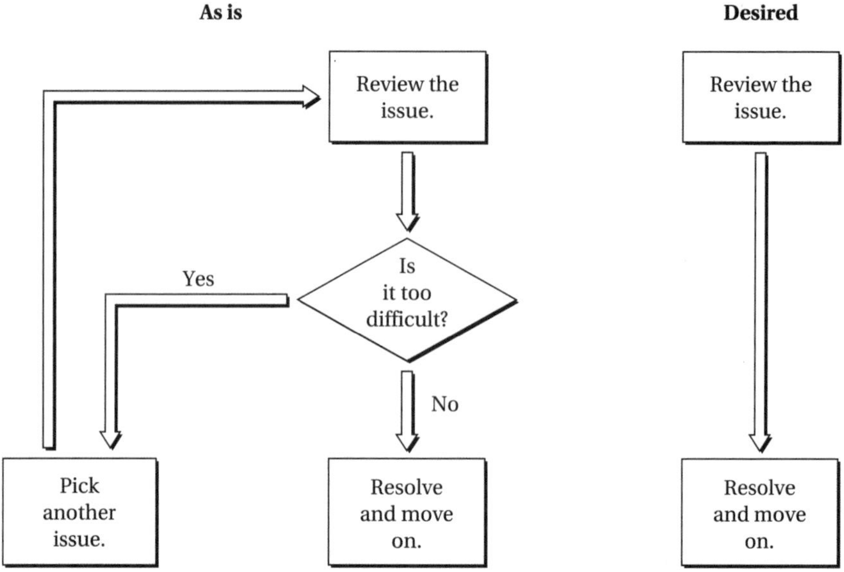

FIGURE 4.8. *Comparison of flowcharts.*

directly beside another. There is a special reason for this. When flowcharts are created, frequently there are questions, comments, or information associated with each box. This might include knowns, like how often an action occurs or exactly who is doing the job, or unknowns. By turning the paper sideways, another column for just such information can be added. This column could also be used to provide cross-reference information to identify specific procedures that may apply (see Figure 4.10).

You have now seen three different ways to do a flowchart. This is just the beginning. Here is where the work really begins.

The exact question that is asked, and the way it is asked, impact the answer. Put it all together, and what you get is a two-step process. First, you ask—roughing out the flowchart as you go. Then, you go back and ask again—showing the rough flowchart. This time, the person both sees and hears the questions, and you often get a clearer result. People will frequently say something like, "Well, that's the way it works *most* of the time, but sometimes . . . ," or "That's the way it's *supposed* to work, but what I really do is. . . ." The value of polling the actual users of a system or process—the ones who are doing the work—cannot be overemphasized. It is frequently this second pass that reveals problems, opportunities, or issues.

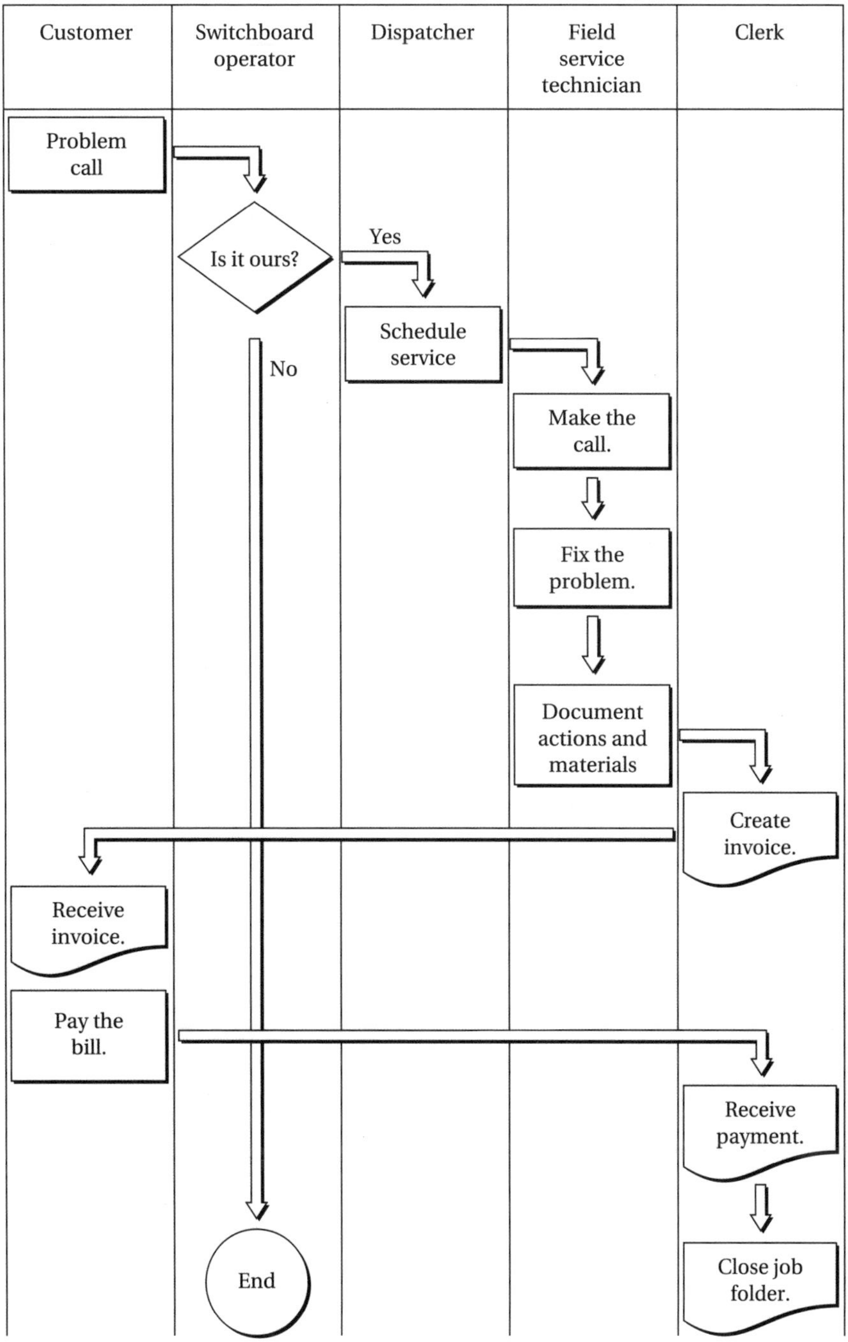

FIGURE 4.9. *Flowchart by organizational units.*

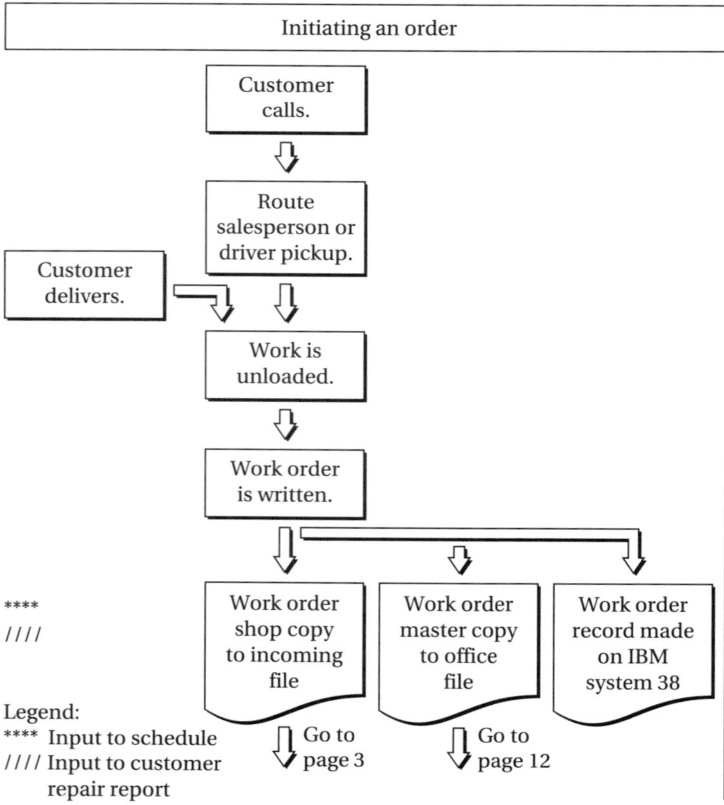

Frequency	Responsibility	Comments
Any time	Staff on call	Business hours—office staff After hours—duty supervisor
Per schedule or callout	Route salesperson or driver and dispatcher	Per customer's requirements
Business hour or by request	Staff on call	Per customer's requirements
At arrival	Customer service clerk	Correct rigging and handling of equipment
As soon as posible on arrival	Customer service clerk	Initiates job in shop and data system, assures that necessary equipment description and customer information is recorded, including standing and special orders, update customer log book
As soon as possible	Customer service clerk	Assures that correct data are shown on all documents and entered into computer system

FIGURE 4.10. *Flowchart with additional comments.*

BOTTOM TO TOP

One way to troubleshoot or improve a flowchart is to review it backwards, or from bottom to top. At each step in the process, all the things necessary to get the job done must be present; that means the people, procedures, information, materials, and equipment. If the equipment is bolted down, it might be taken for granted. Otherwise, the needs at a stage in a process are provided from some other prior step in the process. If the flowchart does not show how the needs for the step in question are satisfied, then there is a problem, either with the process or the flowchart.

EVIL DIAMONDS

One way of looking at a flowchart is that every diamond is a potential source of variation. According to mainstream quality control thinking, variation is wicked and should be driven out. Regardless of the strength of your convictions on this point, it is fair to say that a simple flowchart—one with a few diamonds—is easy to understand. A system that is easy to understand is easy to execute. And a system that is easy to execute is not likely to have problems.

SENGE'S CYCLES

In his book, *The Fifth Discipline,* Peter Senge draws attention to systematic problems.[2] These are frequently overlooked until their consequences demand immediate action.

Of particular importance is the timing of feedback, or information passing, from one stage in a process to the next. In one of Senge's examples, he discusses inventory orders based on forecasts. This system would work perfectly if the forecasts were always accurate. But forecasts are never perfect. If the sales feedback does not come in from the field in a timely way, either excess or inadequate inventory will result. This can result in an expanding cycle of ever-more or ever-less inventory when just the opposite is desired.

Looking at your flowchart from the standpoint of information needed versus information received can shed light on possible problem areas. Although Senge has a unique way to describe flows, you can show the effect of timing or delays on a traditional flowchart by clouding the affected lines.

Figure 4.11 highlights the dangers of strictly linear thinking. In the flowchart, the selling, buying, and forecasting are all occurring continuously as parallel processes. In fact, they do not occur in sequence. Although it may be convenient to show them in sequence, this can get you in trouble.

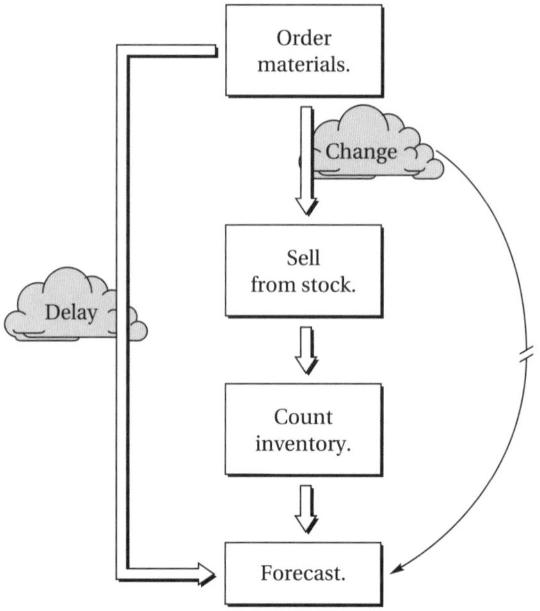

FIGURE 4.11. *Flowchart highlighting a timing problem.*

SUMMARY VERSUS DETAIL

Since one of the primary goals of storyboarding is to communicate, it will be important not to overwhelm viewers with a complicated flowchart. If you are dealing with a complicated system, it may be useful to use a summary flowchart, showing the general areas involved. Each box on the summary flowchart may represent several pages of detail, which can be provided based upon need or interest (see Figure 4.12).

Another way to handle this issue is by dividing the flowchart into pages, with each page representing an identifiable part of the process. Again, you want to communicate, not confuse. A summary flowchart can act like the outline of a book.

The flowchart is one of the first tools you will want to use, because it helps to understand what is happening. Pains should be taken to assure that the customer—the recipient of the output—must be included on the flowchart, or you run the risk of missing the mark. In addition, the sources of inputs—whether inside or outside the organization—must be shown, because the assurance of those sources may be key to the improvement. This explains why many companies develop teams with their suppliers to improve product quality. The flowchart can also lead to the use of other tools, such as the five whys.

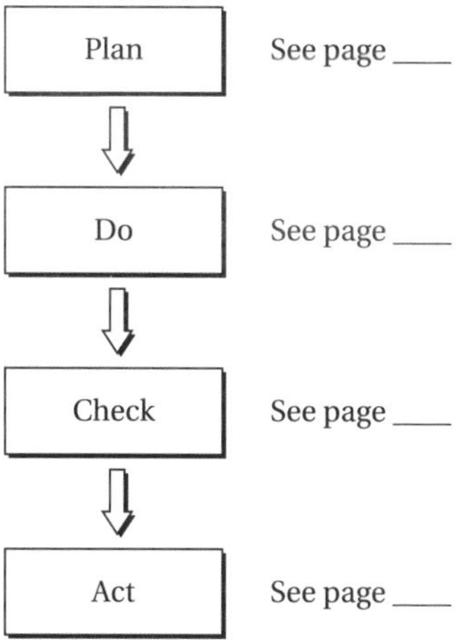

FIGURE 4.12. *Summary flowchart.*

FIVE WHYS

Although not a part of the baseball diamond, the five whys can be useful from start to finish. In fact, the five whys should be asked before you begin any major activity.

The five whys, like the flowchart, cloud, or storyboard itself, can be used for a variety of purposes. Asking why just once can be maddening, because people frequently do things without necessarily questioning them. When you look at a process, you must be aware that you may be looking at a way of doing things that has been built up over time. Ad hoc or temporary remedies to so-called glitches have been installed, and frequently not documented. In some cases, the system or process may never have worked in the first place, but continues to be used because it is too much trouble to correct.

When thinking about the practical application of the five whys, you could hardly pick a better place than the flowchart. Why? Because it contains all the key elements of the process you are considering. If you have done a good job with your flowchart and your mighty clouds, you should have a good idea of where to start asking why. In the clouds, of course.

The purpose of asking why five consecutive times is to get at the root cause of a problem area. It may very well lead you to a tree pattern, with your result at the top and many reasons at the bottom. That's not all bad. Each one of the answers may contain part or all of your solutions. When you have completed the five whys, and have found some possible contributing causes, you may need to gather some data to determine which of these causes has the greatest bearing on the situation.

PARETO CHART

This brings you to the Pareto chart, and its raw material, the check sheet. To solve a problem takes time; time which can be ill afforded, because you are already busy. Taking the time to collect data will only make the situation worse. What should you do?

The check sheet is a simple listing of items you want to count. It is designed for ease of use, and enables you to accumulate a lot of good data without expending a lot of extra time and energy. Since you may be depending on somebody else to get your data, you want to make the check sheet as easy as possible for them.

In order to collect data, then, all you need to do is put a check (✓) or a hash mark (I) for each occurrence. Painless. The users don't even have to total the checkmarks. You can do it for them. If, on the other hand, you have done a good job of communicating, through your storyboard, of why you need these data, check sheet users may want to do even more.

So, you're looking at telephone calls and hope to find out which department is getting the most calls (see Figure 4.13). There is not necessarily a pattern to this, but you need to find out. Say, for example, that your organization is improving its telephone system, and the goal is to improve customer service. Resources, however, are limited. Then, you might be highly motivated to work on the area that handles the most customer calls first. Data, collected over a four-week period, show the distribution of incoming calls illustrated in Figure 4.14.

In order to determine if this distribution shows the Pareto effect, or the 80/20 rule, the data must be arranged in decreasing order (see Figure 4.15). This Pareto chart is drawn lying down, making it easy to read the

Department	Number of calls
Generator department	
Motor department	
Purchasing	
Accounting	
Front office	

FIGURE 4.13. *Check sheet for incoming calls.*

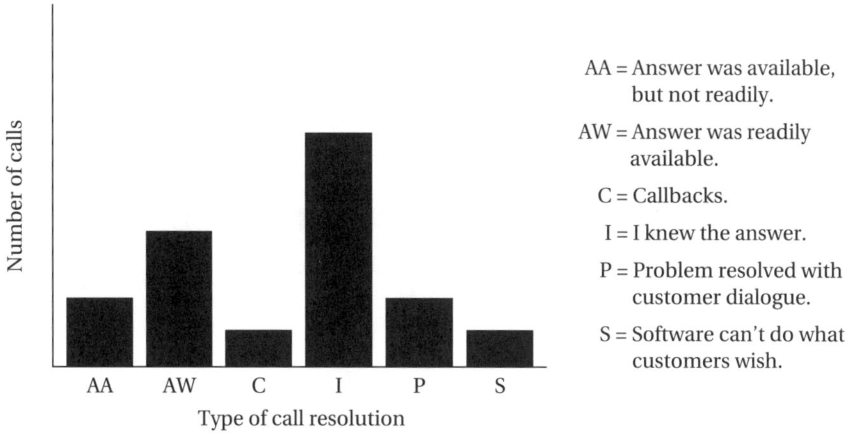

FIGURE 4.14. *Incoming call data.*
Source: PQ Systems/Barbara A. Cleary, Ph.D.

The team considered the status of both complete and incomplete calls to technical support analysts.

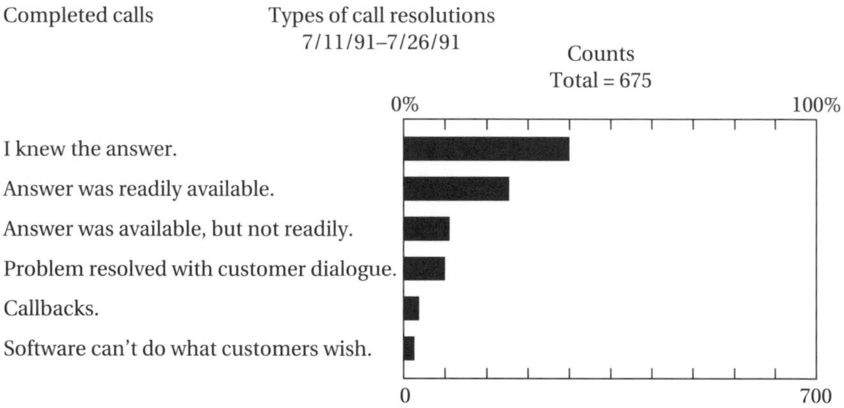

FIGURE 4.15. *Rearranged data.*
Source: Barbara A. Cleary, "Company Cares About Customers' Calls." *Quality Progress* 26, no. 11 (November 1993), 73.

categories. While this may be called a Pareto chart, the one in Figure 4.16 is complete, since it shows the cumulative percentage of complete call resolutions. It can be seen from the Pareto chart that, although the effect is not as dramatic as 80/20, there is still a benefit to working on the first few areas.

Note: While you're doing all this analysis, you continue to track the performance of your key indicator using the run chart. The hope is that

The team considered the status of both complete and incomplete calls to technical support analysts.

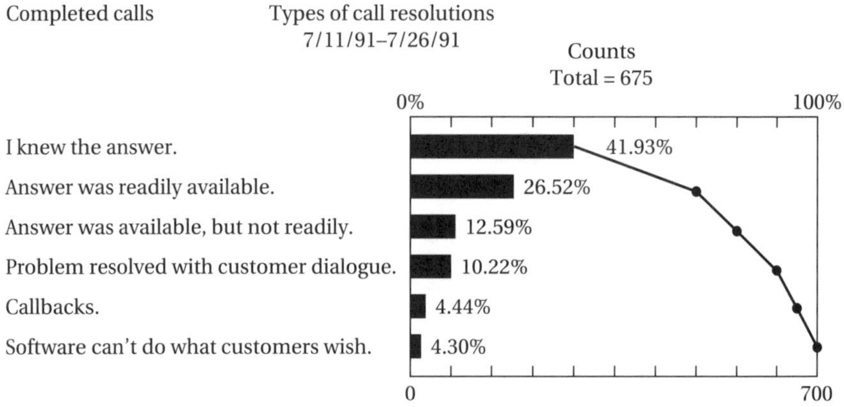

FIGURE 4.16. *Pareto chart.*
Source: Barbara A. Cleary, "Company Cares About Customers' Calls." *Quality Progress* 26, no. 11 (November 1993), 73.

by the time you have developed a good understanding of the situation, you will have sufficient data to establish a baseline for later comparison.

Having applied the five whys to your flowchart boxes is one handy technique. But the five whys have one more application that is even more useful; the cause-and-effect diagram, which is also known as the fishbone diagram or the Ishikawa diagram (after its inventor).

CAUSE-AND-EFFECT DIAGRAM

The fishbone diagram is a visual method for identifying and displaying causes contributing to variation or nonconformance. For purposes of communication, it is useful to use the conventional form. For purposes of this workshop, it is wide open; do anything you want, if it helps.

Look at the example in Figure 4.17. If it seems busy to you, it isn't. Actually, it is about average.

The cause-and-effect diagram can be a creative tool, if you add items you think might be causing a problem. You can always come back later and prove you were wrong. The diagram can be a very messy tool, usually resulting in either a piece of paper with very small scribbles all over it, or an easel pad, also with very small scribbles. What is important is the way it can be used to generate ideas and focus thinking.

The bones of the fish that are commonly used are people, machines, materials, and methods. In addition, information seems to deserve a special place. You could do a fishbone diagram that is organized by work

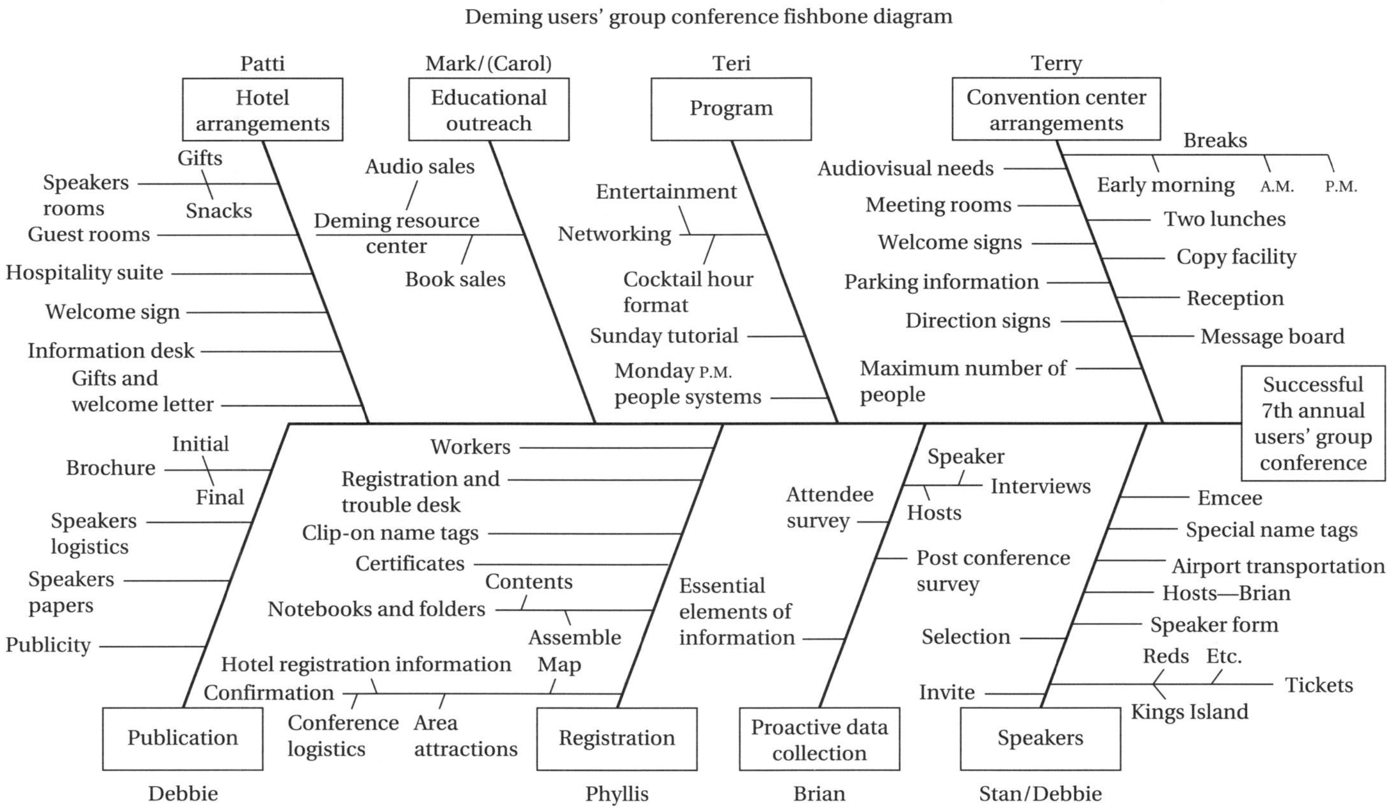

FIGURE 4.17. *Cause-and-effect diagram.*
Used with permission of Ohio Productivity and Quality Council.

group or technical problem sources. There are no limits, except your own, in constructing a diagram.

OTHER QUALITY TOOLS

You are well on your way to solving any problem, and have the potential to hit a home run, if you have done the following:

- Tracked your key indicator using a run chart
- Documented your process using the flowchart
- Identified problems with clouds
- Examined the frequency of various clouds using a check sheet
- Formed those data into a Pareto chart
- Used your cause-and-effect diagram to identify root causes

Rather than digress further into quality tools, I will move on with constructing the storyboard. The tool pages have been provided so that each tool can be understood and referenced as needed.

A NOTE ABOUT THE GRAPHIC EXPLOSION

Software for the personal computer that provides graphic expression for numbers has expanded and improved over the last several years. My personal favorite is Borland's Quattro, from which many of the graphs and charts in this book were originally prepared. Lotus and Microsoft products also have graphic capability. Programs like Harvard Graphics, specializing in graphic presentation only, can also be obtained. Multicolored and multidimensional graphs made possible with this software could enhance any presentation.

Juran, Ja-Dal, IBM, and others now have software specifically made for storyboarding. Recently, multimedia software has become available. Here you can combine sound and color to produce your own animated program. This may very well serve to eventually improve communications, but it takes some time to learn.

One difficult lesson to learn is that you must confine your graphic representation to one idea at a time. The availability of complicated graphic software does not change that fact. You want to be creative and tell a story, not confuse people.

This provides another opportunity to contrast creative thinking with linear thinking. You would like to present each storyboard frame or panel in an interesting way, which requires creativity. At the same time, you want to tell the story in order of occurrence, which requires linear thinking. You need both to do a good job at storytelling. A well-organized, boring story is no better than a highly creative, confused one.

Appendix C contains the tool pages. This is an attempt to list each quality tool, provide the best possible template for its use, and describe the steps in its use.

SUMMARY

Any tool is fair game, provided that it is a means to an end. You can invent a tool. You can combine tools to make a new tool. You can use all of them, if necessary.

It is important to use the tools in a logical progression, with one idea leading to the other, to tell an interesting story. Quality tools serve to define, describe, and amplify ideas presented in your story. But without a story, the tool has no place to be.

Now that you have considered the use of tools, the use of teams, and problem-solving designs, you are ready to continue with your storyboard. On to chapter 5!

Chapter Five

IDENTIFY THE PROBLEM. FIND THE REASON FOR IMPROVEMENT.

Before you begin to deal with the process of improvement, review where you are in your storyboard. Recall that you have provided a cover sheet that identifies the topic, team name (if there is one), and mascot (again, your choice). You have also identified the team members, leaders, or special functions, and people who assisted in other ways. You may also have developed a tentative timetable. In other words, you have covered the "once upon a time" part of the story.

> *Once upon a time (when?), in a land very far away (where?), there was (who?)*

Now, you've come to the reason for improvement.

> *And they had a (problem, opportunity, or issue?), and were very sad, because (why?)*

Does this story sound familiar? It should. This structure has existed for centuries. And it really works. It is just not used to its fullest extent these days.

Why do people want things to change? Probably because something became more of a hassle than it was worth, or because some external threat made it necessary. Humans are creatures of habit. In business, and in person, people frequently do the same thing over and over again, simply because it worked in the past. One of the recent rediscoveries in the world of quality is that angry customers don't always complain; they just go away. In the same way, you can never be assured that your behaviors work for you. All you really know is that nobody is complaining (to you). More companies and individuals are now asking their customers, "How am I doing?" The answers can be frightening.

The fact is that something must be seriously amiss, or there must be a lot to gain, for organizations to get off the dime and do something about it. This is especially true if it means that companies must form teams, which may consist of people who normally don't work together.

What kinds of issues typically raise heads? Here are the big archetypal reasons for improvement.

- Improve customer service.
- Increase value of a product or service.
- Shorten cycle time.
- Reduce variation in the product.
- Reduce variation in a process.
- Simplify a process.
- Reduce or eliminate waste.
- Improve health and safety.
- Decrease environmental impact.
- Recapture lost customers.

In the process of accomplishing these activities, there are two concepts that deserve special attention: the aha experience and low-hanging fruit.

THE AHA EXPERIENCE

Recall from Figure 3.5 that the first step in the process of change is denial. Precisely, it is the overcoming of denial that is the activity of this stage. In many situations, however, people are more the victim of the lack of awareness than the perpetrator of deliberate denial.

Frequently, when teams are formed, or even when meetings are held to discuss issues informally, comments such as the following are made.

- "I didn't know that was a problem."
- "You do *what???*"
- "We have a procedure for handling that situation. You mean nobody is *using* it?"

As the months and years roll by, procedures are often changed or modified without documentation. Without constant focus and attention, a process or system may wind up performing quite routinely, but not accomplishing any purpose at all. Although this is well known to occur in large organizations—the federal government is usually an easy shot—small organizations and groups are by no means exempt.

During the first meeting on a subject, many of these ad hoc changes come to the surface. It is frequently desirable to return to established procedures and stabilize the process right away, thus creating a reliable baseline for performance. It may be the case that the problem has already been solved, and has simply suffered because of lack of documentation, turnover, vacations, or general lack of attention due to other more pressing issues.

Returning the process to its intended design is simple problem solving, but it can be extremely worthwhile. Only you can be the judge of the value of these activities. The need to correct variations must be balanced against the size of the change you are making. If you are going to totally revise a process, then you are probably wasting your time making small corrections. Otherwise, go ahead and make your corrections. It gives the team a feeling of enthusiasm and accomplishment at very little cost.

LOW-HANGING FRUIT

Low-hanging fruit is the term describing easy improvements—solutions waiting to be implemented. Whether this fruit is discovered during your prioritization of issues, or whether it is discovered early in a project, it is still worthwhile to pick.

> *In my backyard, I have three orange trees. Some of the oranges are very high, and must be reached with a pole-mounted clipper. Others are low hanging. When I cut the grass, I take a break under the orange tree, and enjoy one of the oranges. This provides a pleasant break in the otherwise strenuous pace of the day.*

The moral of this little story is that it is not always a good strategy to get all the low-hanging fruit first.

In an organization, low-hanging fruit is like a gift. Enjoy it. Not every problem needs to be strenuous. You will need your energy to tackle the more difficult problems involving multiple departments, groups, or constituencies.

A recognizable breakthrough occurs in an organization once enough individuals have enough confidence to tackle problems that cross departmental lines. It is like reaching a new level of maturity. It is the time at which workers graduate from low-hanging fruit, and invent the teams to go for the high branches. Since most business processes cross organizational boundaries, it is important to get past the low-hanging fruit stage, but not to forget its benefits.

REASON FOR IMPROVEMENT

In this page of your storyboard or storybook, you should explain, in words, numbers, and pictures, the reason why you are looking into this area. As has been mentioned, you want to focus on the pain, the hassle, and the cost; in essence, the thing that is the big symptom. At the same time, it is useful to state the need for improvement and its associated measurement in positive terms. For instance, instead of saying that 2 percent of your repairs are failures, state that there is a 98 percent success rate in repairing equipment. You are then free to establish a target for improvement without sounding critical.

WORDS

Keep it simple for two reasons: (1) You want others to understand; and (2) The act of simplification helps you to clarify your thoughts. For instance, the problem could be stated as follows:

> *Available problem-solving technologies have not been fully integrated, disseminated, and applied, resulting in underutilization of this resource and loss of potential benefits to all people.*

NUMBERS

You want to numerically describe the reason for improvement in order to assure that it is valid. For instance, if I say that one reason for writing this book is that there are no others on the subject, then I should be able to come up with some numerical tally to justify my statement. Here's mine.

Total number of quality-related books	750
Total number of storyboarding books	1

These numbers represent a quick spot check, rather than a comprehensive survey.

Among the three major U.S. publishers of quality-related books there were approximately 750 titles when this process began. There was one book among all three publishers specifically related to storyboarding.

PICTURES

To reinforce a point already made, not enough pictures are used. The recent rise in audio and video training is an improvement. Yet in day-to-day communications, you can really help your stories with pictures.

How can I typify my numerical data in a picture? Figure 5.1 shows one idea. How many other pictures can you imagine?

Now, I'll put together my reason for improvement page.

1. There is only one book on the subject of storyboards that is available to the public.

FIGURE 5.1. *Picture of reason for improvement.*
Note: Actually, this would have to take up three pages to be accurate, but you get the idea.

2. Much of the technology regularly taught in major companies is not available to the general public.
3. This is a good place to check with an organization's goal or value statements.

Many organizations have a form or checklist for determining the acceptability of a potential project. If your organization has one, this is the place for it. If not, develop your own from the tool page example.

Here is where I checked my justification. ASQC Quality Press' mission statement is as follows:

To promote the implementation and advancement of quality thinking and practices using the highest standards of excellence to publish and distribute information to our customers.

Harry Forsha's mission statement is as follows:

To inspire individuals and organizations to the continuous pursuit of excellence.

Does this project agree with both mission statements? Yes!

Here are some sample reasons for improvement from other organizations.

- **Health care**—The issue of payment for medical services is always a sensitive issue, but particularly so when a family is in stress. In order to minimize negative impacts on patients and families, The Hospice of the Florida Suncoast adopted a policy of paying for consulting physician services when the bill was received, then filing for reimbursement with the Medicare/Medicaid intermediaries after receiving required documentation from the providers. This policy was successful in improving the image of Hospice with both patients and physicians. On the other hand, this policy created a $187,000/year problem.
- **Industry**—Equipment has failed to meet customer expectations and has been returned to the shop for rework.
- **Government**—Although several governmental agencies admitted to the productive use of storyboards, none were able to provide copy for publication purposes.
- **Education**—Quality conferencing at the middle school is vital for better educational opportunities for all students. By reviewing the current data for Blueprint 2000, it is obvious that the need for an effective means of conferencing be implemented.

GETTING STARTED

If there is one key phrase in the world of quality improvement, it is *do something.* The initiation of any activity occurs when you finally decide that something must be done, and you make a personal commitment to be the agent of change.

It is at this point that the problem-solving work of the storyboard begins. Of course, it is important to define exactly what it is that you wish to change. The early steps of the storyboard describe your effort to understand the process with which you are working, and to mobilize to create change. Those three steps are (1) Reason for improvement/problem identification; (2) Data gathering/current situation; and (3) Analysis.

REASON FOR IMPROVEMENT/ PROBLEM IDENTIFICATION

This is your first opportunity to use the three types of thinking paradigm. Perhaps you have had the experience of entering into a problem solution, only to find that you solved the wrong problem, or that you addressed the symptom and not the disease. The problem statement is your protection from recreating this type of tragedy. But you need to do some investigation before you can adequately define the problem.

There are two concepts that are particularly useful here. The first is stating the reason for improvement as broadly as possible. This way, at a later point in time, you can narrow the ideas down. If you are only looking at a part of the picture, you run the risk of missing the real point.

The second concept is one I borrowed from my background in experimental psychology—the concept of operational definition. An operational definition can express an abstract idea in terms of the physical realities. For example, anxiety is defined as a 10,000-pound steel ball hanging by a thread directly over my head.

In other words, you can define a problem by using its physical realities. Another term for this is *managing by fact.* Starting with a provisional problem statement, which should be very broad, you can progress by using three types of thought (see Figure 5.2).

CREATIVE THINKING—BRAINSTORMING AND VISUALIZATION

First, you should brainstorm the problem statement, looking at it from every possible angle, and thinking of all the related ideas. The results may suggest that

- You may not have looked at the whole problem. (Your focus is too narrow.)

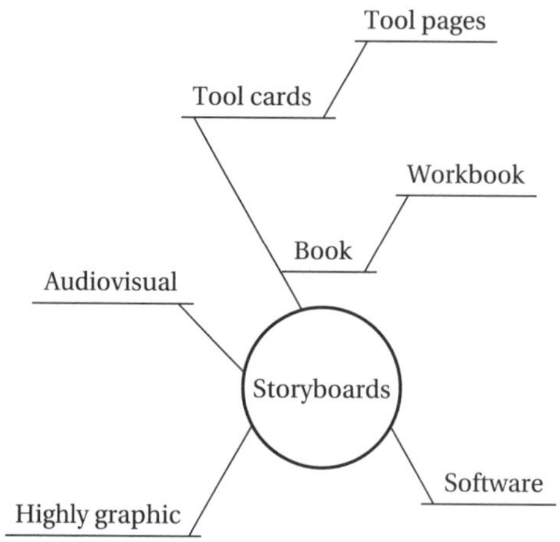

FIGURE 5.2. *Simplified results of brainstorming exercise.*

- You don't have enough data. (Usually you don't, at first.)
- You are not even looking at a problem. (It's all in your attitude.)

You may also wish to visualize the ideal situation relating to your issue. In other words, what would it be like in a perfect world? This may generate another list of ideas.

Remember that you are not looking for the first good idea. You are looking for as many good ideas as you can find, and hopefully for a few great ideas. It is possible that your first idea in a brainstorming session will be your best idea, but collect a few more—the best idea may be just around the corner.

In working with teams of all types, I find that there is a strong tendency to gravitate toward the first idea that seems practical and to stick with it. This happens particularly when there is time pressure. Acting on the first good idea that comes along should definitely be avoided. Always look for at least the second good idea, and preferably the third, fourth, and fifth.

CRITICAL THINKING

Later, in chapter 7, you will take the ideas generated in the creative phase and apply your analytical brain to them. Then you will rip them apart, look at the practicality of the ideas, and consider the options. As you can see, this is a very different kind of thinking, and would have stifled the creative process if you had tried to think critically at the same time.

REFLECTIVE THINKING

Another of my favorite concepts is sleeping on it. In storyboarding that means more than just thinking it over. It means putting the ideas up on the wall where everybody—or at least everybody in your group—sees the thinking and has the opportunity to contribute. This accomplishes several things.

- It announces to all onlookers that this is an issue deserving of at least your personal attention
- It acknowledges all persons who may have interest in the issue.
- By your presentation, it may acknowledge onlookers as valuable people, who may have ideas to contribute.
- It provides you with the opportunity to avoid your personal blind spot, by looking at things from someone else's point of view.

It is a physical fact that there is a blind spot in each eye, where the optic nerve enters the retina. Since most people have two eyes looking at most objects, one eye takes over when the other is in its blind spot.

Psychologically, however, most people are not so fortunate. Everyone develops a world view, which I am more convinced is structured by our early childhood experiences. Since human beings hang ideas upon this tree of consciousness, it is easy for them to dismiss things that do not conveniently fall on a major branch. The risk here is that you will miss something that may be completely obvious to one of your associates. That's quite a risk to take, especially if it is not necessary. Here is one of the powers of the storyboard: You can provide yourself with a nonjudgmental opportunity to collect ideas and put them to use. At this point in the process, you need not be particularly intense; you are still only asking the following questions.

- What is the problem?
- Why is it worth solving?
- Have I adequately defined the scope of the problem?
- Who suffers? What's the point?
- Who is the customer?

How do you know when the creative phase is over? When the ideas dry up or start repeating themselves.

At this point, I would like to raise an issue that I have mentioned, but not emphasized. Among all the other things a storyboard may be, it is a working document. It is constantly in revision until it is finished. After that, it is debatable whether any effort should be expended on spit and polish. There are two key reasons for putting time on a storyboard after the issue is resolved: (1) To train others in the use of the storyboard itself; and (2) To better communicate your process and results to others. If the spit and polish contribute materially to the learning process, fine. Otherwise, cut loose and move on.

Applying that idea to your first problem-solving block, reason for improvement, you should be aware that you have just begun the creative-critical-reflective loop, which will include the next two steps in the storyboard. Unless you have complete understanding of the issue at the start of the project (in which case, you wouldn't need a storyboard), you must come back and gather good data to assure that you truly understand the issue, and you must come up with a clear problem statement that is deserving of your time and effort.

DATA GATHERING

Although most of the data gathering is done later in the process, your improvement project should be linked to at least one key operating indicator. Some organizations call them key results areas, others operating statistics. If, for instance, customer satisfaction is the issue, then you must know where you are now in order to have a basis for comparison later. If you have said the objective is to write a book on the subject, therefore doubling the available literature, then you have a numerical tool for measurement. You may argue that this indicator is rightly included in the current situation section, and you would have a point. Because of its unique place among all numerical indicators, I have chosen to put it right up front, all by itself.

You have now completed your reason for improvement section, as shown in Figure 5.3. You can now move forward.

NOTECARDS

If you used the notecard technique, your brainstorming would have been done on notecards. You could then organize the cards in many ways to consider the possibilities. Notecards are particularly useful during creative activities, because then ideas can be easily moved, mixed, reorganized, and combined.

During the critical thinking phase, you may eliminate those cards with the least merit, creating the strongest possible problem statement. You could also leave the notecards exactly where they are at the end of the session, or put them up where people outside the team can see them, depending on your need or desire to communicate outside the group. You could also choose to make some graphic or picture representation, in order to help others understand what the notecards are all about.

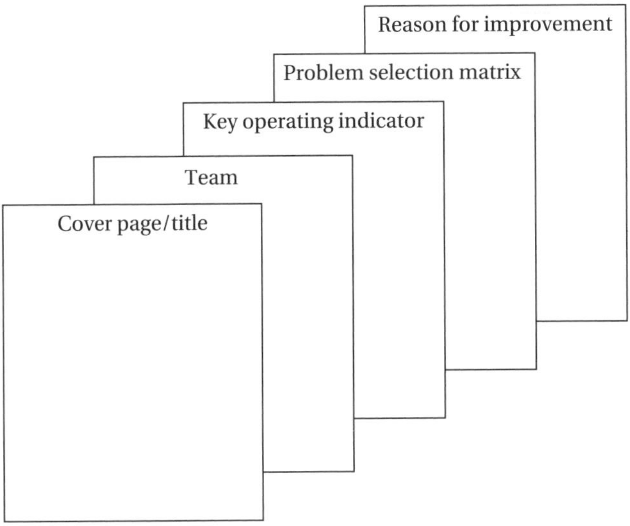

FIGURE 5.3. *Reason for improvement page.*

SUMMARY

Identification and selection of a problem are the first steps in storyboarding. It is essential that you select a project that merits the investment of your time and energy, and that will have value to your organization. The storyboards presented in the next section need little additional justification. This is typical, because many opportunities are commonly acknowledged.

Not all storyboards are perfect, nor are they all intended to be. Some storyboards are done on the fly and never really finished. The intent of the examples used in this and the following chapters is to show the variety of styles and applications. Notably absent are the notecard-style boards because of the difficulty of transporting them.

The reason for improvement panels from selected storyboards are shown in the next section. These are examples from actual case studies. In this chapter, and in each subsequent chapter, the case study storyboards will be expanded to illustrate a single problem-solving step.

REASON FOR IMPROVEMENT PANELS FROM THE CASE STUDY EXAMPLES

HEALTH CARE EXAMPLE: HOSPICE OF THE FLORIDA SUNCOAST

The Hospice of the Florida Suncoast

Synopsis of quality improvement project

The Hospice of the Florida Suncoast is a community-based, nonsectarian, not-for-profit organization dedicated to the care of terminally ill patients and their families. As the largest known hospice program of its type in the world, with an operating budget of $24 million, The Hospice of the Florida Suncoast has served Pinellas County, Florida for 15 years. The Hospice's mission is to provide care for all who need it, regardless of ability to pay. Resources for meeting the costs of care include: Medicare/Medicaid for eligible patients, insurance, personal funds, and charitable contributions.

Reason for improvement The issue of payment for medical services is always a sensitive issue, but particularly so when a family is in stress. In order to minimize negative impacts on patients and families, The Hospice of the Florida Suncoast adopted a policy of paying for consulting physician services when the bill was received, then filing for reimbursement with the Medicare/Medicaid intermediaries after receiving required documentation from the providers. This policy was successful in improving the image of Hospice with both patients and physicians. On the other hand, this policy created a $187,000/year problem.

Problem statement Substantial amounts of money are being written off because claims are not filed within specified billing periods, thus revenues paid for consulting physician services are not reimbursed by Medicare/Medicaid intermediaries. The result has been lost revenue and failure to meet customer expectations.

Planning breakthrough This problem was the focus of the first quality improvement team to be organized at The Hospice of the Florida Suncoast. The problem was selected as part of a training program in which ideas were brainstormed and themes prioritized. Although a group of highly motivated people were aware of this problem, they had never organized as a team to solve it. An interdepartmental team was formed, including members from accounting and finance, medical records, patient care, and quality management, in order to look at all aspects of the problem. Selecting members from multiple departments contributed to the discovery of root causes and effective solutions. Actions were implemented to reduce the backlog of outstanding medical records and to facilitate the timely submittal of claims. Write-offs were reduced and customer satisfaction enhanced.

A storyboard was developed as a training tool for the first quality improvement team. It provided a clear framework for communicating activities and results. This first project was not perfect, yet many valuable lessons were learned along the way. These lessons will be shared with other quality improvement teams and will provide the basis for the continual improvement of our care and services.

"Hospice is a special way of caring"

First quality improvement team

- First quality improvement team at hospice
- Five departments represented
- Developed as part of a TQM training program

Team members

Name	Position	Team function
T. Abrantes	Consulting physician specialist	Team member
M. Farrall	Accounts receivable coordinator	Team member
M. Pruitt	Nursing manager	Team member
G. Case	Patient/family care coordinator	Team member
D. Wise	Medical records	Team member
M. Manrique	Program director	Team member (Added at action plan stage)
V. Wilks	Comptroller	Team leader
B. Oldanie	Director of planning	Facilitator
H. Forsha	Business systems analyst	Consultant, trainer

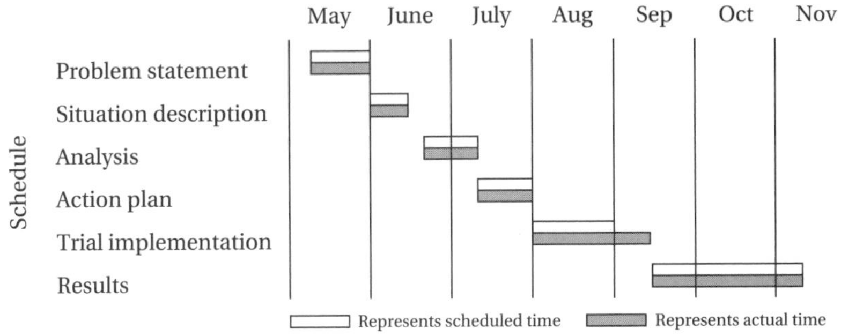

Theme selection process

Managers interviewed for improvement opportunities

⇩

List of ideas brainstormed

⇩

Ideas voted down to a list of three themes

⇩

Data evaluated on a theme selection matrix and selected #1 as our theme

⇩

	Theme name	Impact on customer	Can team solve?	Need for improvement	Score
Theme	1. Consulting physician services claims	4	4	5	13
	2. Delayed admissions	5	2	5	12
	3. Documentation system	3	3	5	11

Scale
Low 1 - 2 - 3 - 4 - 5 High

Theme and customers

From the theme selection matrix we could see that our theme would be

⇩

Low reimbursement rate
for
consulting physician services

Our customers were identified as

⇩

- Attending physicians
- Consulting physicians
- Patients/families
- Case managers
- Billing clerks
- Medicare and Medicaid intermediaries

INDUSTRIAL EXAMPLE: FLOLO CORPORATION SCANNING ROOM

Reason for improvement

Internal customers complain that documents were not available to retrieve as needed.

Indicator 1:	Number of complaints = several per week
Indicator 2:	Backlog in scanner input box
Indicator 3:	Catalogs not updated frequently

Team information

Aileen Cutrara
Alisa Flolo
Jeannine Flolo
Laura McPhee, team leader
Todd Niecikowski
Donna Titzer
Susan Wittke

EDUCATION EXAMPLE: PINELLAS COUNTY (FLORIDA) SCHOOLS

Quality conferencing for an entire grade level in "1" sitting

Conferencing for All

Presented by
Deborah Figg, Aleasha Dees,
and
John Leanes

Carwise Middle School
Pinellas County Schools
Palm Harbor, Florida

Quality conferencing for an entire grade level in "1" sitting . . . Conferencing for All

1993–1994 Team Nomination Criteria

I. Purpose, value, or reason for selecting the project

A. Explain how and why this project was chosen. What was the situation or opportunity?

Quality conferencing at the middle school is vital for better educational opportunities for all students. By reviewing the current data for Blueprint 2000, it is obvious that the need for an effective means of conferencing be implemented. We envision the caring attitude through a positive mode of assessment be done within a minimum time frame. This restructured effort for conferencing is being introduced and developed at our school as a model that we believe could be effective at the middle school level.

B. Describe the techniques used during the project selection process.

1. Deployment flowchart—to determine if customer expectations were aligned with Blueprint 2000 and SCANS report
2. Affinity diagram—to determine customer needs
3. Nominal group technique—to prioritize needs
4. Conferencing
5. Fishbone diagram—to identify two root causes
   a) Negative atmosphere
   b) Time constraints
6. Curriculum development—with outcome of Conferencing for All
7. State, county, and school standards
8. Customer input—for school mission statement (Blueprint 2000) and for benchmarking
9. Pilot programs—including evaluations, benchmark grades, surveys, and process decision program chart

C. Identify the stakeholders in this situation.

1. Students
2. Parents
3. Teachers
4. Administration
5. Volunteers

D. Explain how the project supports the organization's goals.

Conferencing for All is structured so that all sixth-grade students may conference with their parents at the same time and in the same room. Those students with special needs are mainstreamed so that they are included in this quality process.

II. Root cause analysis

A. Identify and explain the root causes of the project.

Parent and student feedback for Blueprint 2000 provided reasons to scrutinize the present conferencing system at the middle school level. Data of grades conclude the individual and group success through the process of whole group quality conferencing. Teachers used the cause-and-effect diagram to identify root causes. (See presentation handouts.)

B. Describe the analysis techniques used. How was the root cause determined?

The root cause was determined by the survey and fishbone diagram. (See presentation handouts.)

III. Data collection
   A. Explain the data-gathering techniques used.
      A deployment survey was used to gather data for Conferencing for All. (See presentation handouts.)

IV. Solution development
   A. Describe the solution/corrective actions considered for this project.
      Corrective actions considered for this project include a process decision program chart and surveys of all participants.
   B. Describe the criteria used to determine the best solutions (e.g., cost, time, and so on).
      1. Gantt charts
      2. Flowcharts
      3. Pilot project
      4. Evaluation of pilot program
   C. Discuss expertise used in reaching this solution. Who was consulted and why?
      To our knowledge, there is no other program of this kind being implemented. Thus, there was no expert advice for us to seek.
   D. Explain how the final solutions affect the root cause.
      The final solution, called Conferencing for All, affected the root cause, identified as the need for effective conferencing, in two ways.
      1. The number of conferences attended increased from 5 percent to 89 percent.
      2. Students displayed a positive attitude toward subjects, evaluation methods, and communication with parents and the school.
   E. State the benefits of the solution.
      One benefit of this concept of quality conferencing recognizes the needs of the whole child. It addresses the essential relationship between the student's affective needs and his or her academic success.

V. Outline of implementation plan, progress, and/or results
   A. Explain your process for getting agreement from stakeholders for implementation of these solutions.
      1. Approval of state and county board officials
      2. Actual count of participants
   B. Define the tracking techniques or follow-up activities that have been developed and/or installed to monitor results.
      1. Surveys
      2. Process decision program chart
      3. Percent of participants
   C. Explain how the results were, or will be, communicated to stakeholders.
      1. School newspaper
      2. Student advisory council
      3. Principal's letter
      4. Class letter
      5. Media coverage
      6. Volunteer training sessions
      7. Countywide training at staff development days
   D. Explain how the solutions have been incorporated into ongoing operations.
      1. Pilot program added three classes of reading students with three new teachers
      2. Training at school level for some teachers
      3. Training at district level for teachers countywide
      4. Training new volunteers in the quality process
      5. Continual development at our school of Conferencing for All

Quality in conferencing

At Carwise we believe:

- All children have value and worth.
- All children need to belong.
- All children need a loving, compassionate environment.
- Cultural diversity is enriching and vital to individuals and society.
- Children have unique backgrounds, talents, interests, and needs that deserve affirmation and support.
- All children can learn.
- Success breeds success.
- High expectations produce high achievement.
- Education is a shared responsibility of the school, home, student, and community.
- All children have the right to be treated equally and fairly.
- Everyone has the right to a healthy and safe physical and mental environment.

Conferencing for All

Carwise Middle School mission statement

The mission statement for JOSEPH L. CARWISE MIDDLE SCHOOL is for students, staff, parents, and community to ensure opportunities for success for ALL students in a caring environment that promotes self-motivation and lifelong learning.

Chapter Six

UNDERSTAND THE PROBLEM AND THE CURRENT SITUATION.

Since you looked at the reason for improvement, you have determined if you need a team to work on the issue. Then you looked at the issue creatively, from a variety of perspectives, to consider what it might be. If it was not already available, you have selected and begun to measure the key quality indicator that will best reflect the success of this project. This key indicator is probably also the link to your customers and to your personal and organizational goals. That's why you watch it.

Now, it's time to present the key facts. Does this seem a slow pace? Of course it does. One of my early storyboarding learnings is to avoid presenting too many ideas at a time. In the reason for improvement section, you looked at only a general area of interest. Now, you will be examining relevant facts.

Remember, you will be trying to communicate your activities to people who are unfamiliar with the breadth and depth of your research. Therefore, clarity is of the utmost importance.

The cloud pattern is a handy device for drawing attention to a particular point. As you present your information using charts, graphs, and visual images, you will want to draw attention to the focal point. You could also use a pointing finger, an arrow or other pointer, a circle, or an oval.

There are two key benefits of the cloud pattern. (1) It is a closed loop, leaving no doubt exactly what is being highlighted. (2) It has been used internationally, and therefore qualifies as common language. As always, I support common language unless I can come up with something better.

Since you are posting your storyboard panels as they are developed, the situation likely changes soon after it is posted. So, don't get hung up on how pretty it looks, but use the tools at your disposal to get the information out, to communicate your message, and to solicit feedback.

As you come to understand the current situation, you may choose to redefine the scope and definition of your work. The current situation should be explained graphically, numerically, and verbally in measurement terms that are pertinent to the improvement. Another way of saying this is that you want to use the same charts and graphs to state the problem, to monitor your activities, and to measure your results. This encourages solid, concise thinking up front, and hopefully avoids a lot of duplicate work.

For instance, the requirements of this text are as follows:

- Describe the science and art of storyboarding in practical, usable terms
- Be user-friendly; that is, easy to read
- Address any and all concerns raised during editorial and peer review
- Be completed within a specified time frame
- Be interesting to the reader
- Be viewed as a good value

In order for the text to be delightful, it

- Should be enriched with specific examples from health, education, industry, and government
- May include a pocketbook companion with key points
- May include a workbook companion with practical exercises
- May include audiovisual companions to facilitate learning
- May include an interactive video companion

The customer could be consulted about these points.

In order to do a thorough job of describing the current situation (remember the baseball diamond in Figure 4.1?), you must have the current status of your key quality indicator. This was started as a run chart, a flowchart of the process you are examining, a fishbone diagram of contributing causes, Pareto charts of key measurable factors you may have observed, and any procedures or documents that relate to the problem.

UNDERSTANDING THE SYSTEM

Peter Senge made crystal clear the importance of understanding the systems in which one is operating.[1] Although there is never complete understanding, you still need to look at least one step upstream, and one step downstream, from the locus of the problem, if you are to have any chance of understanding it. Here's an example.

An accounting department is experiencing transient delays in payment authorizations from the purchasing department. These authorizations are necessary if bills are to be paid on time.

When the system is reviewed, it turns out that there are other issues driving the process. The first is that supplier invoices arrive in a cyclic pattern, which affects the workload of the buyers who prepare the authorizations. Thus, one step downstream is the suppliers. The second issue is that the accounting manager bases his policy on a procedure for monitoring invoice vouchers only once a month, seeing only a glimpse of the complete picture. For invoices that must be paid in less than a month, or, in fact, for any invoice not in the payment process at month end, there is no assurance that it is paid on time. Thus, one step upstream is company policy.

Without those two pieces of information, the problem of prompt payment is unlikely to be resolved. When attacking a problem, one usually begins with only a superficial understanding of the system. Action based on this level of understanding frequently has the opposite effect of that which is desired, since superficial understanding is frequently not reflective of the active system.

NUMERICAL FACTS (STATISTICS)

It is hard to go far into an issue without seeing the effect of Deming. Yet there is a solid need to bridge the knowledge gap between practitioners of statistics and everybody else.

As noted, you know that incoming invoices arrive cyclicly. Yet, how many arrive? And when? What is the pattern that you are trying to change? What are its parameters? How will you measure the process so that you can be assured that it has improved? The answer is numerical facts.

If you start from simple numerical facts, and work your way up to more sophisticated formulas, you have a good chance of success without discouragement along the way. Take the example one step further.

You have counted incoming invoices for a month, and they range from 30 to 170 per day. They come in two waves: one just after the beginning of the month, when suppliers had their month-end billing rush; and one just after the 10th of the month, when many companies have special procedures revolving around the 10th. In between, the flow slacks off. The average number of invoices received daily is 70. If that were all the numbers you had to work with, you could use them. But if you kept an invoice count each day, you have enough numbers to develop a mean and standard deviation (or a median and a range, respectively). This is especially true if you continue counting for more than a month. Every month you get better data.

Instead of old-fashioned mechanical calculators, you can now purchase statistics software that will not only do the analysis for you, but plot it on a graph, which you can then drop into your word processor and publish with your report. You can have a colleague help you. Many companies have statisticians on staff. You can go to the local college for help. Believe it or not, you can also hand crank statistics nearly effortlessly using spreadsheet programs. Finally, if you don't have a monster pile of data, you can work it out with a pencil. It's not that bad, if you're only doing it every now and then. And, it's fun if you're using statistics to discover new information.

FISHBONE DIAGRAM

In this accounting department case, you are working with an issue that has two points of view. Thus, there is no need for a fishbone diagram. The facts are not in dispute. Also in this particular case, the issue has never been resolved.

PARETO CHART

Many times, important information is readily available, and it can be helpful in understanding the situation. Therefore, you could do a Pareto chart by the number of invoices handled in a day or by department. This may very well point to areas of interest. In this case, it was found that one department (out of five) accounted for more than half the outstanding invoices. It was also found that peak flow of invoices came in two specific weeks. These are two pieces of information you gained without really breaking a sweat.

PROCEDURES AND DOCUMENTS

You may find that there are no procedures written down; everything is informal. You may further find, if you haven't already found through your flowcharting, that everybody is doing something a little different, and that there are some special cases where what is normally done is not done, or it is done differently.

Documents have interesting bits of information, like the date when something was done and notes that were written during special handling. Frequently, the dates on documents can aid in identifying cart-before-the-horse situations, where transactions were performed out of sequence. Having been a former inventory control manager, I can speak from experience when I say that a transaction done out of sequence is at least as bad, if not worse, than a transaction not done at all. A cloud pattern is very useful for pointing out problems in procedures and other documents.

ANALYTICAL

In keeping with the concept of doing one thing at a time, avoid for the moment trying to analyze why this problem exists. You must focus on describing the situation as it actually is and from the broadest possible perspective. Analysis is the next step.

REVISED REASON FOR IMPROVEMENT

Based on the facts that you have discovered in this chapter, you may wish to clarify or redefine your reason for improvement. Remember, this is a working document. So change it if you need to. Figure 6.1 shows what you have accomplished in this section of your storyboard.

SUMMARY

In the current situation panels, you want to demonstrate visually, numerically, and verbally, what the current situation is in light of your

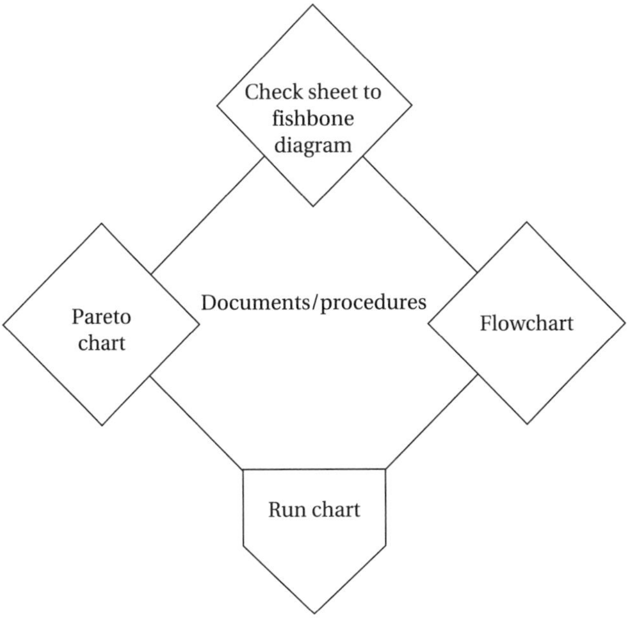

FIGURE 6.1. *Current situation.*

reason for improvement. In order to do this, you must have at least four panels.

1. The current status of your key quality indicator
2. A preliminary flowchart of the system that you are considering, as it actually is now
3. A checklist that shows the contributing factors
4. A Pareto chart that shows the relative occurrences of contributing factors

You will also have collected any documents or procedures that you might need. Armed with a solid understanding of the current situation, you are now ready to analyze it.

CURRENT SITUATION PANELS FROM THE CASE STUDY EXAMPLES

The examples provided here are not intended to be comprehensive. They are presented as they were actually done. In every case, it is important to do what is needed in the situation, rather than to mindlessly conform to a ritual—mine or anybody else's. One of the beauties of this process is that it is so robust; that is, forgiving. You can miss steps, rearrange steps, and in general abuse the concepts, yet still produce improvement because you did enough parts of the process. In order to achieve the best results, however, you should consider doing each step in order. Note that for the education example (Carwise Middle School), the current situation was not described at this storyboard location. Instead, the changes are shown in a results section. Remember that there is no right or wrong way to tell a story. Success is measured by impact on the reader. *Vive la différence!*

HEALTH CARE EXAMPLE: HOSPICE OF THE FLORIDA SUNCOAST

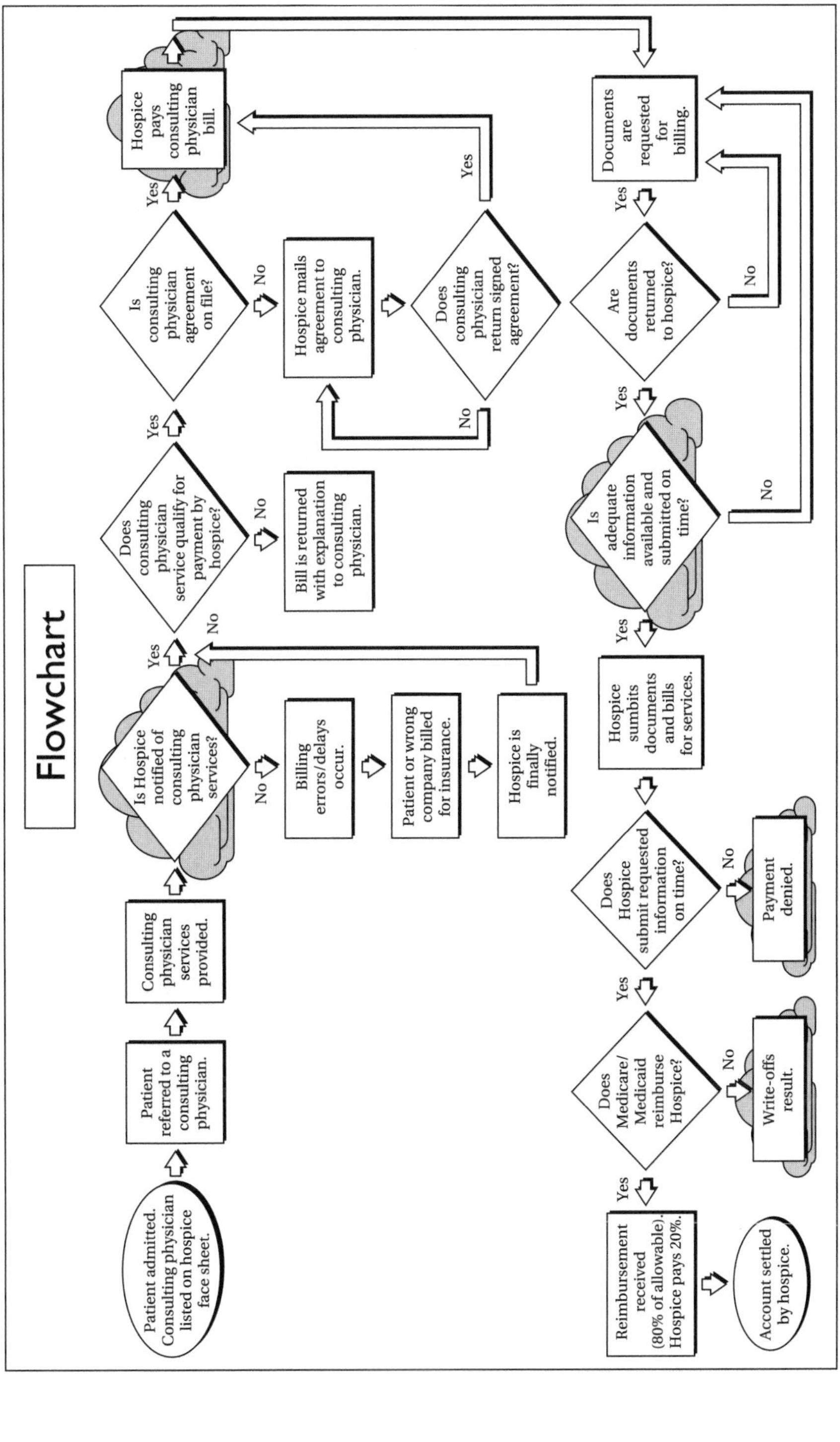

Pareto chart

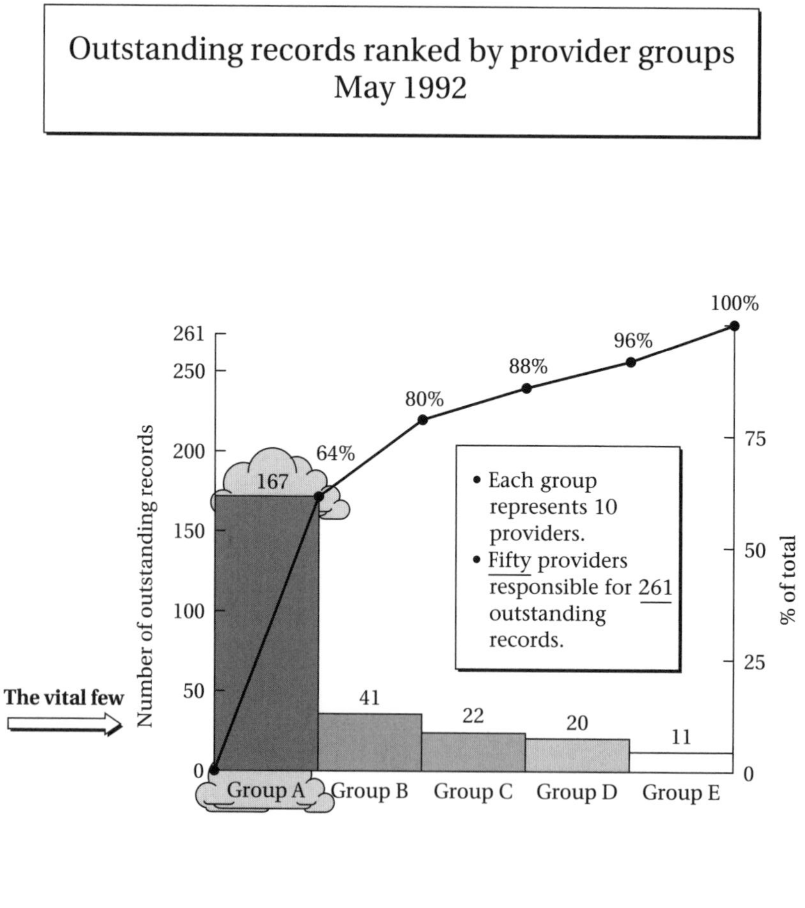

20% of the providers responsible for 64% of the outstanding records.

INDUSTRIAL EXAMPLE: FLOLO CORPORATION SCANNING ROOM

Note: We have enhanced this figure for ease of reading. Storyboards do not need to be "perfect" to be effective.

MANUFACTURING EXAMPLE: ELECTRIC MOTOR SERVICE

Equipment has failed to meet the customer's specifications and has been returned to the shop for rework.

⇩

Improvements over the past few years have *reduced* but *not eliminated* rework, as shown by the chart. The warranty file, which is maintained in the shop to provide for review and evaluation of returned work, was the first of many improvements. It is the database for this *team* project.

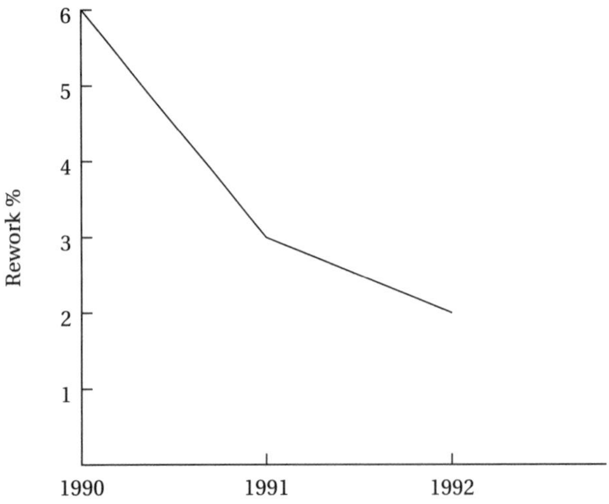

Note: This is a composite example, based upon more than one storyboard. Reason for improvement and current situation have been combined into one graphic.

Chapter Seven

ANALYZE THE PROBLEM.

The objective of this chapter is to come up with the root cause. This is the systemic factor that, if corrected, will result in the desired improvement on a continuous basis. If you have found the root cause, you should be able to construct a clear objective statement that identifies a specific thing to be corrected, shows how it is to be measured, and identifies and prioritizes countermeasures that should be considered.

It took this long to get to the objective statement, because it couldn't be said with certainty that a problem existed. All you had was anecdotal data: a few occurrences you happened to notice; some ideas; or perhaps a handful of complaints. You weren't sure if you were looking at the whole picture, and you hadn't even determined which system you were dealing with.

Since that time, you have formed a team (if needed), looked at the problem creatively and from many angles, conducted some preliminary measurement to determine if your perceptions were factual, and focused on key issues and indicators. Now, it's time for a reality check. Are you still working on something that will create a material improvement from the customer's perspective? Who, indeed, is the customer? When you are finished, will there be celebration, or will your work go unnoticed?

Pause for reflective thinking. You should have gotten some feedback by now on your first few storyboard panels. Do you need to add someone to your team who has a stake in the outcome? Is there new information that will refocus your efforts? Do you still have the support of key people in your organization? Do they see the potential benefits?

This is an area where Masaaki Imai is particularly eloquent.[1] There may be a tendency on the part of the problem-solving persons or teams to analyze the situation from their own perspective. That may be fine, provided that they are the ones who are actually doing the work in the area to be improved.

On the other hand, the members of the team may be supervisors or managers who do not actually perform the work relevant to the problem statement. In this case, they are on dangerous ground. One key lesson learned in the improvement process is that nobody knows the job better than the person who is doing it. So ask. In Japanese, the term used is *gemba*, which roughly translated means *the workforce*. The *gembutsu* are the workplace facts, which may be known only to the members of the workforce. It is essential that you deal with issues on this level in order to assure that data are looked at from a relevant point of view, that the concepts being considered are workable, and that you are looking at the right facts in the first place.

The analysis section is fertile ground for any quality tools that represent data in a way that will enlighten the viewer. You will expect to find cloud patterns demonstrating potential problems or opportunities to improve.

In its simplest form, analysis could consist of returning to the charts and graphs prepared in the current situation section, and inserting cloud diagrams where they apply. Although this may seem like oversimplification, not all problems are complicated. This simple method does serve to illuminate the difference between describing the situation and analyzing it.

At bare minimum, you should have the latest update of your key quality indicator; your analysis of the flowchart, possibly including a proposed revision; Pareto charts identifying the vital few items that are contributing the most to the problem; and fishbone diagrams, with clouds, showing possible root causes. You may go on from there to use any of the other quality tools that will aid in the analysis of the problem and lead to an objective statement.

Tools will be used in combination here. For instance, once a flowchart has been constructed, you could apply the five whys to each step, working from back to front. Once a Pareto chart has been constructed, it may be useful to further break down the vital few by doing a more in-depth Pareto analysis on those top few bars. You only need to ask one why to do that.

Experiment with graphic representations of your information. With the three-dimensional charts and graphs now available on popular software packages, you should be able to find a format that is really eye-catching. At the same time, be sure to select the chart that shows your point most clearly.

The result of this section should be a clear objective statement. You want to standardize something to a specified level, as measured by the key indicator. Be sure you are telling a story.

- **Reason for improvement**—Once upon a time, there was a (your customer's occupation or status) who was (sad, mad, *#@X%&&) because (your group or organization) was (or wasn't) doing (target issue).

- **Team information**—You formed a team to solve the problem. It included all the people you needed to be sure you got it solved for good.
- **Current situation**—You looked at what information you had, and found that . . . Realizing that the information you had was not enough, you identified your key quality indicator, flowcharted the system, identified key factors, and collected the documents and procedures related to the problem.
- **Analysis**—You analyzed the problem from all angles and found that . . . Then you revised your information gathering to assure that you were measuring . . . When you found that the data did (did not) support your initial perceptions, you considered the situation in depth, in order to identify the root cause. If you can eliminate that root cause, then the problem will be solved permanently.

You will notice that each of the following examples approaches analysis in a different way and at varying degrees. One point to keep in mind is the old saying, "You can't argue with success." If your storyboard doesn't work, the models and examples presented should help you to figure out what is missing.

Figure 7.1 summarizes the activities in this part of the story. Now you can say, "Well begun, half done."

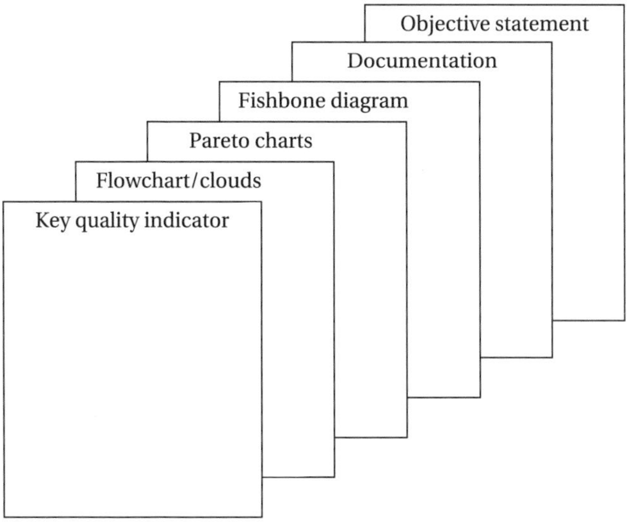

FIGURE 7.1. *Analysis.*

SUMMARY

The better you understand the problem, the better are your chances of solving it. The analysis section is the one that is most consistent among problem-solving models. Rarely is any other wording used. The ideal outcome of a solid problem analysis is a clear objective statement, coupled with a method of measurement. As you see from the examples, a general agreement on the sense of direction is a common outcome, and the specifics may come later. Since teamwork is a dynamic activity, there can and will be a certain fuzziness from one step to another. As long as the pace and action are appropriate to the need, nobody is going to complain because you didn't state one or another problem-solving step in a particular way. As you will see from the examples, this section is frequently the longest section in the storyboard.

ANALYZING THE PROBLEM PANELS FROM THE CASE STUDY EXAMPLES

HEALTH CARE EXAMPLE: HOSPICE OF THE FLORIDA SUNCOAST

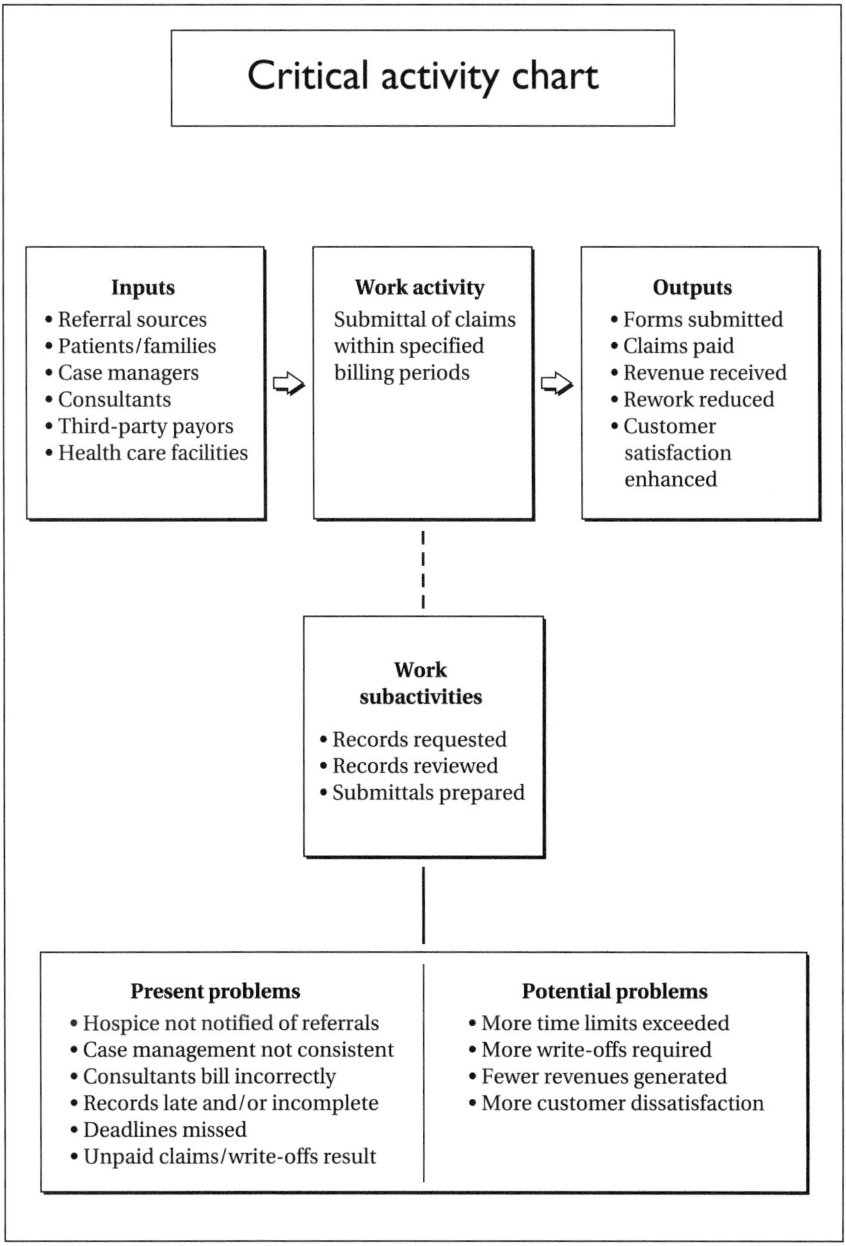

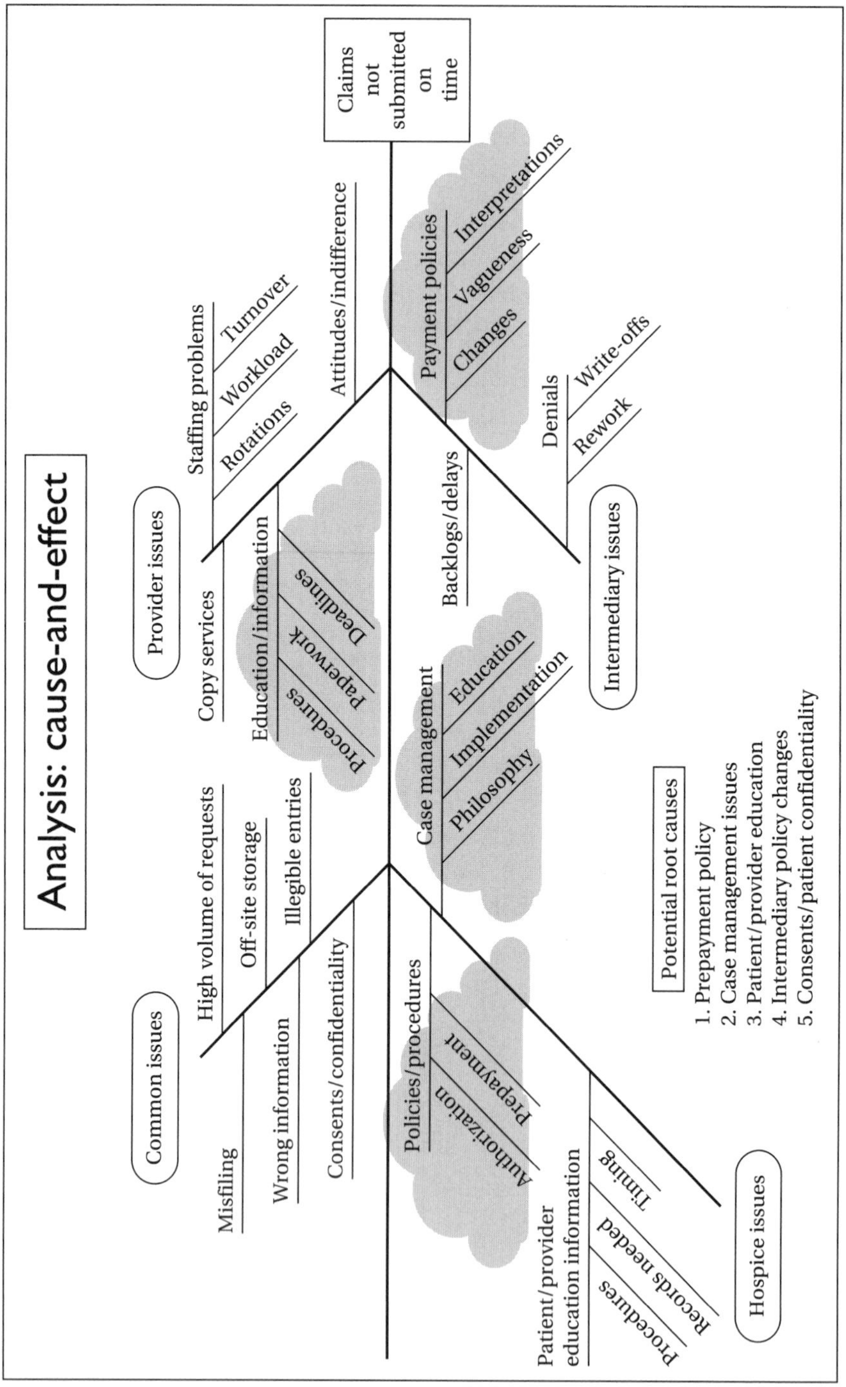

Analysis: cause-and-effect
Claims not submitted on time
Provider issues
Staffing problems
Rotations
Workload
Turnover
Attitudes/indifference
Copy services
Education/information
Procedures
Paperwork
Deadlines
Common issues
High volume of requests
Off-site storage
Illegible entries
Misfiling
Wrong information
Consents/confidentiality
Intermediary issues
Payment policies
Changes
Vagueness
Interpretations
Denials
Rework
Write-offs
Backlogs/delays
Case management
Education
Implementation
Philosophy
Hospice issues
Policies/procedures
Prepayment
Authorization
Patient/provider education information
Timing
Records needed
Procedures
Potential root causes
1. Prepayment policy
2. Case management issues
3. Patient/provider education
4. Intermediary policy changes
5. Consents/patient confidentiality

Problem

Medicare and medicaid claims for consulting physician services are not submitted to the intermediaries within the specified billing periods, resulting in lost revenue and failure to meet customer specifications.

↓

Reason for improvement

- Customers inconvenienced.
- Revenue lost.
- Rework required.

↓

Goals

- Decrease late and incomplete records.
- Increase revenues.
- Increase customer satisfaction.

INDUSTRIAL EXAMPLE: FLOLO CORPORATION SCANNING ROOM

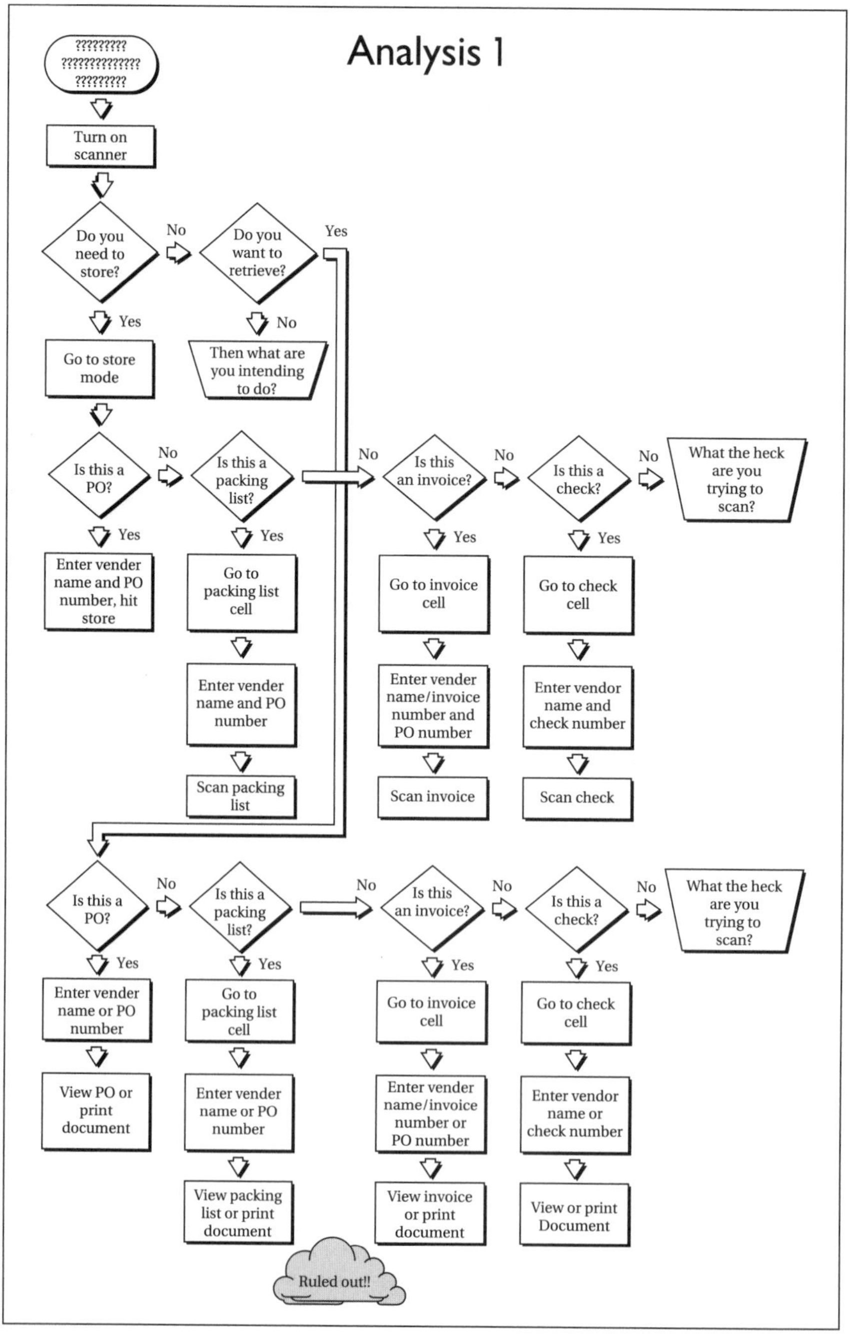

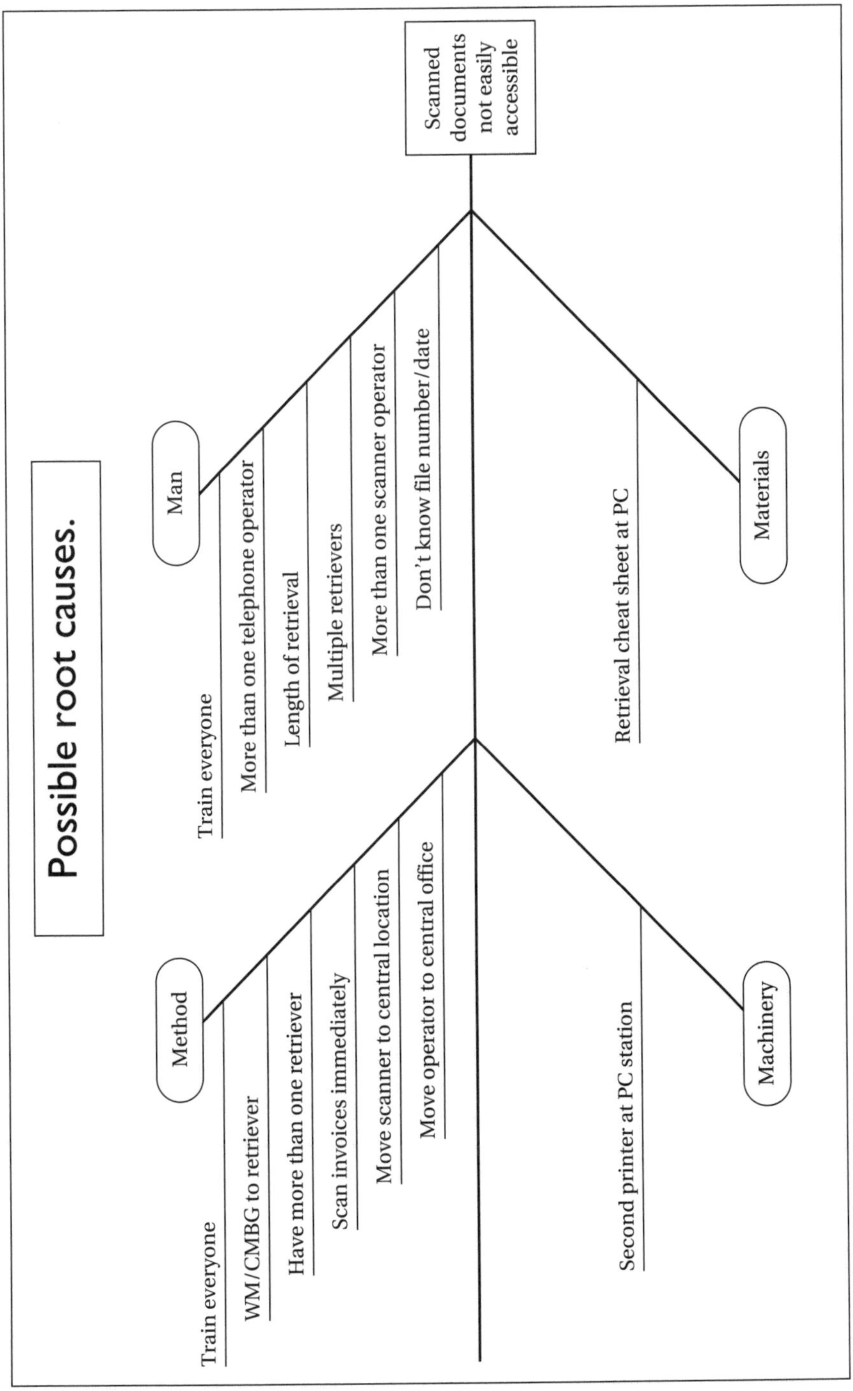
Possible root causes.
Scanned documents not easily accessible
Man
Train everyone
More than one telephone operator
Length of retrieval
Multiple retrievers
More than one scanner operator
Don't know file number/date
Method
Train everyone
WM/CMBG to retriever
Have more than one retriever
Scan invoices immediately
Move scanner to central location
Move operator to central office
Materials
Retrieval cheat sheet at PC
Machinery
Second printer at PC station

Prioritize possible root causes.

	Customer satisfaction	Employee benefits	Cost benefits	Efficiency	Total
Scan inventory immediately	8	9	5	10	32
Multiple retriever	10	10	4	10	34
Don't know file number/date	9	10	10	10	39
Second printer at PC	10	10	3	9	32
Cheat sheet at PC; ask for retriever's input on cheat sheet	10	10	10	10	40
Training	10	10	10	10	40

Document the process flow.

Process flow

Scanning ⇒ Document availability ⇒ Retrieval

Barriers to retrieval

- Documents not scanned in
- Catalogs not updated in a timely manner
- System not available
  - Someone else scanning
  - Someone else retrieving
  - Other

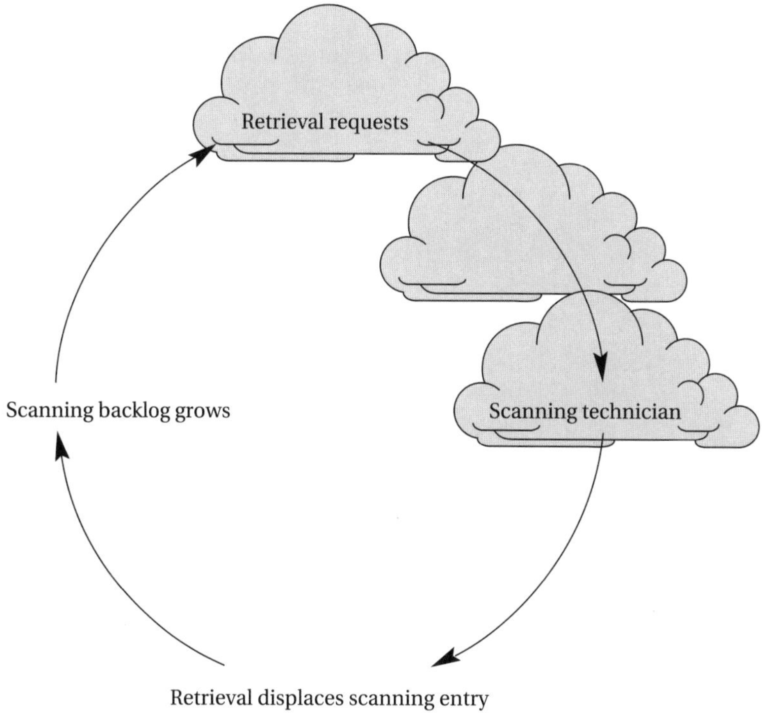

MANUFACTURING EXAMPLE: ELECTRIC MOTOR SERVICE

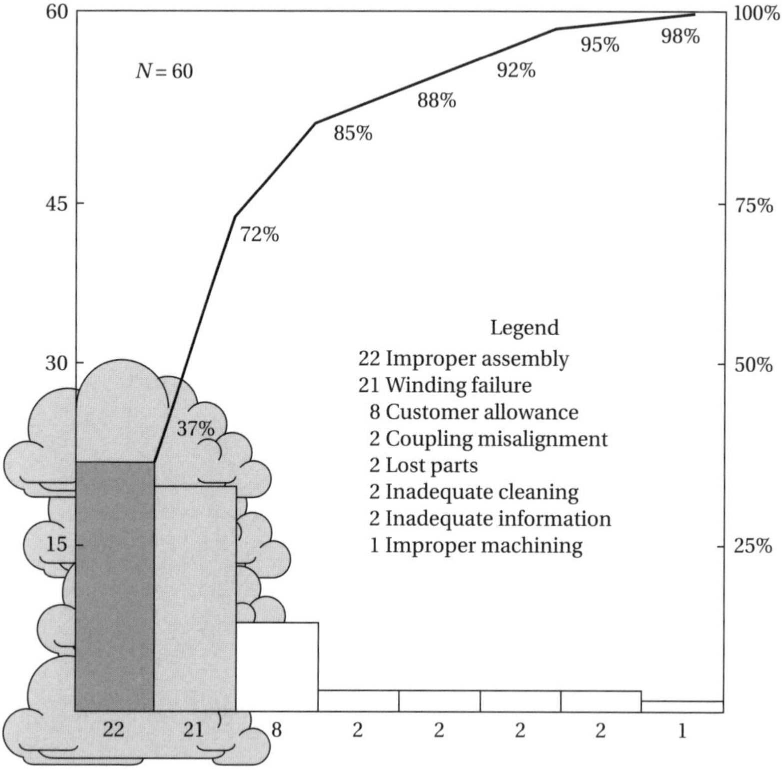

Of the cases of rework, 72% fell into two categories—improper assembly and winding failure. For further description of categories, see figure on next page.

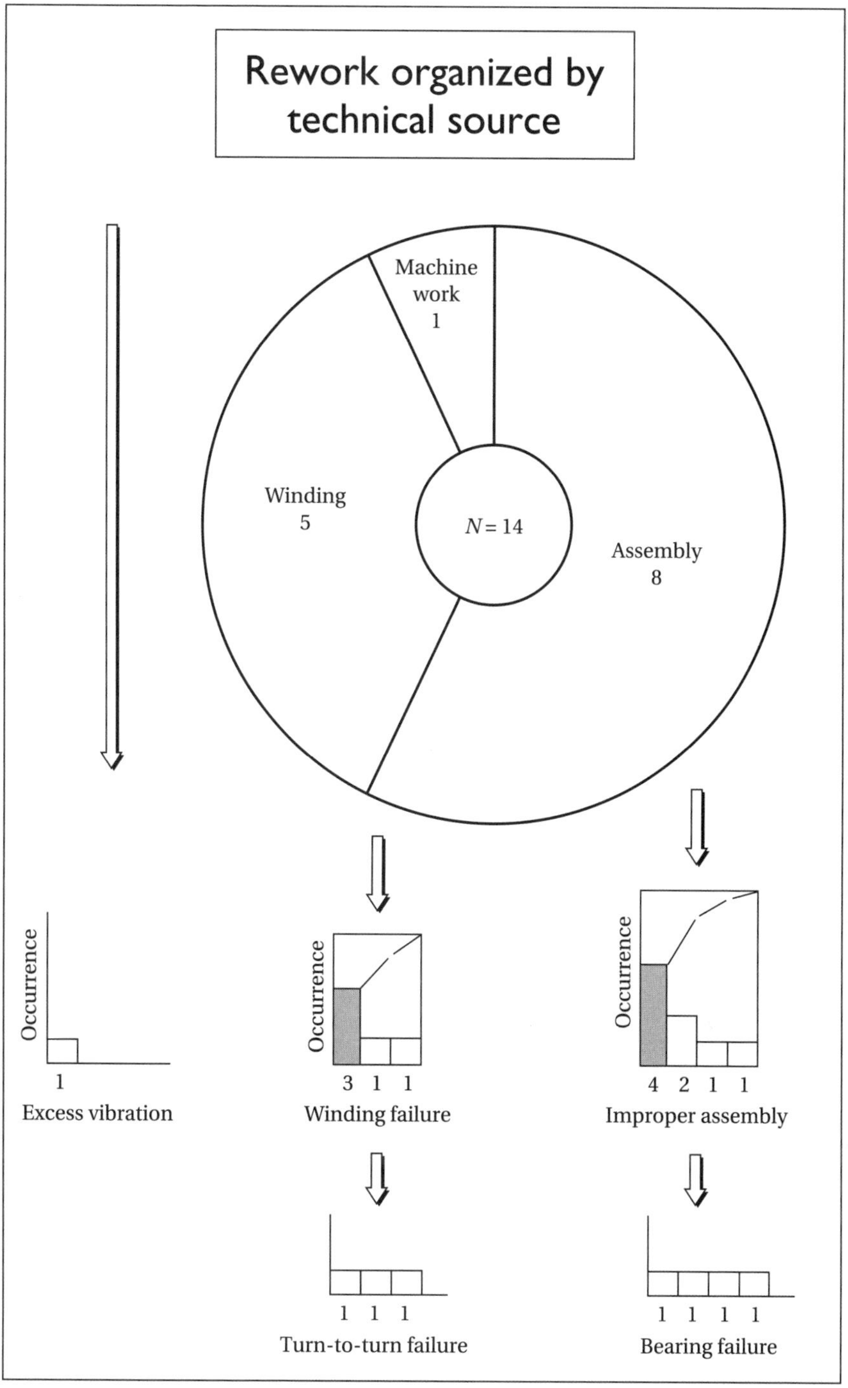
Rework organized by technical source
Machine work 1
Winding 5
N = 14
Assembly 8
Occurrence
1
Excess vibration
Occurrence
3 1 1
Winding failure
Occurrence
4 2 1 1
Improper assembly
1 1 1
Turn-to-turn failure
1 1 1 1
Bearing failure

Of the 14 cases of rework, 11 were within our control.

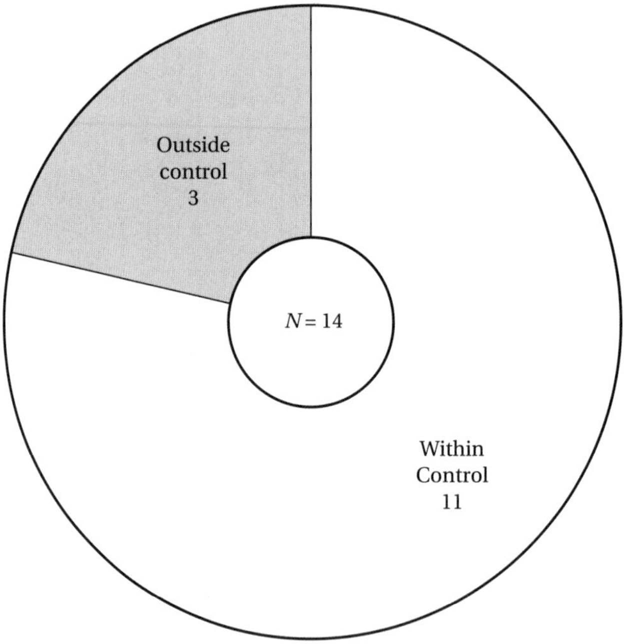

Potential causes of error

The remaining six action items were again examined to determine the actual reason for the failures, in light of the fact that they were

- Within our control
- Preventable or testable
- Not due to a particular repetitive cause
- Not due to a particular person or process

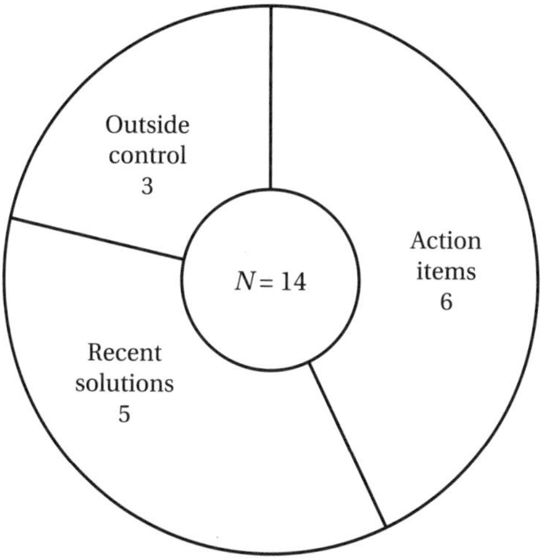

Potential causes of error

	Lack of training	Lack of standard	Wrong equipment	Human error
Improper dip preparation	------------	Not motor shop	------------	------------
Winding stress	No	No	No	No
Materials incompatible	No	No	No	Yes
Failure to test	No	No	No	Yes
Failure to clean	No	No	No	Yes
Assembled backward	No	No	No	Yes

EDUCATION EXAMPLE: PINELLAS COUNTY (FLORIDA) SCHOOLS

Quality in educational conferencing — Why conferencing is necessary.

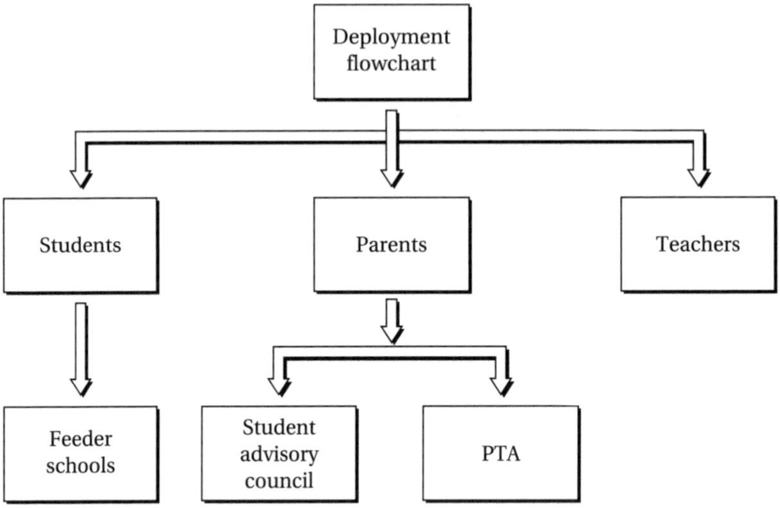

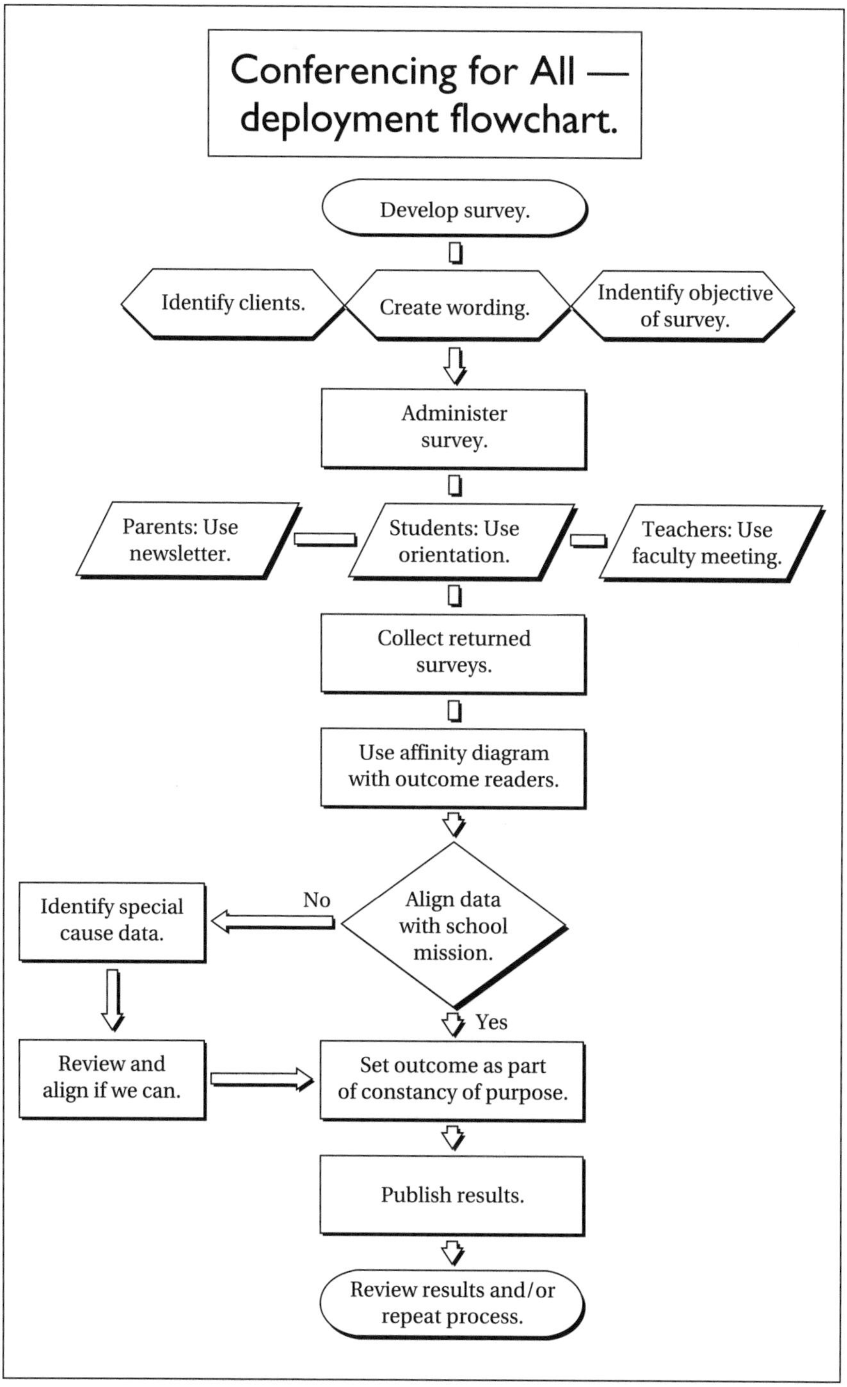
Conferencing for All — deployment flowchart.
Develop survey.
Identify clients.
Create wording.
Indentify objective of survey.
Administer survey.
Parents: Use newsletter.
Students: Use orientation.
Teachers: Use faculty meeting.
Collect returned surveys.
Use affinity diagram with outcome readers.
Align data with school mission.
No
Identify special cause data.
Review and align if we can.
Yes
Set outcome as part of constancy of purpose.
Publish results.
Review results and/or repeat process.

Learner outcomes

- Collaborative workers
- Effective communicators
- Creative thinkers and problem solvers
- Self-directed learners
- Community contributors
- Social interactors
- Quality producers

Parent, teacher, and student survey

Joseph L. Carwise Middle School
3301 Bentley Drive
Palm Harbor, Florida 34684

813-538-0000

John M. Leanes, Principal

Please complete the following statements with one idea.

1. It would be really nice if Carwise would ____________________

____

____

____

____

2. It makes all the difference when ____________________

____

____

____

____

3. Carwise would help my child most by ____________________

____

____

____

____

Please return to student's first period teacher on
Thursday, September 23, 1993.

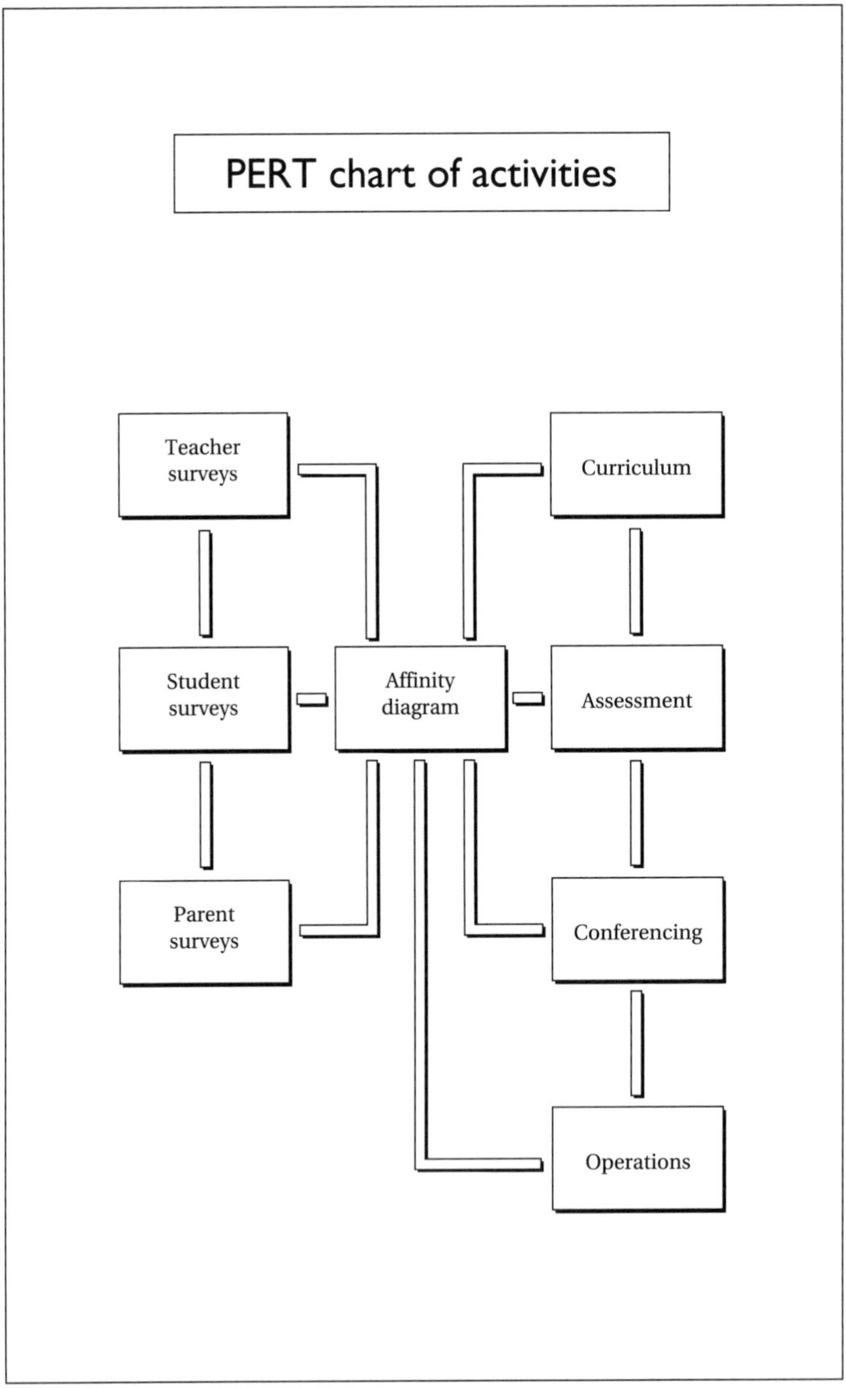
PERT chart of activities
Teacher surveys
Student surveys
Parent surveys
Affinity diagram
Curriculum
Assessment
Conferencing
Operations

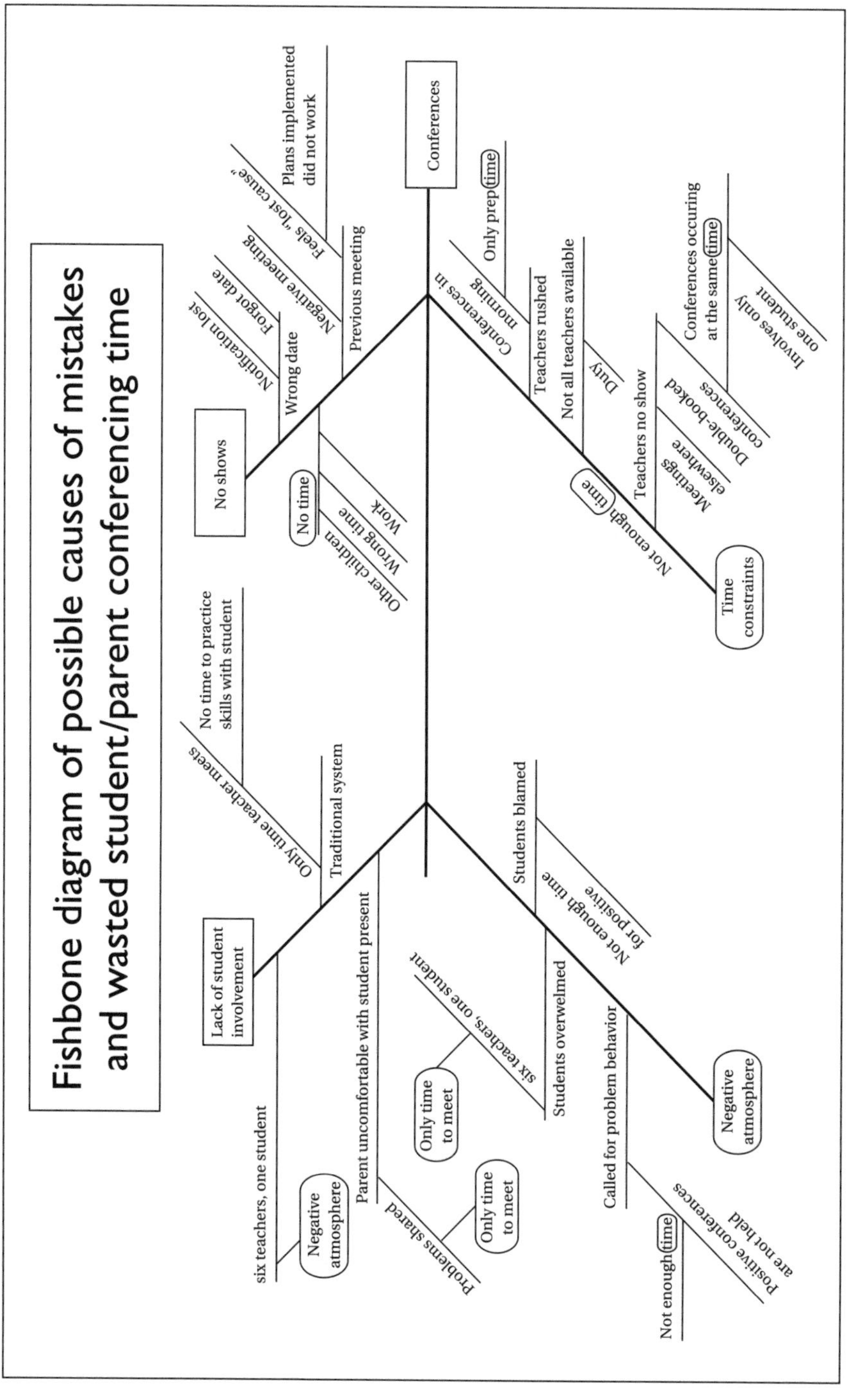
Fishbone diagram of possible causes of mistakes and wasted student/parent conferencing time
Conferences
No shows
Wrong date
Notification lost
Forgot date
Negative meeting
Feels "lost cause"
Plans implemented did not work
Previous meeting
No time
Other children
Wrong time
Work
Time constraints
Not enough time
Conferences in morning
Only prep time
Teachers rushed
Not all teachers available
Duty
Teachers no show
Meetings elsewhere
Double-booked conferences
Conferences occuring at the same time
Involves only one student
Lack of student involvement
Only time teacher meets
No time to practice skills with student
Traditional system
six teachers, one student
Negative atmosphere
Parent uncomfortable with student present
Problems shared
Only time to meet
Only time to meet
six teachers, one student
Negative atmosphere
Students blamed
Not enough time for positive
Students overwelmed
Called for problem behavior
Positive conferences are not held
Not enough time

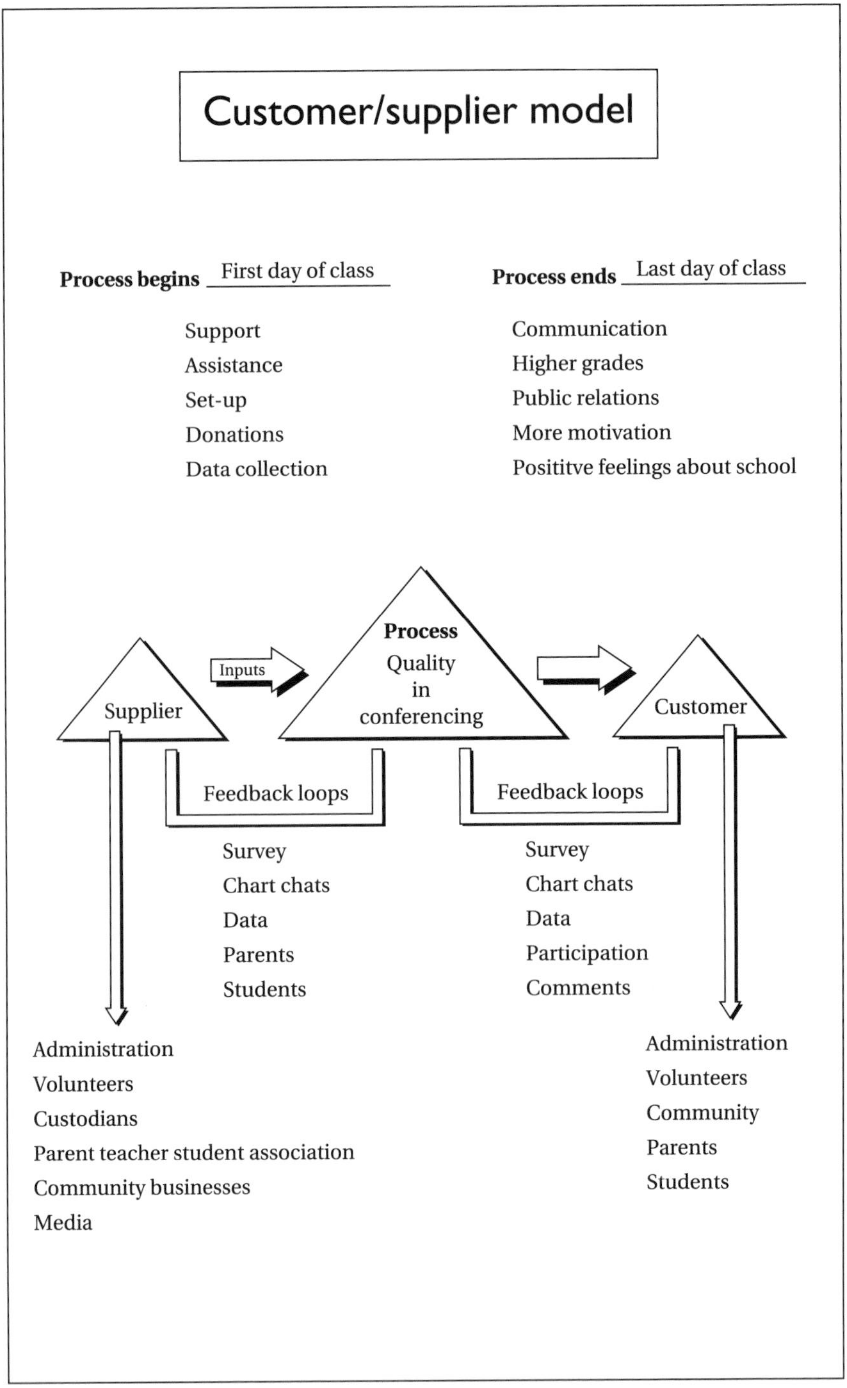

Customer/supplier model
Process begins First day of class
Process ends Last day of class
Support
Assistance
Set-up
Donations
Data collection
Communication
Higher grades
Public relations
More motivation
Posititve feelings about school
Supplier
Inputs
Process
Quality
in
conferencing
Customer
Feedback loops
Feedback loops
Survey
Chart chats
Data
Parents
Students
Survey
Chart chats
Data
Participation
Comments
Administration
Volunteers
Custodians
Parent teacher student association
Community businesses
Media
Administration
Volunteers
Community
Parents
Students

Chapter Eight

GENERATE POTENTIAL ACTIONS.

You have used your creative-reflective-critical-reflective thinking cycle once: to assure that you have clearly defined the problem. Each of the examples is at a decision point. Something must be done about the stated problem. In the case of the book, I am creating something where there was nothing before; in the hospice example, a financial problem is being reduced; in the motor shop example, attempts are being made to eliminate the last few human errors.

It may seem like a long time from the start, but sometimes it takes longer in the telling than in the doing. The total process need not take a long time. If the issue is a small one, and totally under your control, you may very well flip through your seven steps in just a few hours, or perhaps even minutes. For an interdepartmental issue in an average-sized company, and depending upon the scope of the project, the one-meeting-per-step approach typically takes from six weeks to six months. Although at first blush this may seem like a long time, practical experience proves that taking only one step per meeting helps keep the meetings brief, and prevents jumping ahead in the process. Since quality improvement activities are usually done in addition to full-time work requirements, it takes time between meetings to gather data, perform team assignments, and prepare for the next step.

You may have accomplished a great deal by now, even though you have not yet solved the problem. You may have invented a key quality indicator where there was none; you may have created awareness among a wide range of people; you may have standardized procedures, created documentation, learned to understand your team members, and increased your knowledge of your work. You have again reached a new step or a new plateau.

CREATIVITY

During this problem-solving step, you will focus on creative tools. You have already established a base of information in the form of the run chart, the flowchart, the check sheet and fishbone diagram, and the Pareto chart. Now, it's time to have some fun.

The creative process *is* fun. Working with teams and individuals, I have found that most people really enjoy the opportunity to let the ideas flow, to contribute in a nonjudgmental way to improve a situation, and to interact in a less-structured way than usual. Not everybody likes to dance on the skinny branches though, so it is useful at this stage to be sensitive to those needs as well. You might even use a subgroup of people who like to generate ideas, saving the more critical types for the next step in the process.

What is creativity anyway? In this step, you are attempting to encourage a climate in which you can create a new thought—to look at things in a different light and from all points of view, so that you can consider as many solutions as possible.

Since discussing the creative process is difficult for me, I will refer you to a body of literature that deals with creative problem solving. In general, anything that will help compare, contrast, or stimulate ideas will help in this step. Brainstorming in all its forms will be useful. Sometimes a puzzle or exercise not related to the specific problem can be helpful to get people thinking differently.

STRATEGIES

Your strategy will depend on a variety of factors that you have already identified. At this step, however, you want to consider all possible strategies. Some generic strategies that may help you get started include the following:

- Find something that is immediately doable, and do it. Measure results, adjust, and go on to another problem.
- Do clean-up work on all loose ends before moving forward in the problem-solving process.
- Try many approaches at once, using some form of experimental design.
- Use trial implementation with a small group, to work your solution while minimizing risk.
- Be extremely thorough, holding out for the best possible outcome, no matter how long it takes. Then assure that it doesn't take so long next time.
- Select actions that will be supported by key people or by a large group of people, in order to build on success.

- Use total innovation.
- List other strategies that may work for your team.

If you are truly being creative, you will have asked enough questions to at least have flirted with the possibility of total innovation. This is something that has never been done and that will produce a quantum leap in performance.

On the other extreme, you may have spent very little time, money, and energy, but found a small improvement that can be easily implemented right away, saving you time or money. You can then immediately use this newfound time or money to generate an additional improvement.

Somewhere in between the first two strategies is the concept of quantum improvement. In this case you are not innovating, but simply applying known technology to a specific issue to totally eliminate the problem. Do not shrink from this possibility. I see groups, on a weekly basis, accomplishing things they didn't think they could do. For instance, it is possible to not just reduce warranties, but to eliminate them.

SUMMARY

This section of the storyboard deals exclusively with the generation of possible solutions. The purpose of keeping this narrow focus is to avoid confusion, in thought style and objective, between the generation of solutions and their evaluation.

Results of this section will typically be reported on some kind of list, brainstorming sheet, or mind map. The next step, selecting a solution, will apply critical thinking to the ideas to select those that have the most value.

Now return to the examples for a look at how these organizations generated possible solutions. Note that in the case of the Pinellas County (Florida) Schools, there is no demonstration of considering alternatives. This organization had an idea worth trying, and went straight to planning for action.

POSSIBLE SOLUTION PANELS FROM THE CASE STUDY EXAMPLES

HEALTH CARE EXAMPLE: HOSPICE OF THE FLORIDA SUNCOAST

This includes both the thinking and the selection, which are two separate activities. In order not to spoil the fun, I have covered up the selection criteria.

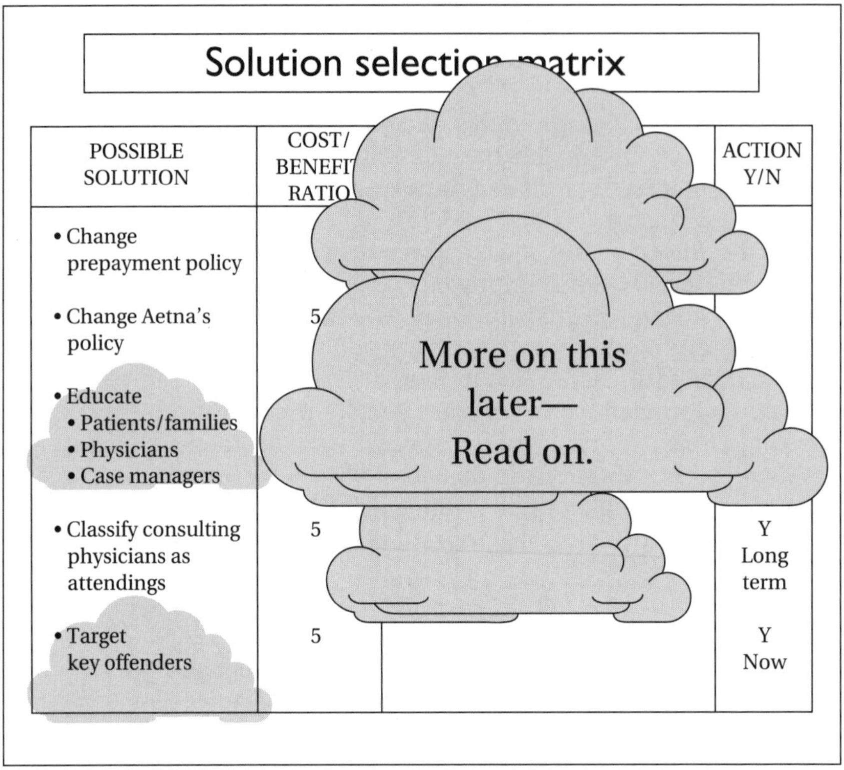

INDUSTRIAL EXAMPLE: FLOLO CORPORATION SCANNING ROOM

Will this group select one option or all of them?

- Training of retrieval system
- Purchase of new software to enable retrievers to have printing functions
- Procedure change: Scanner does not retrieve

MANUFACTURING EXAMPLE: ELECTRIC MOTOR SERVICE

Three possible solutions have been identified.

1. Improved final assembly checklist
2. Manager training
3. Tool box training

Improved final assembly checklist

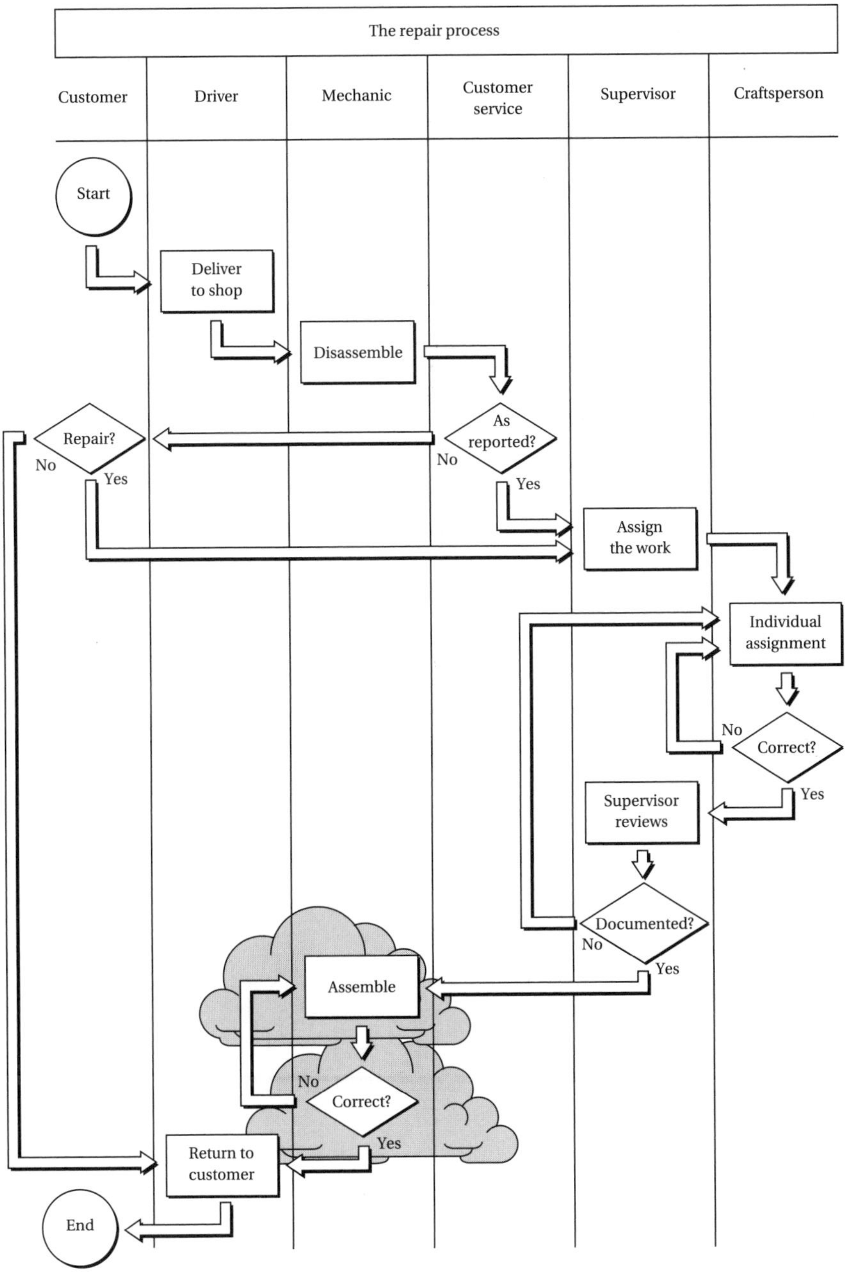

MANAGER TRAINING

Achieving Communications Effectiveness is a 12-hour course that includes video and group exercises. This program will help managers and their employees deal with each other and the situations they face daily. The program is the result of employee feedback.

TOOL BOX TRAINING

Using the existing tool box training sessions, which are held on an as-needed basis, we could

- Share information about rework with all employees.
- Communicate standards and procedures.
- Facilitate teamwork.
- Collect further improvement ideas.

Feedback from recent rework cases can be used to focus the meetings.

Chapter Nine

EVALUATE AND SELECT ACTIONS.

Now that you have generated a list of potential solutions (or actions, if you prefer), you are ready to evaluate them. There are a variety of tools for evaluation. The overwhelming favorite seems to be the evaluation matrix.

Advantages of the matrix include its versatility, you can have as many or as few criteria as you wish; its graphic nature, it is easy to see; and the fact that it provides an opportunity to rate solutions, even the intangible ones, and then discuss the results.

Since you have posted the results of your previous step, and taken time to reflect upon it, you should have a substantial list of possible solutions. Now, you are ready to use your analytical thinking.

The nature of the problem may determine the criteria for evaluation. There are, however, some generic criteria that apply to most situations.

- How effective will this solution be?
- How many of the causes will be covered?
- What is the estimated effect on the key indicator?
- How likely is buy in from management?
- How likely is buy in from those who have to execute the solution?
- How much will it cost?
- How great are the benefits?
- How long will it take?
- How difficult is it?

If the solution is obvious (it usually isn't), then you don't need a matrix. It is theoretically possible that even a large group can achieve consensus without the use of graphic tools. The reality is, however, that you are probably going to need the matrix.

In order to assure that you pick the overall best solution, you should evaluate your top five alternatives. This may mean that you have to apply a group tool such as multivoting or nominal group technique to reduce your list.

The simplest matrix could consist of only two columns. The first column includes a simple, forced numerical rating of options. Members of the team must rank the options from one to five with no ties. The results are totaled, and the total points for each option are presented. Because of the group nature of this exercise, it is still possible to have a tie. In that case, you may wish to discuss the issue further.

The weakness of such simplicity is that it does not force discussion of important success factors. Since the generic criteria factors, and maybe others, will likely weigh in the success of the project, it will be useful to consider them fully.

The next simplest matrix has been used successfully, perhaps because it is a compromise between simplicity and effectiveness. Figure 9.1 shows this matrix. Notice that because there are two criteria, a column needs to be added for the total score. The method is the same as in the simple matrix.

There is one more complexity. You must decide whether to add or multiply. Practical experience shows that the main difference between the two techniques is that multiplication spreads out the scores more than adding, but multiplication does not change the order of the results. In a complicated matrix, with many columns and weighting, the foregoing statement may not be true.

Regardless of the method selected, it is important to achieve consensus from the group on the action to be taken. As a high school friend of mine once said, "You flip the coin. If you agree with the result, proceed. If you disagree, then do what you want to." Since selection factors may involve intangibles, you can't go wrong as long as you consider the evaluation matrix a tool for achieving consensus.

You may wish to use other tools at this point, including the consideration of barriers and aids to implementation. This is a great place to be

Solutions	Effectiveness	Feasibility	Total

FIGURE 9.1. *Simple decision matrix.*

on the lookout for indications of nonsupport. You want the best possible consensus so that your implementation will be free of team trouble.

A trial implementation may be used if you have strong support for conflicting solutions. By trying a few selected alternatives, you provide the opportunity for each one to stand on its own merits.

Now examine how the sample organizations fared in selecting their solutions.

SUMMARY

This section of the storyboard shows how the actions, or countermeasures, were selected. It is particularly important to show the reasoning used so that others will understand it. In the absence of understanding, people frequently think the worst. The better you show your logic and the better you have communicated, the better you will promote both the results and the process.

This is another area where pictures can be extremely beneficial. With the use of expensive equipment, you can now take digitized photographs in the workplace, download them directly into your personal computer, and work them into a storyboard using over-the-counter software. In time, the total price for all the goodies necessary will make them practical for most companies.

EVALUATION AND SELECTION OF ACTION PANELS FROM THE CASE STUDY EXAMPLES

HEALTH CARE EXAMPLE: HOSPICE OF THE FLORIDA SUNCOAST

Solution selection matrix

Possible solution	Cost/ benefit ratio	Effectiveness	Feasibility	Total score	Action Yes/no
• Change prepayment policy	5	3	1	9	No
• Change Aetna's policies	5	4	2	11	Yes Long term
• Educate • Patients/families • Physicians • Case managers	4	4	5	13	Yes Now
• Classify consulting physicians as attendings	5	4	3	12	Yes Long term
• Target key offenders	5	5	5	15	Yes Now

Scale
Low 1 - 2 - 3 - 4 - 5 High

Barriers	Aids
• Attitudes/opinions • Lack of information • Complex procedures • Reliance on external informants • Resistance to change	• Administrative support • Additional staff person • Improved computer system • High cost of write-offs • Reimbursements available

INDUSTRIAL EXAMPLE: FLOLO CORPORATION SCANNING ROOM

Action

- Training on retrieval system
- Purchase of new software to enable retrievers to have printing functions
- Procedure change—scanner does not retrieve

MANUFACTURING EXAMPLE: ELECTRIC MOTOR SERVICE

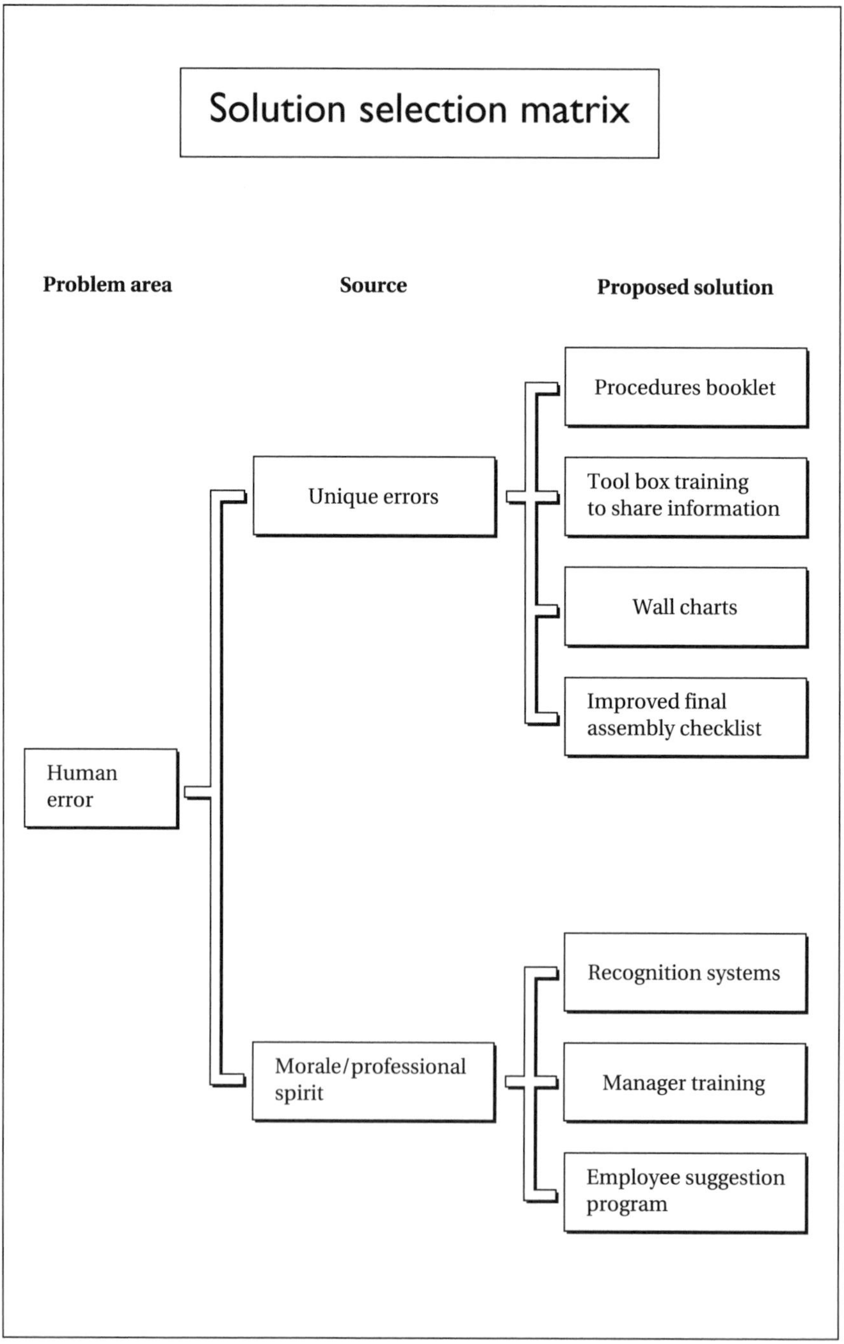

We believe that prevention of errors can have a positive effect on rework and should be pursued. But, it is the checking procedure that will save the customer from the pain of lost production and additional cost of rework that is caused by human error. Accordingly, solutions were ranked by the estimated impact on rework.

Proposed Solution	Effect ×	Feasibility =	Total	Order
Procedures booklet	1	2	2	
Tool box training to share information	3	3	9	3
Wall charts	2	2	4	
Improved final assembly checklist	3	3	9	1
Recognition systems	1	1	1	
Manager training	3	3	9	2
Employee suggestion program	1	3	3	

EDUCATION EXAMPLE: PINELLAS COUNTY (FLORIDA) SCHOOLS

Outcomes for students through a process of conferencing for quality

1. **Self-value**—Students will set expectations.
2. **Cooperative value**—Students will demonstrate group processing skills.
3. **Designing rubric**—Students will set goals and purpose for learning, and will constantly seek information and learn.
4. **Communicate**—Students will discuss, share, and communicate ideas clearly. They will implement technology in their processes.
5. **Peer conferencing**—Students will think critically, use experiences, share, rethink, and reason for improvement.
6. **Teacher conferencing**—Students will identify, define, and explore means to quality while evaluating the results.
7. **Conference with parent**—Students will seek new ways to tackle problems and to meet challenges.
8. **Continuing the process**—Students will maintain a sense of wonder and appreciate cooperative efforts as well as individual perspectives.

Gantt chart of teacher activities

Portfolio night	Before school	Week 1	Week 2	Week 3	Week 4	Week 5	Week 6
1. Analyze existing method of conferencing at middle school.							
2. Survey a need for conferencing.							
3. Devise a plan to meet with stakeholders.							
4. Prepare system for process.							
5. Create a flowchart of functions and structure of conferencing techniques.							
6. Create a rubric for process of portfolio conferencing.							
7. Add to portfolio with quality pieces of work.							
8. Use portfolios with peers.							
9. Revise conference procedures to conference with peers.							
10. Do whole group presentation.							
11. Have one-to-one conferencing with parents.							
12. Evaluate process.							

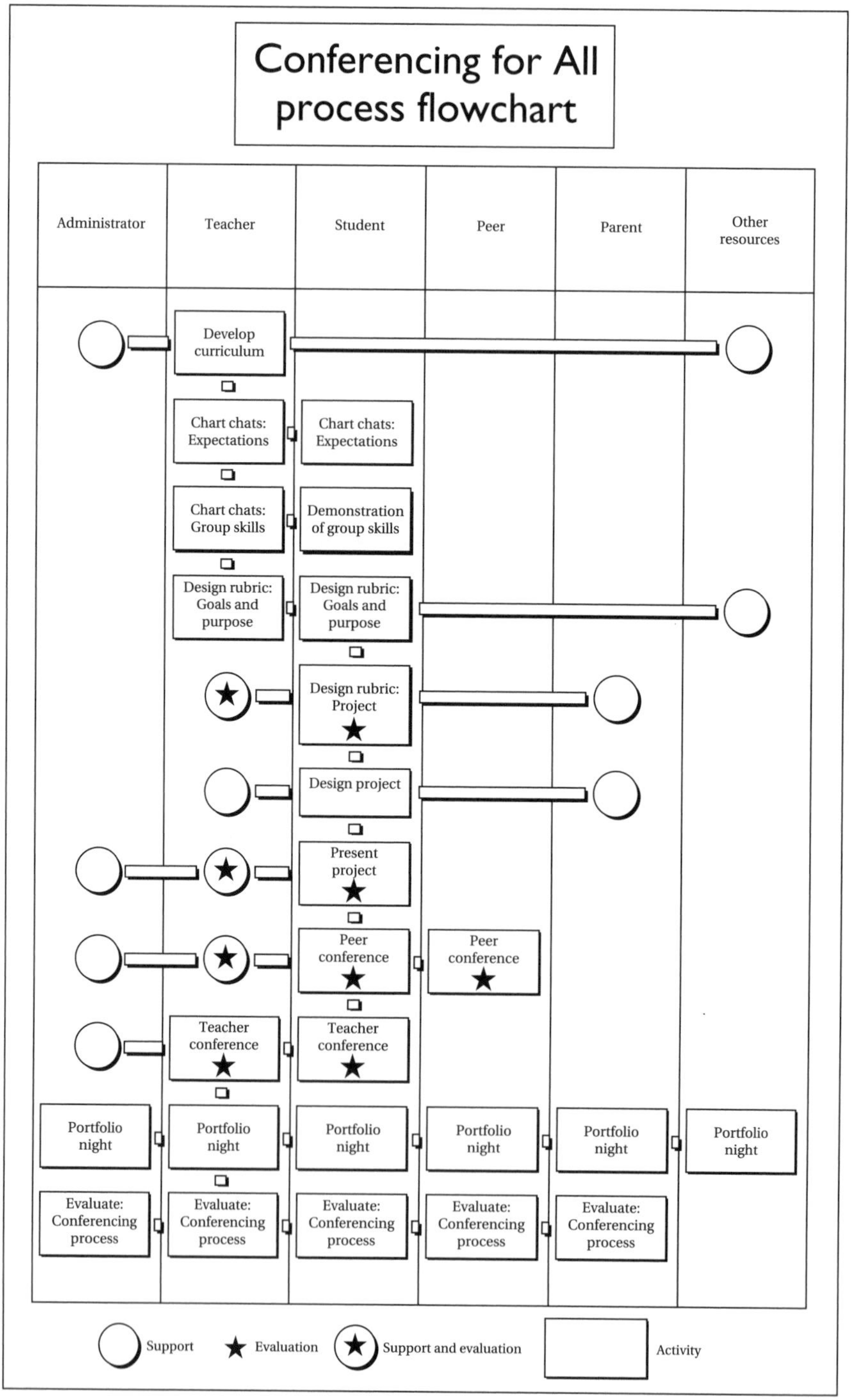
Conferencing for All process flowchart
Administrator
Teacher
Student
Peer
Parent
Other resources
Develop curriculum
Chart chats: Expectations
Chart chats: Expectations
Chart chats: Group skills
Demonstration of group skills
Design rubric: Goals and purpose
Design rubric: Goals and purpose
Design rubric: Project
Design project
Present project
Peer conference
Peer conference
Teacher conference
Teacher conference
Portfolio night
Portfolio night
Portfolio night
Portfolio night
Portfolio night
Portfolio night
Evaluate: Conferencing process
Evaluate: Conferencing process
Evaluate: Conferencing process
Evaluate: Conferencing process
Evaluate: Conferencing process
Support
Evaluation
Support and evaluation
Activity

Gantt chart of student activities

Portfolio night	Week 1	Week 2	Week 3	Week 4	Week 5	Week 6
1. Develop a rubric.						
2. Design a portfolio.						
3. Design a project.						
4. Read the book.						
5. Create a class mummy.						
6. Present project.						
7. Have student evaluation.						
8. Have student conferencing.						
9. Participate in portfolio night.						
10. Evaluate portfolio night.						

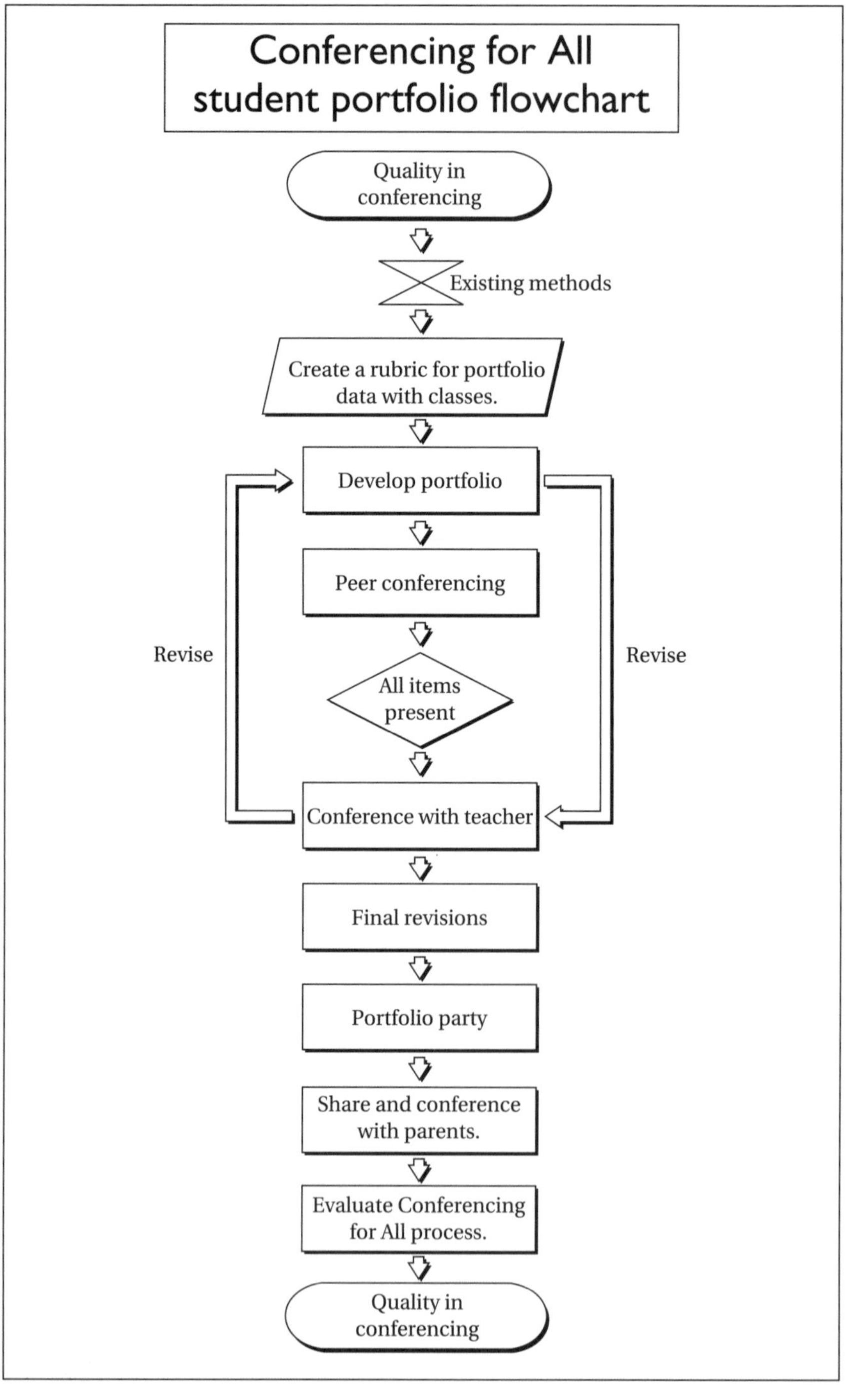
Conferencing for All student portfolio flowchart
Quality in conferencing
Existing methods
Create a rubric for portfolio data with classes.
Develop portfolio
Peer conferencing
All items present
Revise
Revise
Conference with teacher
Final revisions
Portfolio party
Share and conference with parents.
Evaluate Conferencing for All process.
Quality in conferencing

Name ______________________________

Pyramid flowchart

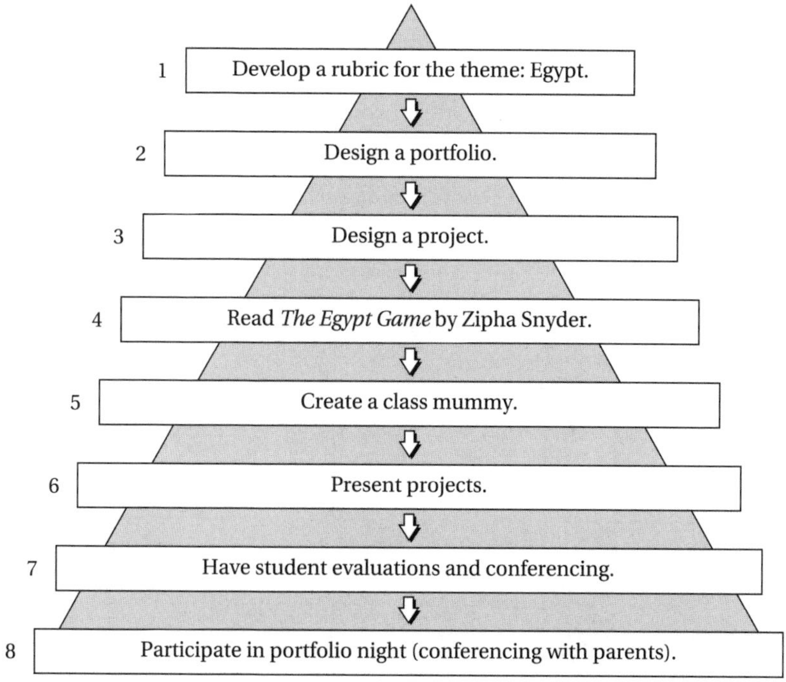

Student evaluation form for peer conferencing

Student's portfolio ____________________

Student evaluator ____________________

Date of conference ____________________

Theme's title ____________________

Please check if material is present and of good quality.

Portfolio items

______ Cover
______ Word search
______ Mummification paper
______ King Tut paper
______ Hieroglyphics
______ Mummy on black paper
______ Travel brochure
______ Mummy invitation
______ Final short story
______ Illustration
______ Project summary and/or grade sheet
______ Flowchart

What positive comments can you say about this portfolio?

1. ____________________

____

2. ____________________

____

Continue to strive to ____________________

____

Portfolio night: This is important because ____________________

____

I am proud of my work!

Student ____________________ Teacher ____________________

Conferencing for All
Evaluation methods: process decision program chart

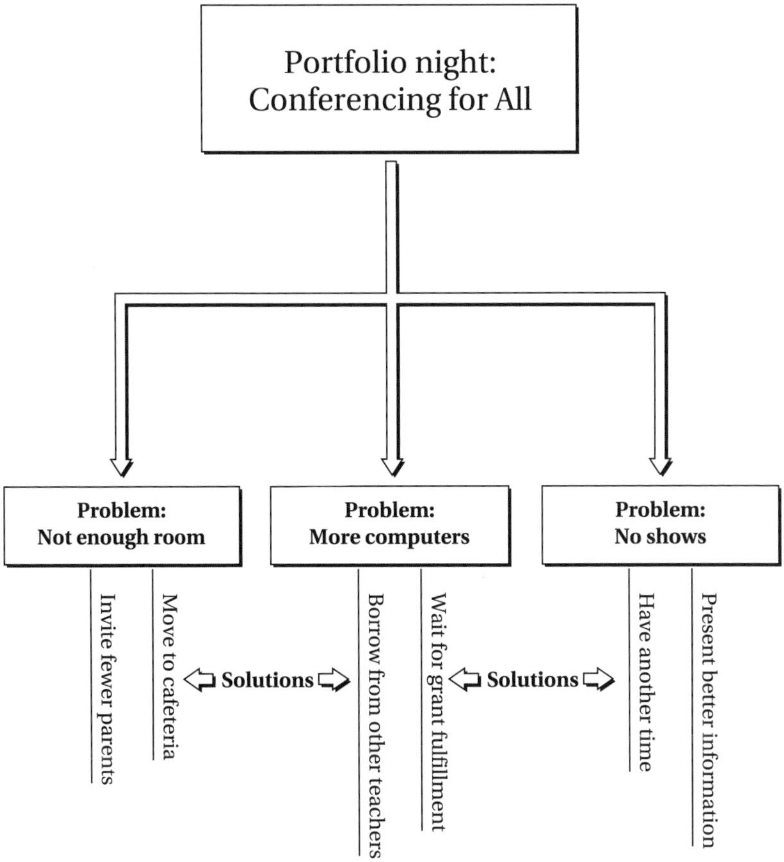

Traditional bell curves

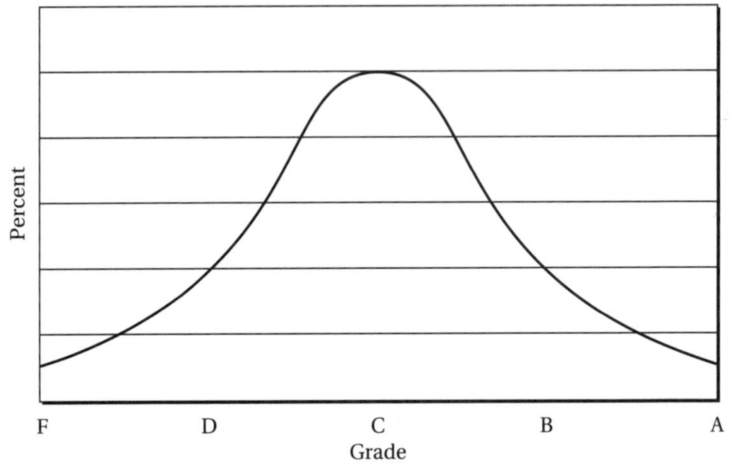

Pinellas County school

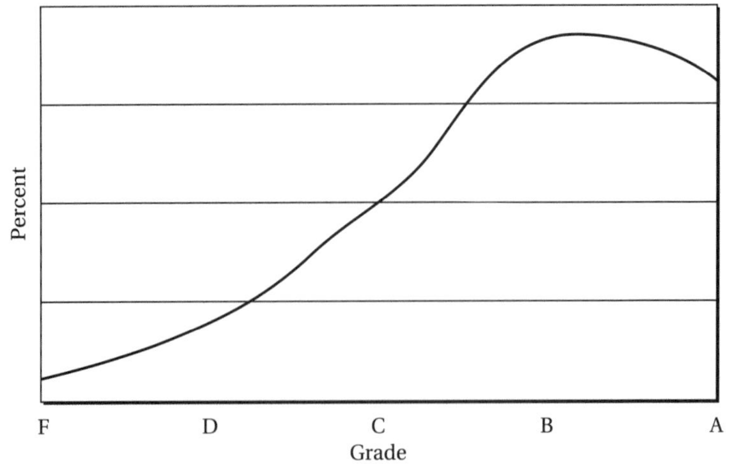

Chapter Ten

ACTION

PLANNING

Before doing anything, you may wish to organize specific actions. It could be argued that the first four steps of the problem-solving process are planning. The more complicated your action is, however, the more important it will be to have a specific order of actions in place. A Gantt chart, for example, could be handy at this point. Be sure that you have thought through the details before you take any action.

Among the details is one thing that deserves special mention—communication. It is vitally important that you communicate your plan to others who will be affected by your actions. If you don't, you are asking for trouble. No matter how good your storyboard is, you can't assume that everybody has read it. Memos are helpful, but again, you can't assume that they will be read. If a person or group is critical to your implementation, be sure that you have warned it in advance.

Well look at this. You finally *did* something. If this has been a small project, you may not have spent a lot of time on it. The greater the benefit or risk, the more careful you will have been, and the more time you will have spent on the project.

This is the place where you find out if you were thinking clearly when you selected the reason for improvement, when you described the current situation and did the analysis, when you planned the action, and when you actually did what you had planned. This is the big kahuna, the whole enchilada. This is what you have been working for all this time. Right?

Well, almost. Not every effort meets with success. An important part of storyboarding and problem solving is learning the process itself. If you don't get the desired results, you examine the process and improve it, so that you will produce the desired results next time. Some would argue that people only learn when they don't achieve the expected results. The more I see this concept in action, the more respect I have for it.

There continues to be a debate between those who believe in process-oriented reward systems and those who embrace results-oriented reward systems. There is a place for both. Too much emphasis on one alone will produce shortcomings. In the same way that too much emphasis on the income statement may cause management to sacrifice valuable assets, too much emphasis on results could cause teams to cheat on the method in order to produce something that looks good right now, while sacrificing long-term gains. By the same token, too much emphasis on process-oriented rewards could produce lack of pace (energy) and loss of focus.

REPORTING RESULTS

Bearing all that in mind, you will observe, chart, and monitor your key indicator(s) using the same charts and graphs you constructed earlier, to see if your actions produced results. It will be important to show on the chart or graph where each action took place. Hopefully, you have avoided multiple implementations, assuring that you can see the benefit of each solution, since solutions are implemented one at a time.

If you have discovered that you cannot show results on your present graph or chart, you have a very serious problem. This means that you have lost the link between your activities and your key indicator. It's time to go back to square one.

The results section of the storyboard may be very cut-and-dried. Here you simply report the results of your activities, showing the point of intervention on the same charts and graphs that were developed early in the process. Absence of demonstrable change is just as much a result as change itself. It just demonstrates a different consequence.

Using the same diagram as before, Figure 10.1 demonstrates the concept. Notice how the same charts and graphs that were used in the beginning of the process continue to serve your needs now.

If your solution is a solid hit to center field, you showed the changes to your flowchart and simplified the system. Now you gain speed, find the root causes, and pick the best area to work on using the Pareto chart. Rounding third base, you're going for the home stretch. Yes, the results are clearly shown on the (home) run chart.

The most significant result, of course, is the effect on your key quality indicator. See Figure 10.2.

CELEBRATION

Ritual is an important part of people's lives, and should not be overlooked. Yet, the intensity of U.S. society is frequently such that workers are immediately distracted by the next issue. This is a real danger. It is vitally important to celebrate successes, and indeed to provide for success.

In the team section of this book, pacing of the project was discussed. An important part of that pacing was providing an adequate amount of positive reinforcement along the way; that is, encouragement.

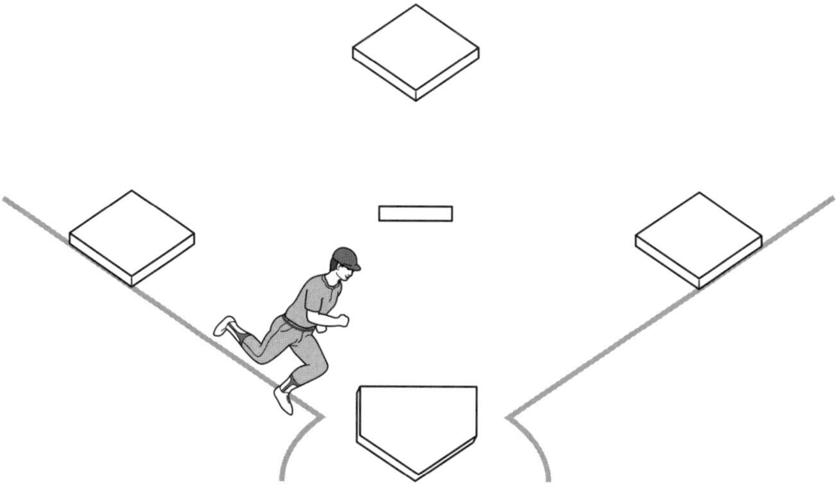

FIGURE 10.1. *Reporting results using original indicators.*

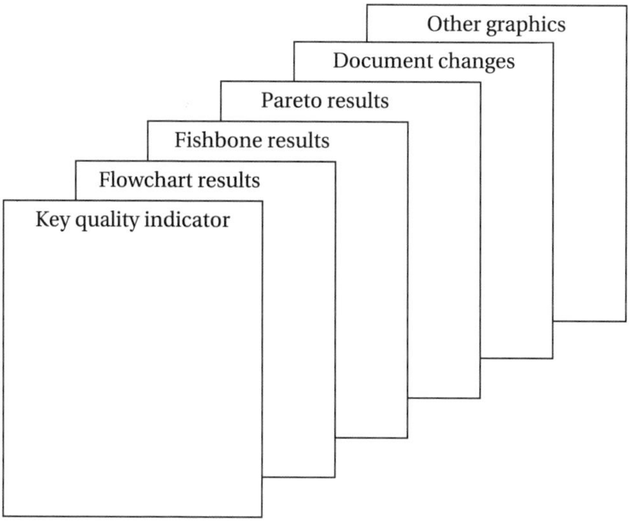

FIGURE 10.2. *Results section.*

Now is the time to celebrate results. Experience has proven that the celebration need not be expensive, but it must be of personal value. Companies have chosen to celebrate with awareness items like pens, coffee mugs, coasters, or formal plaques, awards, and gift certificates. Even in the absence of a company reward system, people still have the capacity to reward themselves. In fact, it would be argued by most psychologists that this system is far more important—yet sometimes harder to come by—than a company award system. Yet it is essential to improvement.

Here are some ways that individuals celebrate their accomplishments, either individually or as a group.

- Take a vacation, even if only a day.
- Have a favorite dinner.
- Plan a group outing, such as a day at the beach.
- Buy a special gift or treat.
- Thank your team.
- Thank yourself.

Experience with teams of all types suggests that you must take the time to celebrate before you evaluate your results. To stifle the celebration is to take the fun out of the process, and this is certain to discourage future participation. Once the applause has died down, it is time to review your entire process to consider its merits and any remaining causes for improvement. If you are a team leader, please don't overlook the simplest, most powerful, and yet frequently forgotten forms of celebration with your team—a sincere expression of your appreciation.

SUMMARY

The results section of the storyboard is where the rubber meets the road. If you have prepared well up front, by being well organized, by establishing measurements, by having clear objectives, and by understanding the system you are working with, then you have increased the odds of success.

Even if change is not shown, your team still wins. No change is good information. Edison discovered the carbon filament for the electric light bulb by systematically trying all the possibilities, including those that didn't work.

Finally, celebration is an important part of accomplishment. Don't forget to celebrate.

Now examine how the paradigm stacks up with the real world. Here are the examples.

IMPLEMENTATION OF ACTION PANELS FROM THE CASE STUDY EXAMPLES

HEALTH CARE EXAMPLE: HOSPICE OF THE FLORIDA SUNCOAST

Implementation

Monthly collections
for consulting physician services

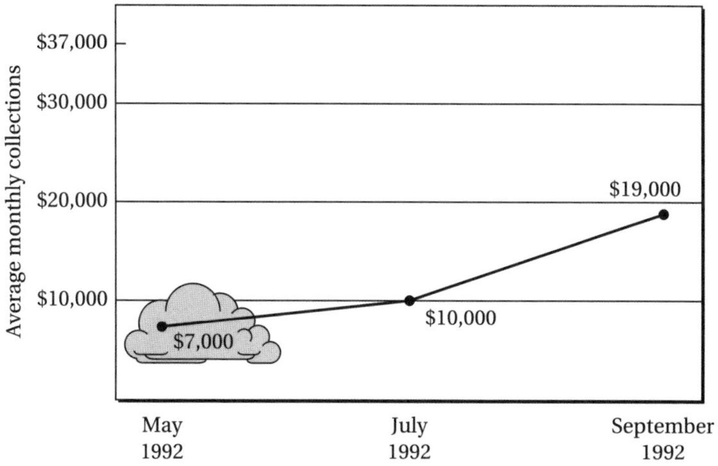

- Claims for consulting physician services totaled $410,000 for the past 12 months.
- Average monthly charges for consulting physician services totaled $37,000/month.

- Collections rose from $7,000 in May 1992 to $19,000 in September. This is an increase of $12,000.
- Collections increased 170% in the four-month period.

Results

Outstanding records ranked by provider groups
September, 1992

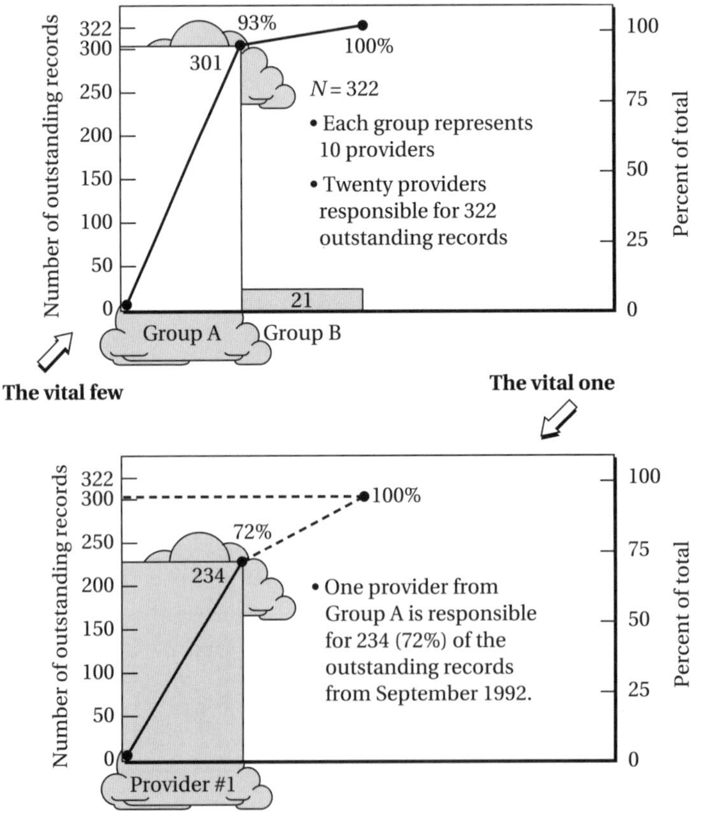

Scope of problem
One provider = 72% of the problem

INDUSTRIAL EXAMPLE: FLOLO CORPORATION SCANNING ROOM

Appraisal 1

Results

Complaint level = zero

Backlog = zero

MANUFACTURING EXAMPLE: ELECTRIC MOTOR SERVICE

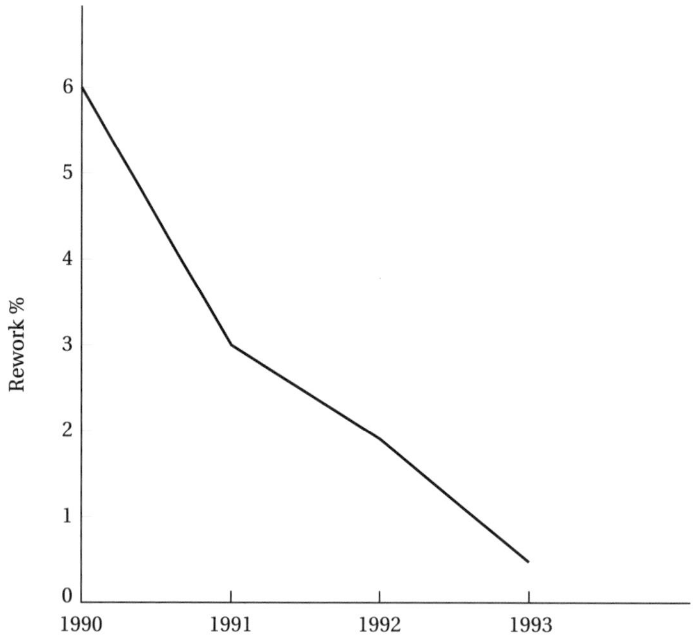

Rework has been reduced.

EDUCATION EXAMPLE: PINELLAS COUNTY (FLORIDA) SCHOOLS

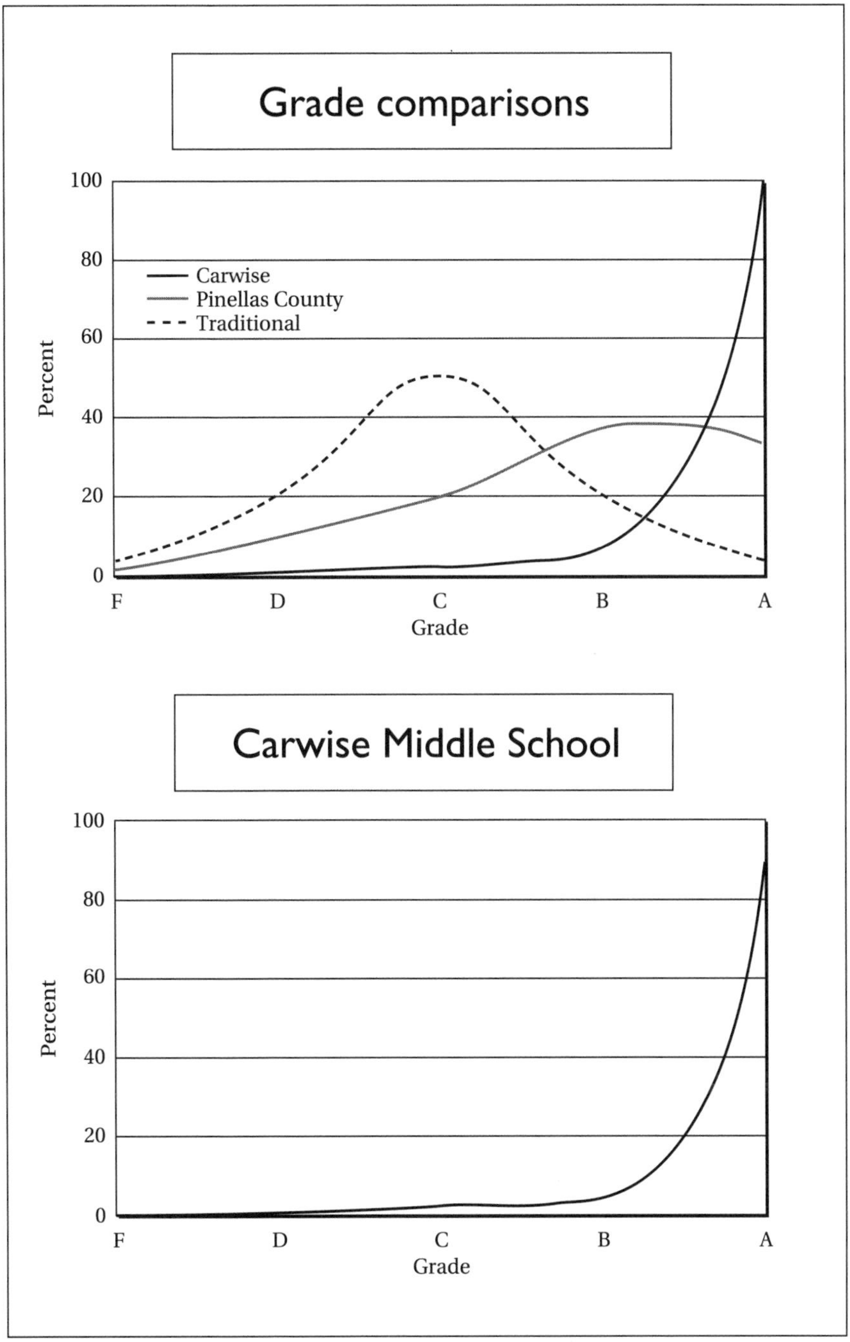

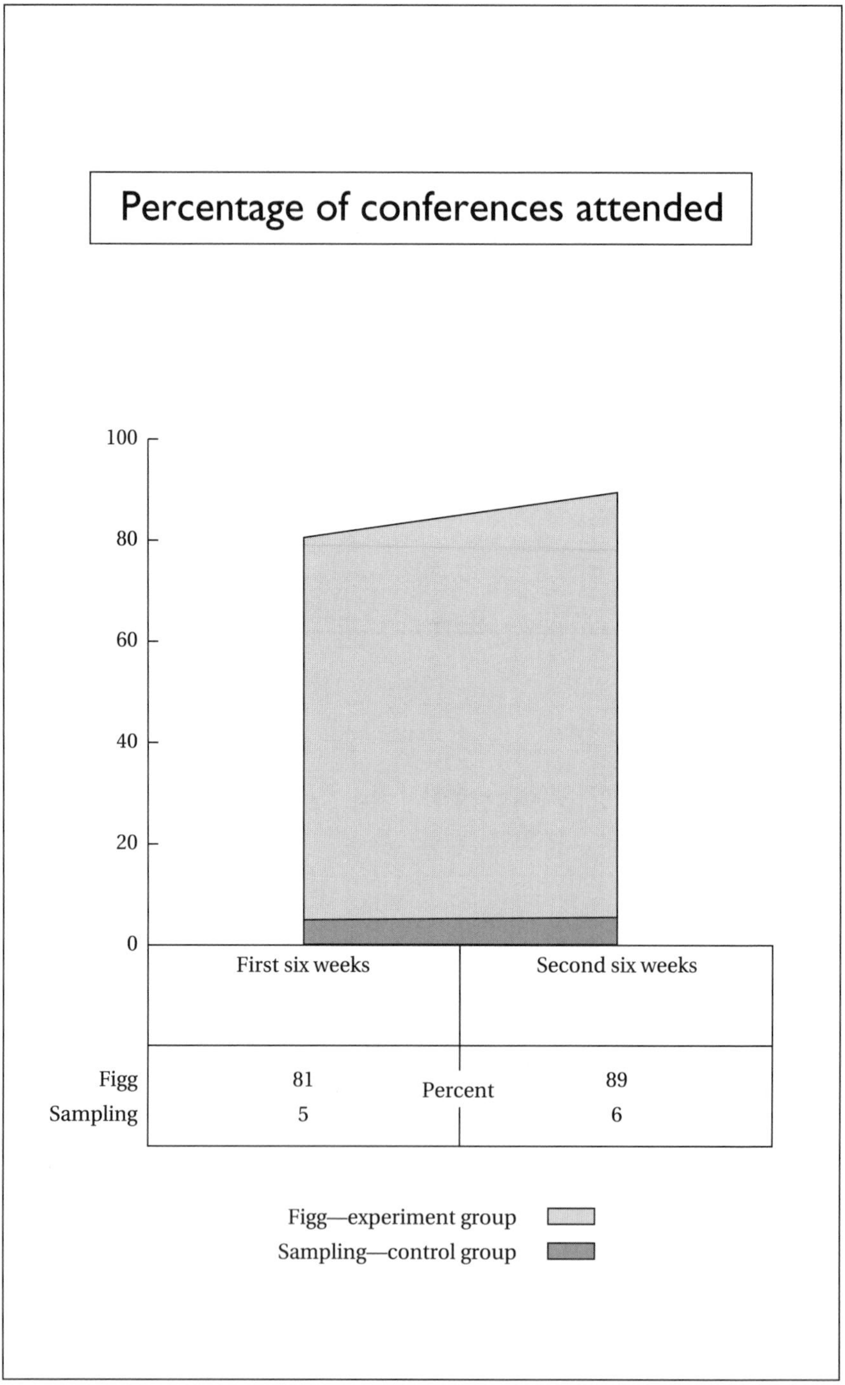
Percentage of conferences attended
100
80
60
40
20
0
First six weeks
Second six weeks
Figg
Sampling
81
5
Percent
89
6
Figg—experiment group
Sampling—control group

Chapter Eleven

APPRAISE OR EVALUATE.

The improvement project is essentially completed, but the storyboard is not quite finished. Some degree of celebration, proportional to your achievement of expectations, has been completed, and you have recuperated from the merriment. (My experience with celebrations in the workplace is that the recuperation won't take too long.)

There are three levels upon which you may evaluate your storyboards.

1. **Results**
    a. Did you achieve the results you set out to achieve?
    b. Did you gain more?
    c. Did you gain less?
2. **Process**
    a. Did you follow the problem-solving steps?
    b. Did you apply the tools appropriately for the situation?
    c. Could the process itself be improved next time?
    d. Should a step or section of the storyboard be redone?
    e. Did misapplication of the process affect results?
3. **Communication**
    a. Did you tell a story?
    b. Was it interesting?
    c. Was it in chronological order?
    d. Was it clear and understandable?
    e. Did you use words, numbers, and pictures?

Figures 11.1–11.3 show some forms that may be helpful in conducting this evaluation. Use them if you like or invent your own. There is no limit to the depth and breadth of self-evaluation, either as an individual or as a team. The most important guideline is that you stay focused on the situation. Never let evaluation destroy the goodwill generated in the effort.

Feature	Check
Please state the objective. Was it achieved? (Y/N)	
What was the total cost of this project? Was it worth the money? (Y/N)	
Please indicate the percent improvement of your key quality indicator.	
Please itemize additional benefits.	
Were procedural changes documented?	

FIGURE 11.1. *Results-based appraisal checklist.*

Step	Measurement	Tools
Reason for improvement		
Current situation		
Problem analysis		
Action		
Results		
Appraisal		
Future plans		
Overall rating		

FIGURE 11.2. *Process-based appraisal checklist.*

For each step, please indicate which tools were used.

	Words	Numbers	Pictures
Reason for improvement			
Current situation			
Problem analysis			
Action			
Results			
Appraisal			
Future plans			

Please rate your story on each of the following questions. Use 0 to 10, with 10 being the highest score.

Was it chronological? ______________________

Was it clear and understandable?______________________

Did it describe important changes? ______________________

Did it use words, numbers, and pictures?______________________

Was it interesting?______________________

TOTAL SCORE ______________________

FIGURE 11.3. *Communication appraisal.*

SUMMARY

As you see, many teams did not use an appraisal form. That is not horrible. Like the other tools and techniques discussed here, it is just another opportunity to increase the odds of success. If you begin with a clear idea of what should be done, the chances are greater that you will do it. The evaluation can have much of its benefit long before it is ever performed. This is because individuals and groups are working to the evaluation standard all along. At the risk of seeming repetitive, this is just another example of what gets measured gets done.

People are always evaluating themselves. But it is when they start evaluating gains as a team that they begin to experience the benefits of continuous improvement.

RESULTS PANELS FROM THE CASE STUDY EXAMPLES

Only the education example used an evaluation page. Other teams evaluated as a part of their normal management procedures. The results from the other examples are summarized as follows:

- **Health care example**—This was the first effort by this hospice to use the storyboard technique. The evaluation was by acclamation. Results were far beyond expectations. There was a group celebration, and this storyboard has been displayed across the country as an example.
- **Industrial example**—This group solved the problem. Evaluation was done as a part of further training, which followed the guidelines in Figure 11.3.
- **Manufacturing example**—This exercise was a composite of more than one storyboard. In this case, the customer is the one whose evaluation counts. One organization began this project in 1984, and continues to monitor the percent of rework. A zero-defects condition has been achieved and maintained for periods of up to three months.

EDUCATION EXAMPLE: PINELLAS COUNTY (FLORIDA) SCHOOLS

Again, the evaluation is not seen, but a form has been put in place. Comparative data are presented.

Portfolio assessment: Reflections of a self-directed learner

3. Three important things I've learned are:

2. Two applications that help me to achieve the above:

1. One action I will continue to improve:

Parent response:

I am proud of:

I will help you by:

Benchmarking Carwise's total grades to reading

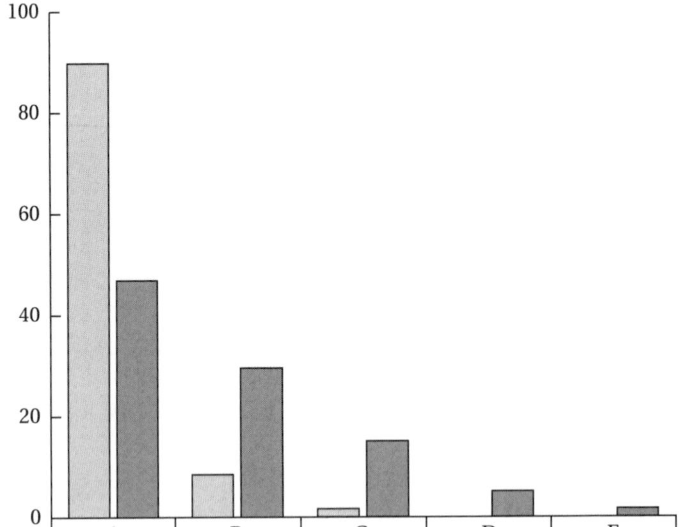

	A	B	C	D	F
Figg average	89.5	7.3	2.6		
Carwise average	46	30	16	5	2

Figg average
Carwise average

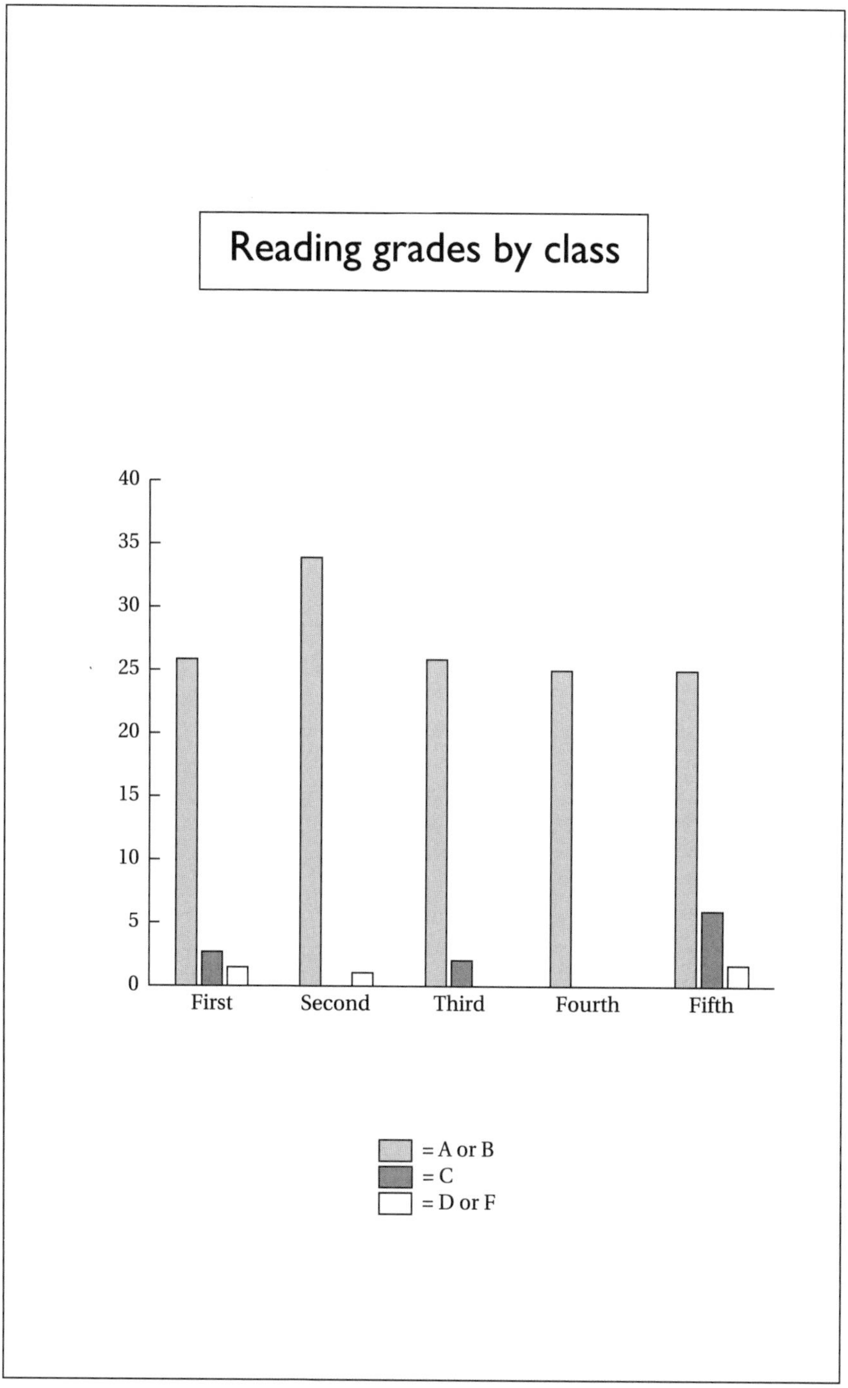
Reading grades by class
40
35
30
25
20
15
10
5
0
First
Second
Third
Fourth
Fifth
= A or B
= C
= D or F

Chapter Twelve

DOCUMENTATION, FUTURE PLANS, AND LESSONS LEARNED

You've essentially finished the project. Congratulations . . . almost. As it is often said, the job is not over until the paperwork is finished.

DOCUMENTATION

Most improvements include changing an existing procedure or inventing a new procedure. These must be discussed with the people involved, reviewed, and perhaps reworded. Training must be provided, and the procedure formalized so that others who need it in the future will know where to find and apply it.

If you have no documentation standard, an example is shown in Figure 12.1. As ISO 9000 continues to gain international strength, it will be useful to use those standards for documentation.

NONCONFORMANCES

Nonconformance is becoming a big word these days. What is done when things do not occur as they are supposed to? This is a key part of every procedure. It is required for ISO 9000 documentation, as well as other business and governmental standards. No procedure is complete without this section.

ACTING TO HOLD THE GAINS

You have essentially two choices: Go back and clean up any remaining problems with your original project; or go on to something else. If you elect to clean up your first project, you may still need to solidify the improvements you have already made, by assuring that procedures are drafted and that people are trained.

If you elect to go on to something else, then you need to first assure that the improvements you have made will hold. That may mean that you revisit the data once a quarter, or maybe only once a year. It may

Procedure name: Page ____ of ____

Procedure number: Revision number:

Date of revision:

Purpose: (Why does this procedure exist?)

Scope: (What does this procedure cover?)

Procedure: (What should be done?)

Nonconformance: (What should be done if a violation of this procedure is discovered?

Authority: Who is the owner of this procedure?

References to other procedures:

Signature block

FIGURE 12.1. *Documentation example.*

mean that you record the procedure for review in six months. You are the best person (or group) to decide what needs to be done, because you are the experts.

FUTURE PLANS

Your project has accomplished its objective. Is it something that will be useful to somebody else who is facing the same situation?

If your storyboard relates to operating equipment, could other operators of the same equipment use it? For example, a storyboard about a quicker way to change the setup on a lathe could be applied by all lathe operators.

Could your solution be generalized to a broader category of equipment? For example, a storyboard about preventive maintenance scheduling for computer equipment could be useful for other types of electrical or mechanical equipment.

If your storyboard is safety related, could it have other benefits beyond the scope of your specific actions? For example, a storyboard about removing a leaking underground gasoline storage tank resulted in decreasing cost, thus eliminating a hazard and decreasing governmental inspection activities. One additional effect was to improve the quality of the regional water supply.

Are there certain aspects of your process that can be generalized? For example, a storyboard about decreasing warranties in an electric motor shop could be used as a guide by another electric motor shop. Although there would be some differences, much of the storyboard would require just filling in new numbers.

LESSONS LEARNED

Finally, you should take time to consider what you have learned from this storyboard experience. Here are some things that others have learned from theirs.

- There was a lot of data, but it was never organized for use.
- The issue had many small contributing causes.
- Procedures that had been standard for a long time were no longer followed.
- Somebody changed a form without advising the rest of its users.
- The team didn't know it was that easy.
- The team should have gotten (person) involved at the start.
- The team could have made better use of the tools.

Here's what I learned while developing this book.

- Ask more questions.
- Listen to the answers.
- Follow your heart.
- Have fun. If you don't enjoy it, you shouldn't be doing it.

Now take a last look at the examples.

FUTURE PLANS AND LESSONS LEARNED PANELS FROM THE CASE STUDY EXAMPLES

Only the panels from the health care and industrial examples are shown. The future plans and lessons learned panels from the manufacturing example do not appear in the source material.

The educational project is ongoing in the Pinellas County (Florida) schools. It appears that the trial implementation was quite successful. As a parent of (former) middle school students, I can appreciate the potential impact of this project. It should be broadly applied.

HEALTH CARE EXAMPLE: HOSPICE OF THE FLORIDA SUNCOAST

Graduate TQM

Lessons learned

- Difficulty of improving a process that is partially controlled by external customers
- Inconsistency of conformance with established policies and procedures
- Inadequacies of current management information system
- Rewards gained by eliminating shotgun approach and focusing on the vital few
- Effectiveness of a structured problem-solving process utilizing TQM tools

Future plans

- Share storyboard with hospice staff and physicians.
- Develop plan for educating employees and physicians.
- Propose change in prepayment policy as related to providers identified as the vital few.
- Design management information system capable of tracking key indicators.
- Perform ongoing monitoring and evaluation of established criteria.
- Lobby for changes in reimbursement regulations.

INDUSTRIAL EXAMPLE: FLOLO CORPORATION SCANNING ROOM

Lessons learned

1. Data gathering is essential to planning.
2. Minimizing retrieval by scanning technician allows more time to scan documents.
3. Having several retrievers allows scanning technician to avoid backlog.
4. By working together we can accomplish our goal.
5. All group members learned how to retrieve themselves.

Documentation

Procedure change

- Scanning technician does not retrieve documents.
- Accounts payable documents are being scanned as they are approved.

BOOK SUMMARY

Following my own advice, I am now taking a reflective look at what has been presented here. You have traveled through the process of creating a storyboard, and have attempted to follow each step outlined in the actual preparation of this book.

Most fascinating to me were the questions that I asked when I forced myself to apply the tools as I have described; when I did things differently than I had in the past; and when the tools led me to ask questions I'm not used to asking. In summary, here are my lessons learned.

STRUCTURE FOR CLEAR THINKING

Having a structure for problem solving, issue resolving, or opportunity optimizing can help get the best out of a situation; however, it must be used appropriately. You don't want a team of 20 elephants to kill one flea. Yet the flea, with the right equipment, could bring down 20 elephants.

TRAINING TOOL

The storyboard is a training tool of the first order. I knew it was good the first time I was exposed to it. Now, after applying it in many organizations, my admiration for the process grows. People want to learn by doing. They like to get their hands on things and make things happen. Armed with a structure, you can dramatically improve the odds of making the right things happen and can achieve what Juran calls stretch goals.

ROBUST SYSTEM

Storyboarding is a robust system, meaning that it is strong and resistant to variation while producing consistently good results. It is forgiving. You can make many technical mistakes and still produce excellent results. I have yet to see any team, regardless of experience, persist to the end of the process without substantial, measurable results.

CREATIVITY

The recent history of storyboarding and problem solving has been weighted heavily toward the scientific side—structure, linearity, and technical tools. Yet there is an extremely rich world of creative problem solving that I have tried to bring into the picture here. No writer could ever do justice to the creative richness that exists in each of your minds. Yet the creative side is frequently stifled. No great discovery or advance has ever been made without an element of creativity. So take it out and play with it.

COMMUNICATION TOOL

Structured problem solving is one thing; communications is another. In every company that I interviewed, communication, both inside the company and with customers, is a key issue. Frequently it is the number-one issue. The storyboard is a way to communicate. It has been underexploited. Organizations have not taken the best advantage of it, but the advantage is there to be taken.

In order to produce the best storyboard, you must not lose sight of the fact that it is a communication tool, not a problem-solving tool. Its purpose is to communicate, so you must use all the visual, numeric, and word skills you can muster to show your concepts clearly and concisely and to make your story interesting. Nobody wants to read a boring story. Yet nested within your story are the steps of an organized problem-solving process; that is, a logical flow.

SDCA

One of the most common variations of the Deming wheel principle (plan-do-check-act) is the standardize-do-check-act cycle. One of the most common outcomes of a storyboard is the fact that other groups, either inside or outside the original organization, can use the results of the storyboard. This is so because the groups are performing exactly the same functions elsewhere, or because, although their functions are different, *the process is the same.*

In *The Pursuit of Quality Through Personal Change,* the ever-increasing value of improvements to higher-level processes was discussed. If you can improve a process that is a general one and that applies to many cases, you can multiply the value of your improvement by the number of times it is used. The next person or group does not have to reinvent the wheel. Therefore it frees the group to invent the transistor—another multiplicative effect.

RESULTS

Results are why problem solving is done in the first place. By being organized, you have made useful results relatively painless. As Vince Lombardi is frequently quoted as saying, "Winning is not a sometime thing . . . it's an all-the-time thing." In the same way that he was organized around his goals, you can become better organized to produce winning results every day. That sounds like fun to me.

WORLDWIDE COMMON LANGUAGE

As a result of the efforts of Crosby, Deming, Feigenbaum, Ishikawa, Imai, Juran, and the just-emerging generation of their followers, a worldwide language based on continuous improvement has evolved. You can look at a storyboard from Japan, Israel, Sweden, Brazil, or the United States, and visually understand it without understanding the words. Perhaps this common visual language contains the seeds of hope that humans will not revisit the Tower of Babel in this generation.

UNDERUTILIZED

It is possible that continuous improvement is the most underutilized technology in the history of the human race. While its recent development has been focused largely on industry, there is every reason to apply storyboarding and the other quality tools to improvement of the quality of life worldwide. If Buckminster Fuller was right, it will be 25 years before the positive contributions of this generation will be generally applied. At the same time, there is evidence that key areas such as public health, government, and philanthropy are picking up on quality tools and using them advantageously.

BENEDICTION

It is my hope and vision that you will find storyboarding as useful a tool as I have, and that this process will help you make your own visions become reality.

The ability to imagine is the largest part of what you call intelligence. You think the ability to imagine is merely a useful step on the way to solving a problem or making something happen.

But imagining is what makes it happen.

—From *Sphere* by Michael Crichton

Appendix A

STORYBOARD EXAMPLES FOR HEALTH CARE AND EDUCATION

The purpose of this appendix is to look at one storyboard in depth, in order to explore the things that were done, those that were not done, and the reasons for those decisions. The storyboard prepared by the Hospice of the Florida Suncoast was selected because it provides the greatest opportunity for discussion.

The storyboard prepared by the Pinellas County (Florida) Schools is included because quality professionals have been looking forward to applying quality tools for the benefit of the public through education. This is offered as an example of a successful implementation in this important area.

The hospice storyboard was done as a follow-up to training in quality, problem solving, and storyboarding. It was the first attempt by this group to do a storyboard. The group was coached during the first five meetings by an outside consultant. Then it finished the project on its own. The copy you see in this book was a part of the hospice's submission for consideration of the Florida Governor's Sterling Award.

The Hospice of the Florida Suncoast

Synopsis
of
Quality Improvement Project

October 1992

EXECUTIVE SUMMARY

While not discussed in this book, the executive summary can be a useful tool, especially if you are presenting your story outside your group or organization. It is a variation of the old saw, "tell 'em what you're going to tell 'em, tell 'em, then tell 'em what you told 'em." The executive summary tells the audience what you are getting ready to tell them by briefly summarizing the entire story. This approach allows the casual viewer the opportunity to understand your accomplishment without reading the whole book. It gives interested readers a frame of reference for what they are about to see. If you are making others in your organization aware of your activities by presenting your storyboard as it is developing, then you won't be able to do an executive summary until you are finished.

The Hospice of the Florida Suncoast

Synopsis of quality improvement project

The Hospice of the Florida Suncoast is a community-based, nonsectarian, not-for-profit organization dedicated to the care of terminally ill patients and their families. As the largest known hospice program of its type in the world, with an operating budget of $24 million, The Hospice of the Florida Suncoast has served Pinellas County, Florida for 15 years. The Hospice's mission is to provide care for all who need it, regardless of ability to pay. Resources for meeting the costs of care include: Medicare/Medicaid for eligible patients, insurance, personal funds, and charitable contributions.

Reason for improvement The issue of payment for medical services is always a sensitive issue, but particularly so when a family is in stress. In order to minimize negative impacts on patients and families, The Hospice of the Florida Suncoast adopted a policy of paying for consulting physician services when the bill was received, then filing for reimbursement with the Medicare/Medicaid intermediaries after receiving required documentation from the providers. This policy was successful in improving the image of Hospice with both patients and physicians. On the other hand, this policy created a $187,000/year problem.

Problem statement Substantial amounts of money are being written off because claims are not filed within specified billing periods, thus revenues paid for consulting physician services are not reimbursed by Medicare/Medicaid intermediaries. The result has been lost revenue and failure to meet customer expectations.

Planning breakthrough This problem was the focus of the first quality improvement team to be organized at The Hospice of the Florida Suncoast. The problem was selected as part of a training program in which ideas were brainstormed and themes prioritized. Although a group of highly motivated people were aware of this problem, they had never organized as a team to solve it. An interdepartmental team was formed, including members from accounting and finance, medical records, patient care, and quality management, in order to look at all aspects of the problem. Selecting members from multiple departments contributed to the discovery of root causes and effective solutions. Actions were implemented to reduce the backlog of outstanding medical records and to facilitate the timely submittal of claims. Write-offs were reduced and customer satisfaction enhanced.

A storyboard was developed as a training tool for the first quality improvement team. It provided a clear framework for communicating activities and results. This first project was not perfect, yet many valuable lessons were learned along the way. These lessons will be shared with other quality improvement teams and will provide the basis for the continual improvement of our care and services.

"Hospice is a special way of caring"

OUTLINE

This is not usually seen in a storyboard. It is, however, another way to communicate.

Quality improvement storyboard outline

I. Team information
  A. First quality improvement team at Hospice.
  B. Five departments represented.
  C. Team developed as part of a TQM training program.
II. Theme selection
  A. Theme selection matrix utilized.
  B. Theme selected dealt with claims for consulting physician services.
  C. Six customers were identified.
III. Problem statement
  A. Claims for consulting physician services not submitted on time.
  B. Reasons for improvement identified.
    1. Customers inconvenienced.
    2. Revenue lost.
    3. Rework required.
  C. Goals included decrease in number of late records and increase in revenue collected.
IV. Analysis of root causes
  A. Flowchart of current situation.
  B. Cause-and-effect diagram.
  C. Critical activity chart.
  D. Pareto analysis of current situation.
    1. Twenty percent of providers responsible for 64 percent of outstanding records.
    2. Collection rate for consulting physician services = 19 percent; write-offs = 81 percent.
V. Solution selection
  A. Selection matrix utilized.
  B. Solutions selected included targeting the vital few, revising prepayment policy, and educating key persons.
  C. Barriers and aids identified.
VI. Implementation/results
  A. Proactive and reactive solutions implemented.
  B. Achieved 60 percent reduction in number of providers with outstanding records; 32 percent increase in percentage of revenues collected; and 170 percent increase in actual amount of dollars collected.
VII. Future plans
  A. Share results with staff and physicians.
  B. Propose change in prepayment policy as related to targeted providers.
  C. Design management information system capable of tracking key indicators.
  D. Lobby/advocate for changes in reimbursement regulations.
VIII. Lessons learned
  A. The value of using TQM tools to understand problems and monitor results.
  B. Inadequacies of current management information systems.
  C. Difficulty of improving a process that is partially controlled by external customers.
  D. Areas of nonconformance with established policies/procedures.
  E. Rewards to be gained by reducing shotgun approach and focusing on the vital few.

TEAM SELECTION

Since this was the organization's first storyboarding attempt, the team included a broad cross section of individuals from throughout the hospice. Some team members were recruited while others were volunteered. They often worked with others in their departments to identify and develop information used in the storyboard.

In many organizations there is a thin line between volunteerism and recruitment. Frequently people volunteer because they know they will be needed. They may not have excess time to devote to a new project, and may, in fact, spend personal time on it. Many fine organizations have developed a culture that makes recruitment relatively easy. All you have to do is ask.

In other organizations people will volunteer because they know they will be recruited anyway. Finally, there are organizations where people lie in the weeds, hoping not to be selected for extra work. In this case, you may need to work hard to get the help you need, until the overall culture changes.

TEAM PAGE

This team page is very well laid out. The addition of a photograph is a nice touch, making the work personal. The center section, with team member names, is essential for further communication with readers. The Gantt chart at the bottom shows the activity going according to schedule. It is unusual for a group to stick to a schedule so well. In this case, contributing causes included the following:

- Meetings were held on time and scheduled in advance.
- No delays or exceptions occurred. I attribute this to the overall culture of the hospice.
- The team leader was skilled, determined, and believed in the process.
- There was a strong consensus that this issue was worth the effort.

First quality improvement team

- First quality improvement team at hospice
- Five departments represented
- Developed as part of a TQM training program

Team members

Name	Position	Team function
T. Abrantes	Consulting physician specialist	Team member
M. Farrall	Accounts receivable coordinator	Team member
M. Pruitt	Nursing manager	Team member
G. Case	Patient/family care coordinator	Team member
D. Wise	Medical records	Team member
M. Manrique	Program director	Team member (Added at action plan stage)
V. Wilks	Comptroller	Team leader
B. Oldanie	Director of planning	Facilitator
H. Forsha	Business systems analyst	Consultant, trainer

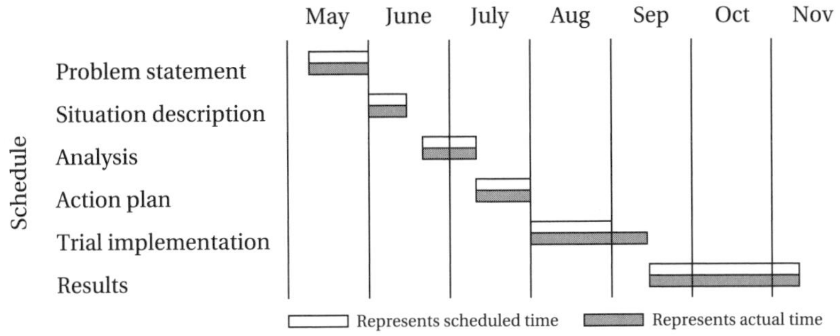

THEME SELECTION

The top three issues were recommended by a group consisting of managers and other key persons. This team developed and applied its own criteria for problem selection.

Especially in organizations where storyboarding has not been done before, there are many issues worth the work. Multivoting was relatively easy, because there was consensus on the top issue. This is common. People working together know what the problems are; they just need a vehicle to get them up to the surface for action.

Theme selection process

Managers interviewed for improvement opportunities

⇩

List of ideas brainstormed

⇩

Ideas voted down to a list of three themes

⇩

Data evaluated on a theme selection matrix and selected #1 as our theme

⇩

Theme	Theme name	Impact on customer	Can team solve?	Need for improvement	Score
Theme	1. Consulting physician services claims	4	4	5	13
	2. Delayed admissions	5	2	5	12
	3. Documentation system	3	3	5	11

Scale
Low 1 - 2 - 3 - 4 - 5 High

THEME AND CUSTOMERS

This group took the time to examine who the customers were, and found broad involvement throughout the organization. As it turned out, the hospice had already solved this problem for its external customers, the people they serve and their families. There was, however, a costly internal problem.

Theme and customers

From the theme selection matrix we could see that our theme would be

⇩

Low reimbursement rate
for
consulting physician services

Our customers were identified as

⇩

- Attending physicians
- Consulting physicians
- Patients/families
- Case managers
- Billing clerks
- Medicare and Medicaid intermediaries

PROBLEM STATEMENT

In order to understand this statement, you need to know that an *intermediary* is an insurance company that distributes funds to health care organizations as reimbursement for Medicare and Medicaid claims. There are strict time limits during which claims must be processed. If the claims are not made during that time limit, they will not be paid, and the health care organization loses the money.

This problem statement does a good job of zeroing in on a specific problem. Claims are not being submitted on time, thus creating additional costs.

Problem

Medicare and medicaid claims for consulting physician services are not submitted to the intermediaries within the specified billing periods, resulting in lost revenue and failure to meet customer specifications.

↓

Reason for improvement

- Customers inconvenienced.
- Revenue lost.
- Rework required.

↓

Goals

- Decrease late and incomplete records.
- Increase revenues.
- Increase customer satisfaction.

THE MISSING PAGE

Purists would argue that you can't tell for sure if you have a problem until you have established a measurement system, and have documented it. Mostly, I agree.

Yet when you first look at an issue or a problem, you frequently do not have a measurement system in place. Developing a measurement system is often one of the first jobs of problem solving. As you come to understand the problem, you frequently have to improve the measurement system as well.

In this case, it was necessary to hand crank the numbers, taking a recent time period and auditing the records. No average over time was taken, and variation around an average could not be determined. It was well known that the computer system was scheduled for an upgrade, which would be able to accumulate the needed data, and it was a consensus that this issue had broad effects on the organization. I would rather have a team get started learning the problem-solving process, and accomplish some improvements, than wait until it had a new computer system to accumulate better data.

FLOWCHART

The hospice team found the flowcharting process to be a very useful tool. It was during this process that many problem areas were identified. In other words, there were several places in the process where improvements could be made.

By the way, a consulting physician is called in by the primary physician in order to provide special services. The primary physician is the family doctor or specialist managing a patient's overall care.

This flowchart is clean and easy to understand. As is typical, each box could be expanded to show more details.

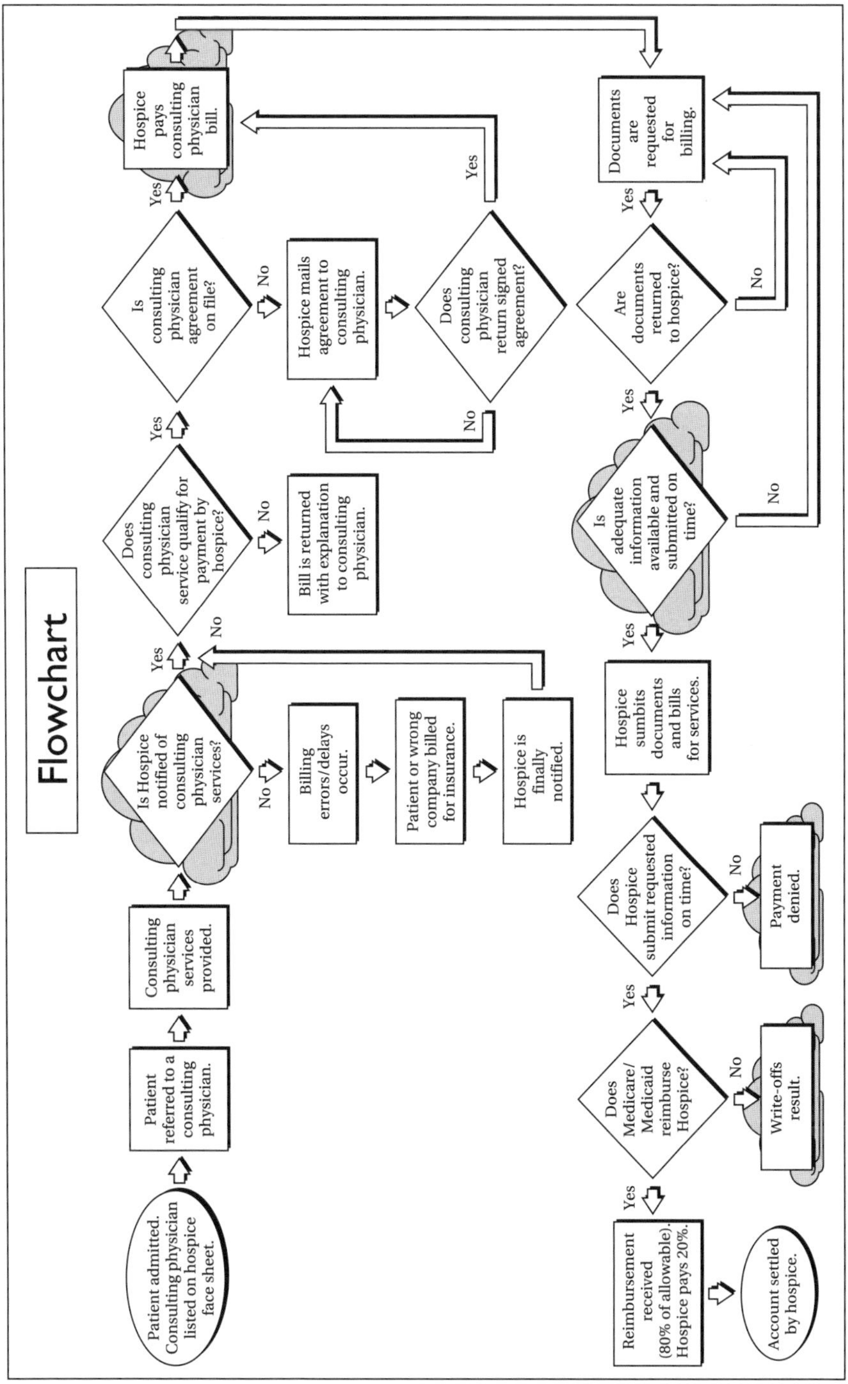
Flowchart
Patient admitted. Consulting physician listed on hospice face sheet.
Patient referred to a consulting physician.
Consulting physician services provided.
Is Hospice notified of consulting physician services?
No
Billing errors/delays occur.
Patient or wrong company billed for insurance.
Hospice is finally notified.
No
Yes
Does consulting physician service qualify for payment by hospice?
No
Bill is returned with explanation to consulting physician.
Yes
Is consulting physician agreement on file?
No
Hospice mails agreement to consulting physician.
Does consulting physician return signed agreement?
No
Yes
Yes
Hospice pays consulting physician bill.
Documents are requested for billing.
Yes
Are documents returned to hospice?
No
Yes
Is adequate information available and submitted on time?
No
Yes
Hospice sumbits documents and bills for services.
Does Hospice submit requested information on time?
No
Payment denied.
Yes
Does Medicare/ Medicaid reimburse Hospice?
No
Write-offs result.
Yes
Reimbursement received (80% of allowable). Hospice pays 20%.
Account settled by hospice.

FISHBONE DIAGRAM

This particular fishbone diagram shows a variety of problem areas. Some are policy issues; and some are cleanup activities, where activities were in place, but execution could be improved. Finally, there was the actual work issue selected, which will be explained later in this appendix.

Frequently, the cleanup issues can be delegated and worked on while the major work is moving forward. This can provide some, and maybe even substantial, improvement in the key indicator. So cleanup issues should not be ignored.

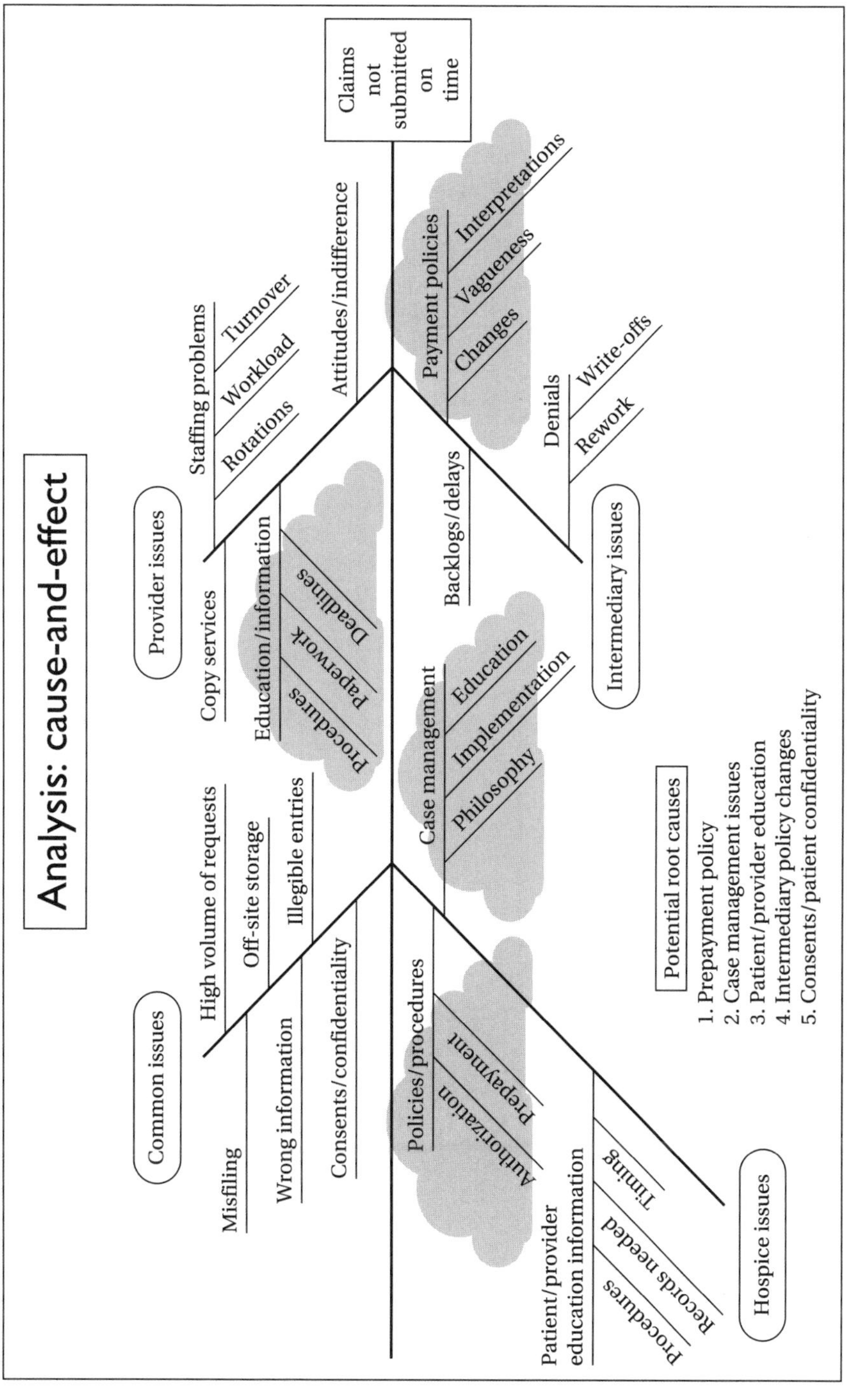
Analysis: cause-and-effect
Claims not submitted on time
Provider issues
Staffing problems
Rotations
Workload
Turnover
Attitudes/indifference
Copy services
Education/information
Procedures
Paperwork
Deadlines
Common issues
High volume of requests
Off-site storage
Illegible entries
Misfiling
Wrong information
Consents/confidentiality
Intermediary issues
Backlogs/delays
Denials
Rework
Write-offs
Payment policies
Changes
Vagueness
Interpretations
Case management
Philosophy
Implementation
Education
Hospice issues
Policies/procedures
Authorization
Prepayment
Patient/provider education information
Procedures
Records needed
Timing
Potential root causes
1. Prepayment policy
2. Case management issues
3. Patient/provider education
4. Intermediary policy changes
5. Consents/patient confidentiality

CRITICAL ACTIVITY CHART

There are two types of critical activity charts. This type looks at the big picture, identifying the key process involved, and the inputs, activities, and outputs. It also defines the key problems in the present system.

The second type of critical activity chart deals with critical activities of the corrective actions. Both types of charts are beneficial.

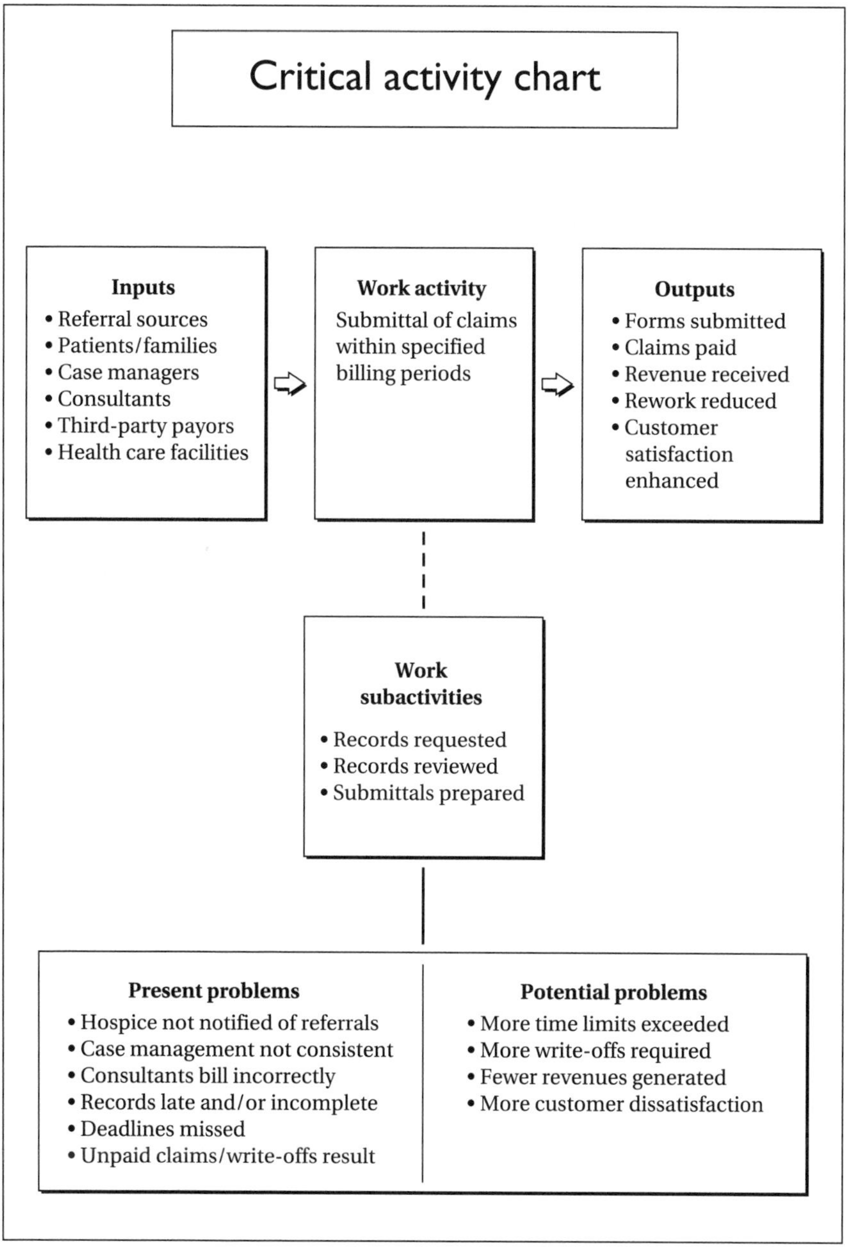
Critical activity chart
Inputs
• Referral sources
• Patients/families
• Case managers
• Consultants
• Third-party payors
• Health care facilities
Work activity
Submittal of claims within specified billing periods
Outputs
• Forms submitted
• Claims paid
• Revenue received
• Rework reduced
• Customer satisfaction enhanced
Work subactivities
• Records requested
• Records reviewed
• Submittals prepared
Present problems
• Hospice not notified of referrals
• Case management not consistent
• Consultants bill incorrectly
• Records late and/or incomplete
• Deadlines missed
• Unpaid claims/write-offs result
Potential problems
• More time limits exceeded
• More write-offs required
• Fewer revenues generated
• More customer dissatisfaction

PARETO CHART

The revealing of this information made my problem-solving spine tingle. One person on the team had this information firmly in mind—but only that one person. In order to get this information where it could be used, there had to be a team; this person had to be on the team; and the right questions had to be asked. The day this information was revealed was an *aha* experience for the whole team.

As you can see, there are a lot of doctors serving hospice patients. This team did a smart thing in presenting its data. After the team members arranged their data in descending order, they classified providers into groups of 10 so that it would be easy to present the data graphically. That does not change the overall shape of the distribution, and it makes for a clear presentation.

Notice the clarity of the bulleted statement and the remarkable contribution of the first group to the problem. This is common. It is 64/20. Frequently the 80/20 rule is more like 90/10. Every case is different.

Pareto chart

Outstanding records ranked by provider groups
May 1992

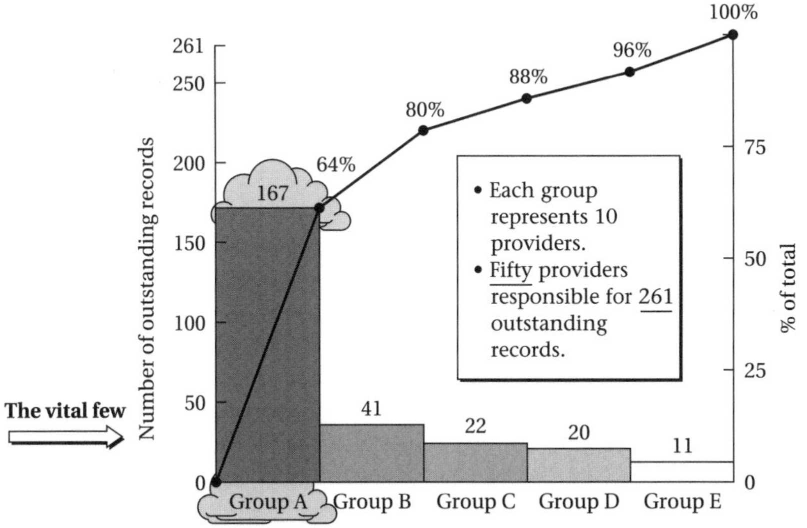

20% of the providers responsible for
64% of the outstanding records.

SOLUTION SELECTION MATRIX

While this matrix is clean in its presentation, do not be deceived. It takes a lot of work to get to these decisions. Also, notice how the item "target key offenders" evolved from the information in the Pareto chart.

BARRIERS AND AIDS

This is an excellent tool for planning, and for considering the problems that may occur during implementation.

Solution selection matrix

Possible solution	Cost/ benefit ratio	Effectiveness	Feasibility	Total score	Action Yes/no
• Change prepayment policy	5	3	1	9	No
• Change Aetna's policies	5	4	2	11	Yes Long term
• Educate • Patients/families • Physicians • Case managers	4	4	5	13	Yes Now
• Classify consulting physicians as attendings	5	4	3	12	Yes Long term
• Target key offenders	5	5	5	15	Yes Now

Scale
Low 1 - 2 - 3 - 4 - 5 High

Barriers	**Aids**
• Attitudes/opinions	• Administrative support
• Lack of information	• Additional staff person
• Complex procedures	• Improved computer system
• Reliance on external informants	• High cost of write-offs
• Resistance to change	• Reimbursements available

IMPLEMENTATION

Here is the key indicator that the team had been waiting for. The real objective was to minimize uncollected funds; or stated positively, maximize collected funds. This information could be placed in the results section of the storyboard.

Notice that the record keeping was still based on a hand-cranked audit. It was the decision of the team to use this method until the new computer system was installed. Yes, it's nice to have more frequent reporting, but it is not always necessary, and it may be more expensive than can be justified.

THE REAL WORK

Note that this storybook doesn't spend any time on the real work; that is, educating patients and staff, calling on doctors' office managers, building relationships, and improving materials.

Implementation

Monthly collections
for consulting physician services

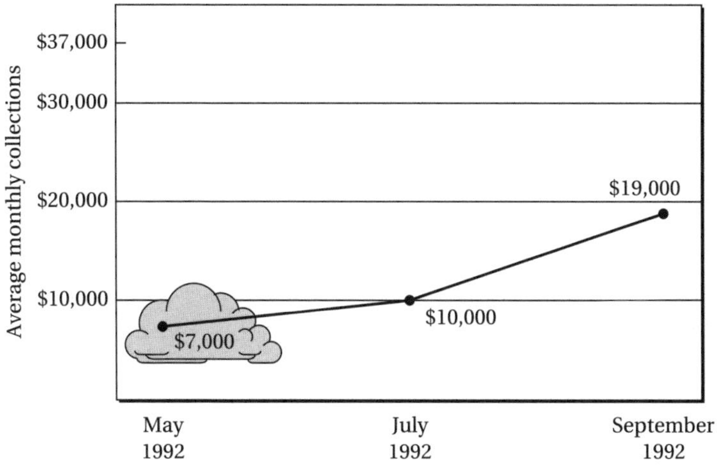

- Claims for consulting physician services totaled $410,000 for the past 12 months.
- Average monthly charges for consulting physician services totaled $37,000/month.

- Collections rose from $7,000 in May 1992 to $19,000 in September. This is an increase of $12,000.
- Collections increased 170% in the four-month period.

RESULTS

Beyond the results achieved on the key indicator already described, there is a secondary effect. Look at how the Pareto chart shows the change in scale and the dramatic decrease in the number of problem providers. This is not an unusual change of scale, when the actual roots of a problem are discovered. You can also imagine that the flowchart would show a lot fewer clouds.

Results

Outstanding records ranked by provider groups
September, 1992

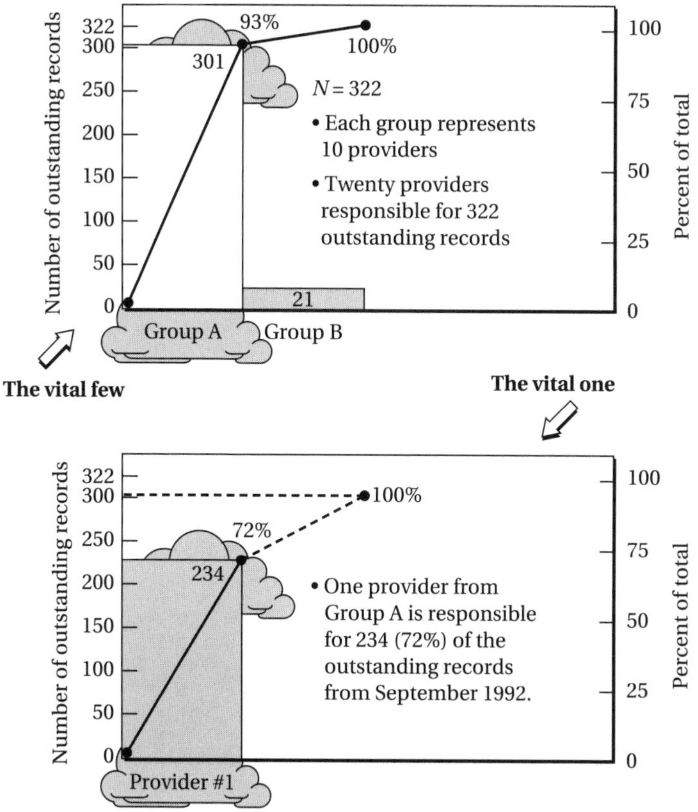

Scope of problem
One provider = 72% of the problem

LESSONS LEARNED

These are clear and concise in presentation. Notice how even small pictures or graphics make this panel interesting.

FUTURE PLANS

Notice how the seeds for future projects are contained in the future plans section. At this point no one knows which, or how many, of these plans will come to pass. It is up to the team to decide if, or when, it wants to tackle another project. At this point, the team should

- Celebrate success.
- Consider its own plans.
- Present the results to management.
- Achieve consensus with management on future plans.

Graduate TQM

Lessons learned

- Difficulty of improving a process that is partially controlled by external customers
- Inconsistency of conformance with established policies and procedures
- Inadequacies of current management information system
- Rewards gained by eliminating shotgun approach and focusing on the vital few
- Effectiveness of a structured problem-solving process utilizing TQM tools

Future plans

- Share storyboard with hospice staff and physicians.
- Develop plan for educating employees and physicians.
- Propose change in prepayment policy as related to providers identified as the vital few.
- Design management information system capable of tracking key indicators.
- Perform ongoing monitoring and evaluation of established criteria.
- Lobby for changes in reimbursement regulations.

COMMENTS ON OTHER STORYBOARD EXAMPLES

Of all the examples in this book, the Hospice storyboard is the most finely produced. There was a reason for that. The team was competing, and it was presenting its story outside the organization. This is neither good nor bad.

The other examples used were primarily for internal activities, and did not use the latest software, if any. This is good or bad only in the context of the objective.

I had the good fortune to work for an organization for many years that would overlook an occasional spelling error and move on. If you like to use computers, and it helps you to cost-effectively generate charts and graphs, use computer graphics. If you don't have a computer, make a conscious judgment about the costs and benefits before you buy expensive software. The objective of storyboarding is to solve problems, not to generate graphics.

Finally, you will observe missing steps, varying use of tools, and different approaches. This is great! The processes discussed in this book are robust. They are forgiving primarily because they contain so many ways to increase your odds of solving or improving a problem, so that it is actually difficult *not* to achieve results. The best odds, however, are to use the process to its fullest, and that will only come with experience and, yes, a little luck from time to time.

This brings you back to rule number one: There are no rules.

Happy storyboarding.

Pinellas County (Florida) Schools

Quality conferencing for an entire grade level in "1" sitting

Conferencing for All

Presented by
Deborah Figg, Aleasha Dees,
and
John Leanes

Carwise Middle School
Pinellas County Schools
Palm Harbor, Florida

Quality conferencing for an entire grade level in "1" sitting . . . Conferencing for All

1993–1994 Team Nomination Criteria

I. Purpose, value, or reason for selecting the project

A. Explain how and why this project was chosen. What was the situation or opportunity?

Quality conferencing at the middle school is vital for better educational opportunities for all students. By reviewing the current data for Blueprint 2000, it is obvious that the need for an effective means of conferencing be implemented. We envision the caring attitude through a positive mode of assessment be done within a minimum time frame. This restructured effort for conferencing is being introduced and developed at our school as a model that we believe could be effective at the middle school level.

B. Describe the techniques used during the project selection process.

1. Deployment flowchart—to determine if customer expectations were aligned with Blueprint 2000 and SCANS report
2. Affinity diagram—to determine customer needs
3. Nominal group technique—to prioritize needs
4. Conferencing
5. Fishbone diagram—to identify two root causes
   a) Negative atmosphere
   b) Time constraints
6. Curriculum development—with outcome of Conferencing for All
7. State, county, and school standards
8. Customer input—for school mission statement (Blueprint 2000) and for benchmarking
9. Pilot programs—including evaluations, benchmark grades, surveys, and process decision program chart

C. Identify the stakeholders in this situation.

1. Students
2. Parents
3. Teachers
4. Administration
5. Volunteers

D. Explain how the project supports the organization's goals.

Conferencing for All is structured so that all sixth-grade students may conference with their parents at the same time and in the same room. Those students with special needs are mainstreamed so that they are included in this quality process.

II. Root cause analysis

A. Identify and explain the root causes of the project.

Parent and student feedback for Blueprint 2000 provided reasons to scrutinize the present conferencing system at the middle school level. Data of grades conclude the individual and group success through the process of whole group quality conferencing. Teachers used the cause-and-effect diagram to identify root causes. (See presentation handouts.)

B. Describe the analysis techniques used. How was the root cause determined?

The root cause was determined by the survey and fishbone diagram. (See presentation handouts.)

III. Data collection
   A. Explain the data-gathering techniques used.
      A deployment survey was used to gather data for Conferencing for All. (See presentation handouts.)

IV. Solution development
   A. Describe the solution/corrective actions considered for this project.
      Corrective actions considered for this project include a process decision program chart and surveys of all participants.
   B. Describe the criteria used to determine the best solutions (e.g., cost, time, and so on).
      1. Gantt charts
      2. Flowcharts
      3. Pilot project
      4. Evaluation of pilot program
   C. Discuss expertise used in reaching this solution. Who was consulted and why?
      To our knowledge, there is no other program of this kind being implemented. Thus, there was no expert advice for us to seek.
   D. Explain how the final solutions affect the root cause.
      The final solution, called Conferencing for All, affected the root cause, identified as the need for effective conferencing, in two ways.
      1. The number of conferences attended increased from 5 percent to 89 percent.
      2. Students displayed a positive attitude toward subjects, evaluation methods, and communication with parents and the school.
   E. State the benefits of the solution.
      One benefit of this concept of quality conferencing recognizes the needs of the whole child. It addresses the essential relationship between the student's affective needs and his or her academic success.

V. Outline of implementation plan, progress, and/or results
   A. Explain your process for getting agreement from stakeholders for implementation of these solutions.
      1. Approval of state and county board officials
      2. Actual count of participants
   B. Define the tracking techniques or follow-up activities that have been developed and/or installed to monitor results.
      1. Surveys
      2. Process decision program chart
      3. Percent of participants
   C. Explain how the results were, or will be, communicated to stakeholders.
      1. School newspaper
      2. Student advisory council
      3. Principal's letter
      4. Class letter
      5. Media coverage
      6. Volunteer training sessions
      7. Countywide training at staff development days
   D. Explain how the solutions have been incorporated into ongoing operations.
      1. Pilot program added three classes of reading students with three new teachers
      2. Training at school level for some teachers
      3. Training at district level for teachers countywide
      4. Training new volunteers in the quality process
      5. Continual development at our school of Conferencing for All

Conferencing for All

Carwise Middle School
Pinellas County Schools
Palm Harbor, Florida

Quality in conferencing

At Carwise we believe:

- All children have value and worth.
- All children need to belong.
- All children need a loving, compassionate environment.
- Cultural diversity is enriching and vital to individuals and society.
- Children have unique backgrounds, talents, interests, and needs that deserve affirmation and support.
- All children can learn.
- Success breeds success.
- High expectations produce high achievement.
- Education is a shared responsibility of the school, home, student, and community.
- All children have the right to be treated equally and fairly.
- Everyone has the right to a healthy and safe physical and mental environment.

Conferencing for All

Carwise Middle School mission statement

The mission statement for JOSEPH L. CARWISE MIDDLE SCHOOL is for students, staff, parents, and community to ensure opportunities for success for ALL students in a caring environment that promotes self-motivation and lifelong learning.

Quality in educational conferencing — Why conferencing is necessary.

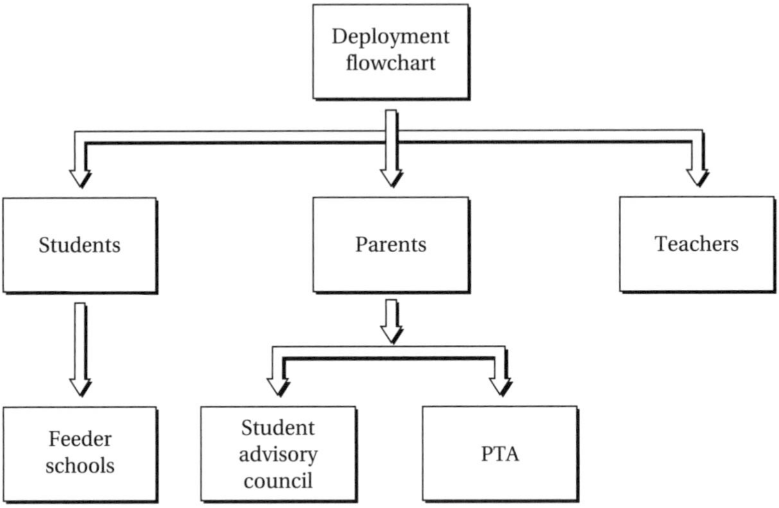

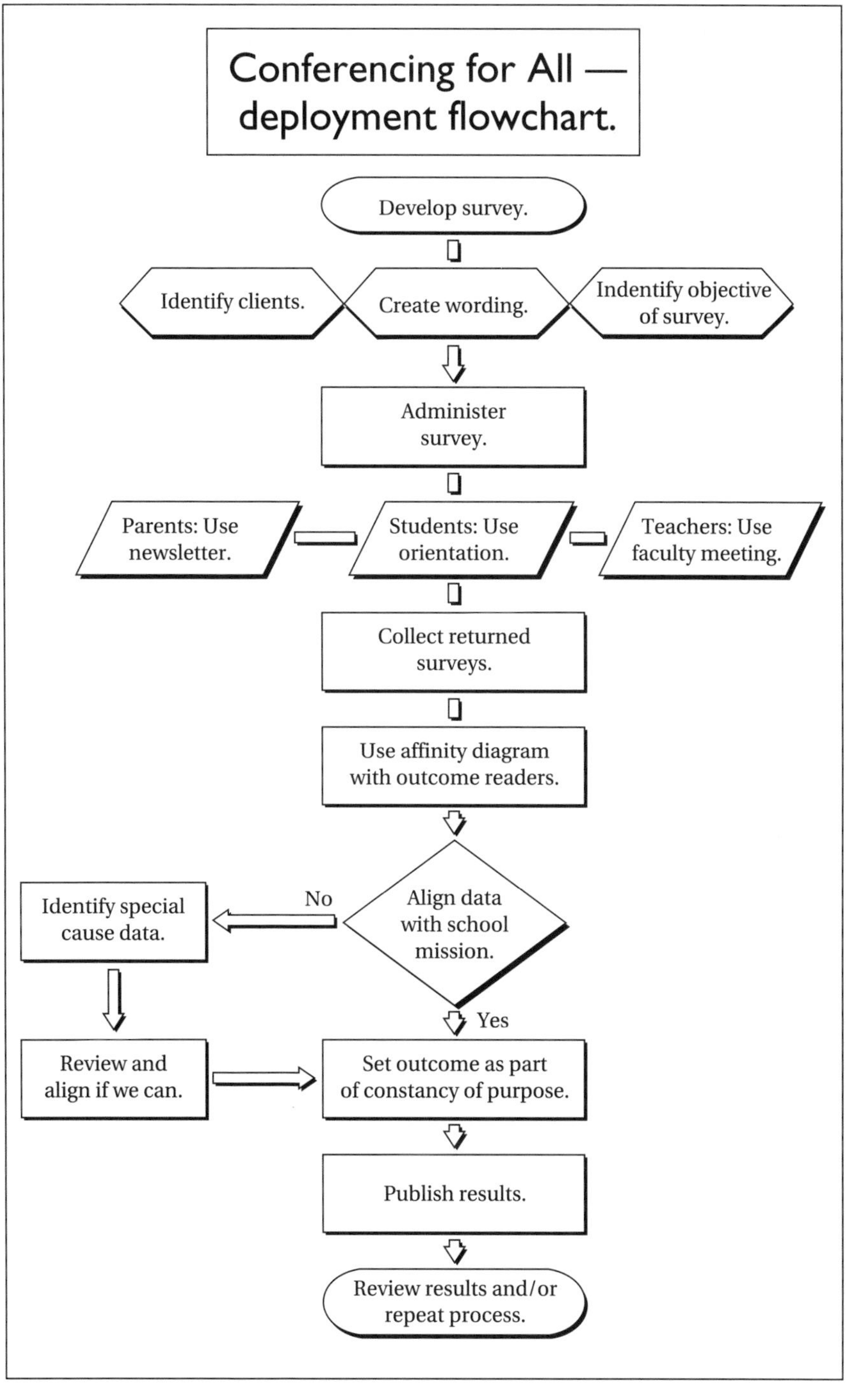
Conferencing for All — deployment flowchart.
Develop survey.
Identify clients.
Create wording.
Indentify objective of survey.
Administer survey.
Parents: Use newsletter.
Students: Use orientation.
Teachers: Use faculty meeting.
Collect returned surveys.
Use affinity diagram with outcome readers.
Align data with school mission.
No
Identify special cause data.
Review and align if we can.
Yes
Set outcome as part of constancy of purpose.
Publish results.
Review results and/or repeat process.

Learner outcomes

- Collaborative workers
- Effective communicators
- Creative thinkers and problem solvers
- Self-directed learners
- Community contributors
- Social interactors
- Quality producers

Conferencing is necessary so that

- Collaborative workers who effectively use leadership and group skills can productively work with others in culturally and organizationally diverse settings.
- Effective communicators who develop and integrate reading, language, math, art, and technology skills can effectively acquire, exchange, and express information, ideas, and feelings.
- Creative thinkers and problem solvers can identify, interpret, evaluate, and use available resources and information to formulate solutions to complex problems.
- Self-directed learners can formulate and use positive values to
  —Examine options.
  —Create a positive vision for their future.
  —Set achievable goals.
  —Initiate actions.
  —Monitor progress.
  —Evaluate their results.
- Community contributors can dedicate their time, energies, and talents to helping others and to improving the quality of their life in the home, school, community, and world.
- Social interactors can consistently demonstrate behavior patterns based on the following concepts.
  —Fairness
  —Honesty
  —Kindness
  —Compassion
  —Respect
  —Empathy
- Quality producers can create intellectual, practical, and artistic products that reflect originality and high standards and that use advanced technologies.

Parent, teacher, and student survey

Joseph L. Carwise Middle School
3301 Bentley Drive
Palm Harbor, Florida 34684

813-538-0000

John M. Leanes, Principal

Please complete the following statements with one idea.

1. It would be really nice if Carwise would ________________

____

____

____

____

2. It makes all the difference when ________________

____

____

____

____

3. Carwise would help my child most by ________________

____

____

____

____

Please return to student's first period teacher on Thursday, September 23, 1993.

PERT chart of activities

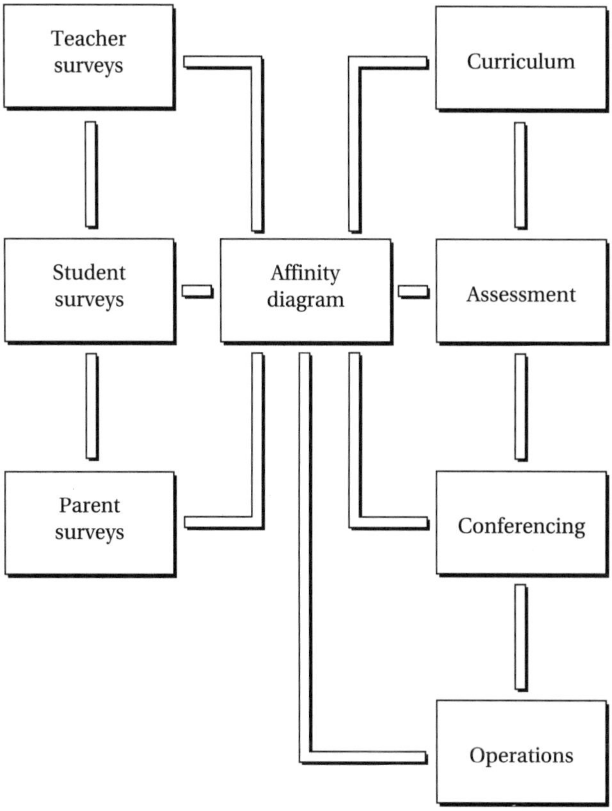

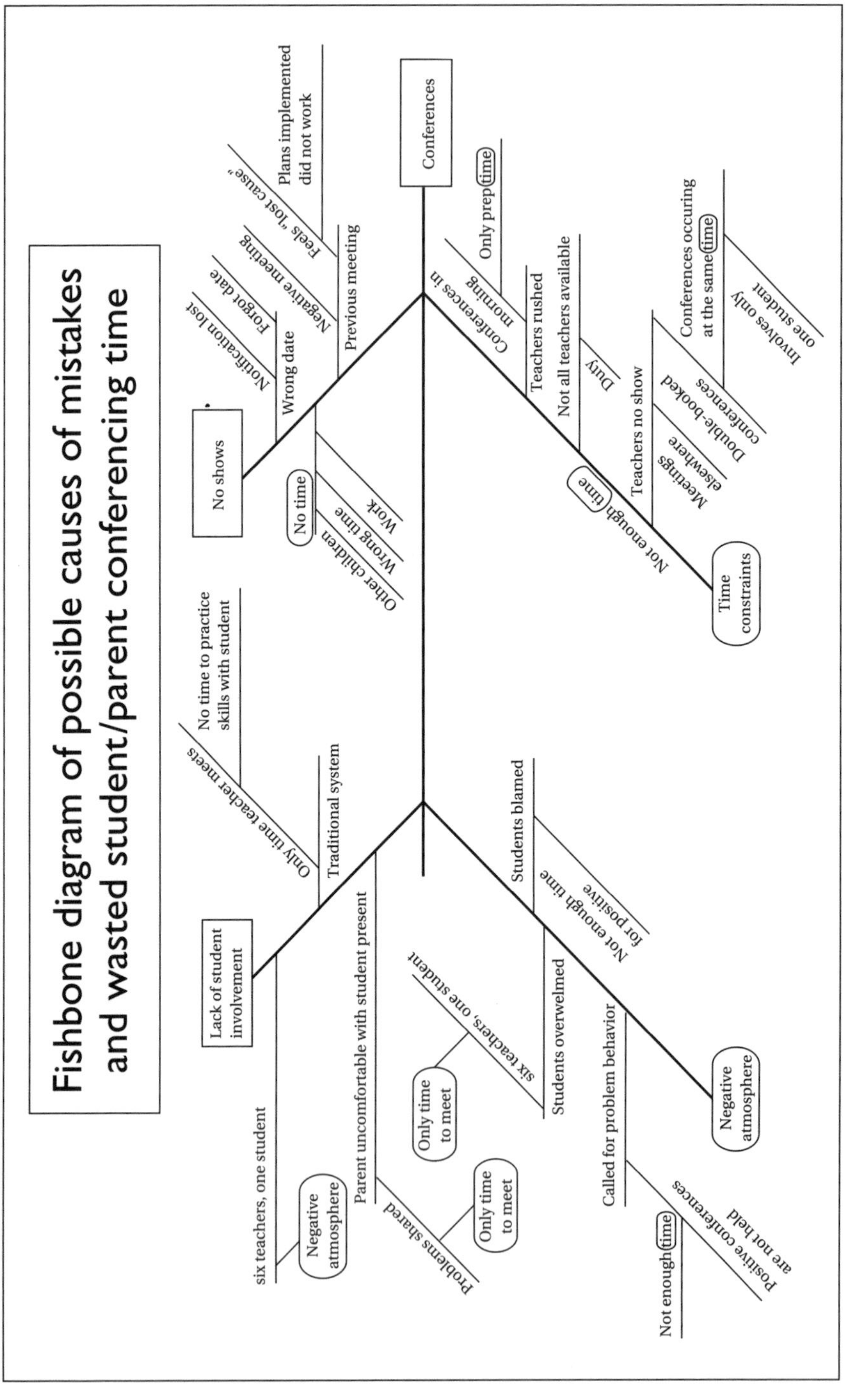

Fishbone diagram of possible causes of mistakes and wasted student/parent conferencing time
Conferences
No shows
Wrong date
Notification lost
Forgot date
Previous meeting
Negative meeting
Feels "lost cause"
Plans implemented did not work
No time
Work
Wrong time
Other children
Time constraints
Not enough time
Conferences in morning
Only prep time
Teachers rushed
Not all teachers available
Duty
Teachers no show
Meetings elsewhere
Double-booked conferences
Conferences occuring at the same time
Involves only one student
Lack of student involvement
Only time teacher meets
No time to practice skills with student
Traditional system
six teachers, one student
Negative atmosphere
Parent uncomfortable with student present
Problems shared
Only time to meet
six teachers, one student
Only time to meet
Negative atmosphere
Students blamed
Not enough time for positive
Students overwelmed
Called for problem behavior
Positive conferences are not held
Not enough time

Customer/supplier model

Process begins First day of class

Support
Assistance
Set-up
Donations
Data collection

Process ends Last day of class

Communication
Higher grades
Public relations
More motivation
Posititve feelings about school

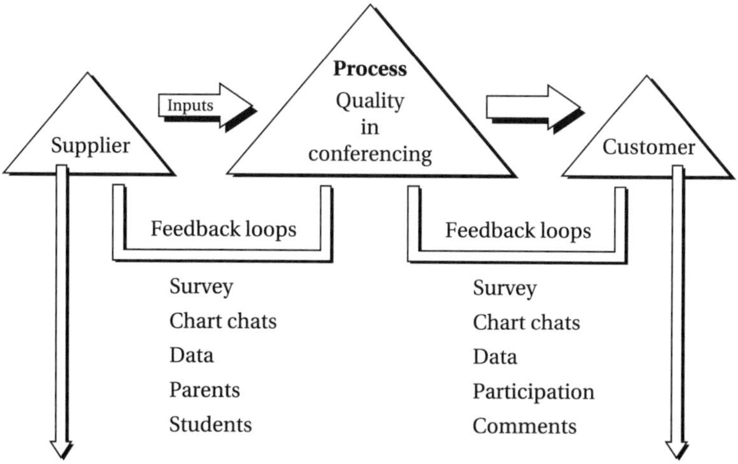

Administration
Volunteers
Custodians
Parent teacher student association
Community businesses
Media

Administration
Volunteers
Community
Parents
Students

Outcomes for students through a process of conferencing for quality

1. **Self-value**—Students will set expectations.
2. **Cooperative value**—Students will demonstrate group processing skills.
3. **Designing rubric**—Students will set goals and purpose for learning, and will constantly seek information and learn.
4. **Communicate**—Students will discuss, share, and communicate ideas clearly. They will implement technology in their processes.
5. **Peer conferencing**—Students will think critically, use experiences, share, rethink, and reason for improvement.
6. **Teacher conferencing**—Students will identify, define, and explore means to quality while evaluating the results.
7. **Conference with parent**—Students will seek new ways to tackle problems and to meet challenges.
8. **Continuing the process**—Students will maintain a sense of wonder and appreciate cooperative efforts as well as individual perspectives.

Gantt chart of teacher activities

Portfolio night	**Before school**	**Week 1**	**Week 2**	**Week 3**	**Week 4**	**Week 5**	**Week 6**
1. Analyze existing method of conferencing at middle school.							
2. Survey a need for conferencing.							
3. Devise a plan to meet with stakeholders.							
4. Prepare system for process.							
5. Create a flowchart of functions and structure of conferencing techniques.							
6. Create a rubric for process of portfolio conferencing.							
7. Add to portfolio with quality pieces of work.							
8. Use portfolios with peers.							
9. Revise conference procedures to conference with peers.							
10. Do whole group presentation.							
11. Have one-to-one conferencing with parents.							
12. Evaluate process.							

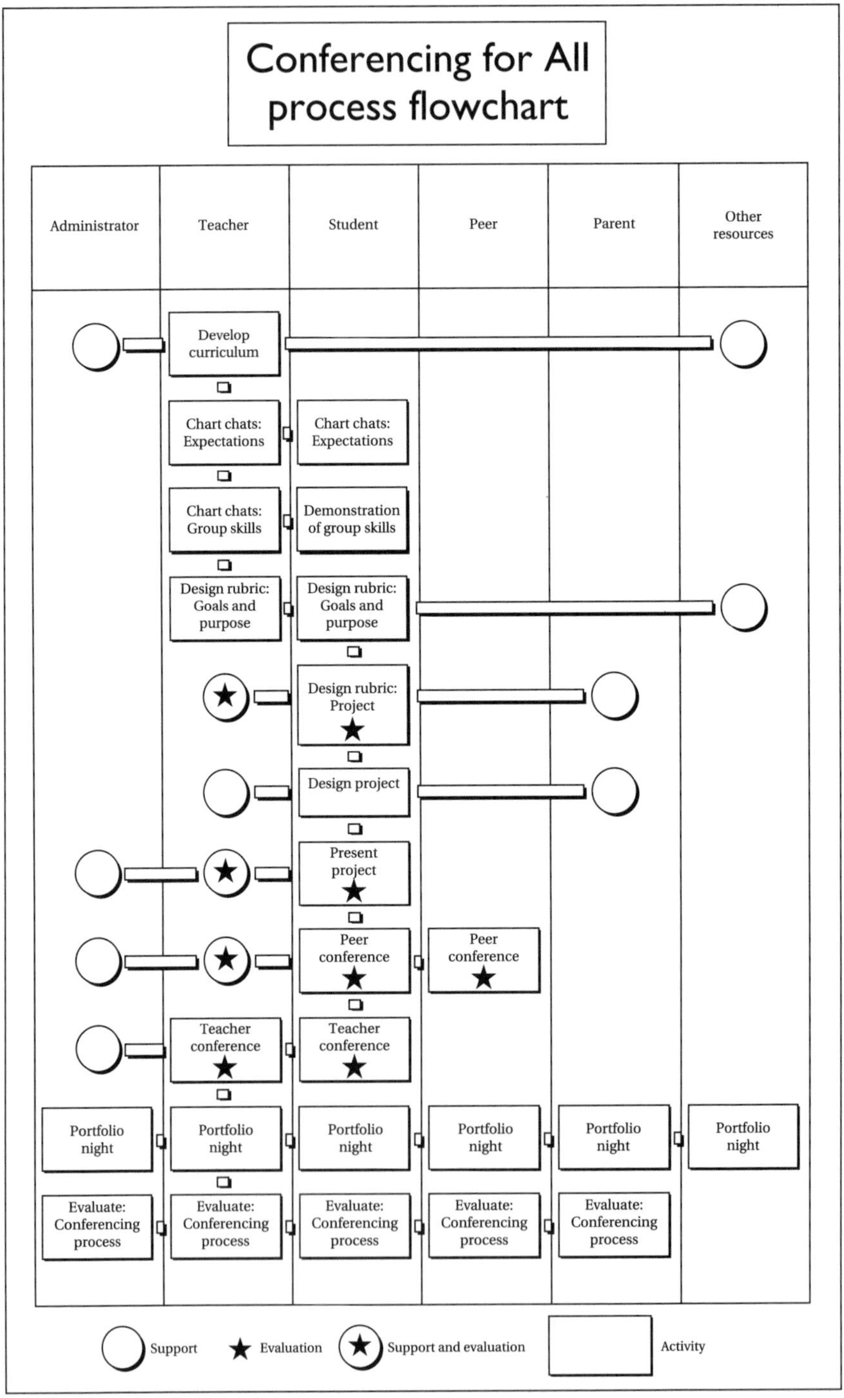
Conferencing for All process flowchart
Administrator
Teacher
Student
Peer
Parent
Other resources
Develop curriculum
Chart chats: Expectations
Chart chats: Expectations
Chart chats: Group skills
Demonstration of group skills
Design rubric: Goals and purpose
Design rubric: Goals and purpose
Design rubric: Project
Design project
Present project
Peer conference
Peer conference
Teacher conference
Teacher conference
Portfolio night
Portfolio night
Portfolio night
Portfolio night
Portfolio night
Portfolio night
Evaluate: Conferencing process
Evaluate: Conferencing process
Evaluate: Conferencing process
Evaluate: Conferencing process
Evaluate: Conferencing process
Support
Evaluation
Support and evaluation
Activity

Gantt chart of student activities

Portfolio night	**Week 1**	**Week 2**	**Week 3**	**Week 4**	**Week 5**	**Week 6**
1. Develop a rubric.						
2. Design a portfolio.						
3. Design a project.						
4. Read the book.						
5. Create a class mummy.						
6. Present project.						
7. Have student evaluation.						
8. Have student conferencing.						
9. Participate in portfolio night.						
10. Evaluate portfolio night.						

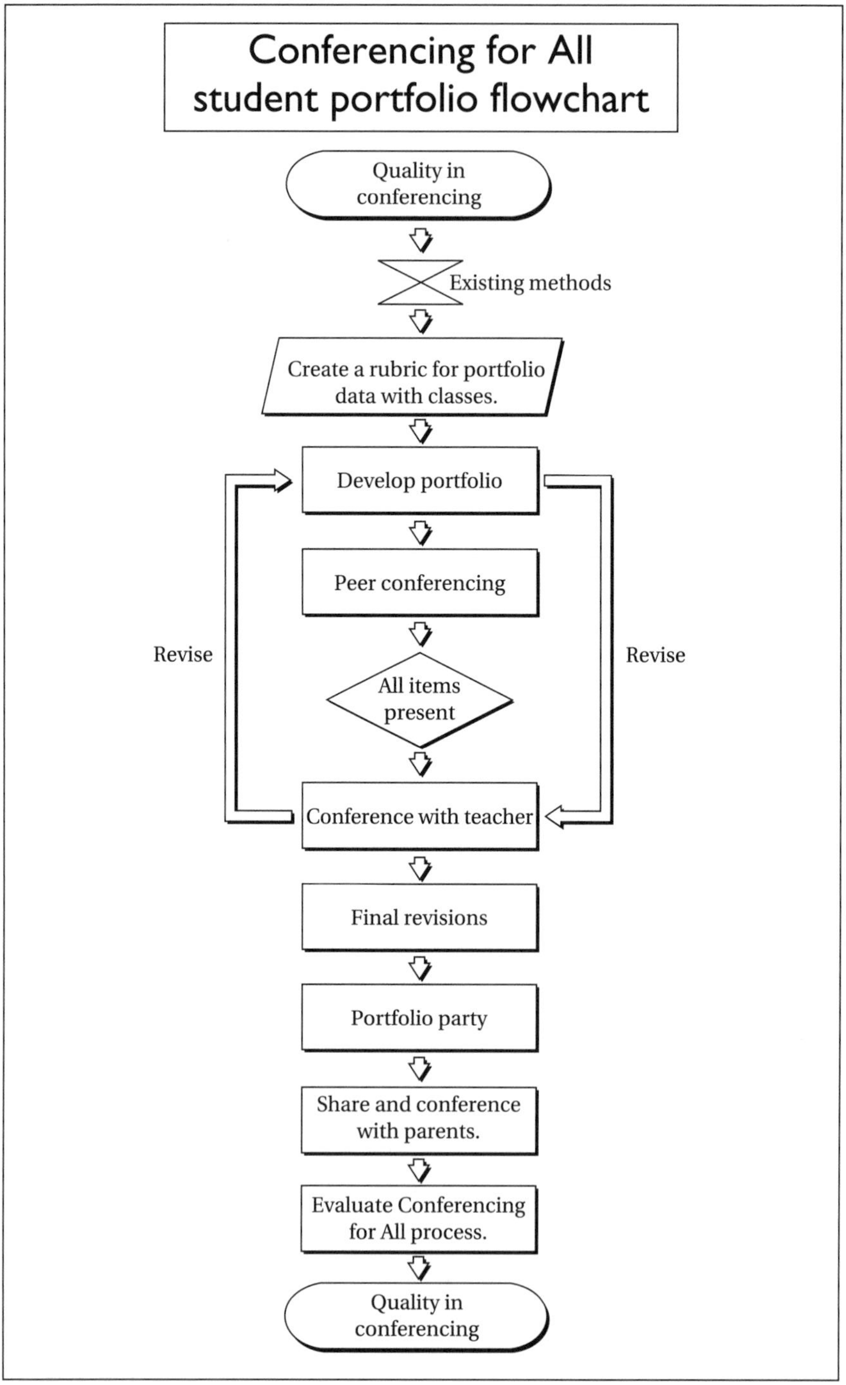
Conferencing for All student portfolio flowchart
Quality in conferencing
Existing methods
Create a rubric for portfolio data with classes.
Develop portfolio
Peer conferencing
All items present
Conference with teacher
Revise
Revise
Final revisions
Portfolio party
Share and conference with parents.
Evaluate Conferencing for All process.
Quality in conferencing

Name ________________________________

Pyramid flowchart

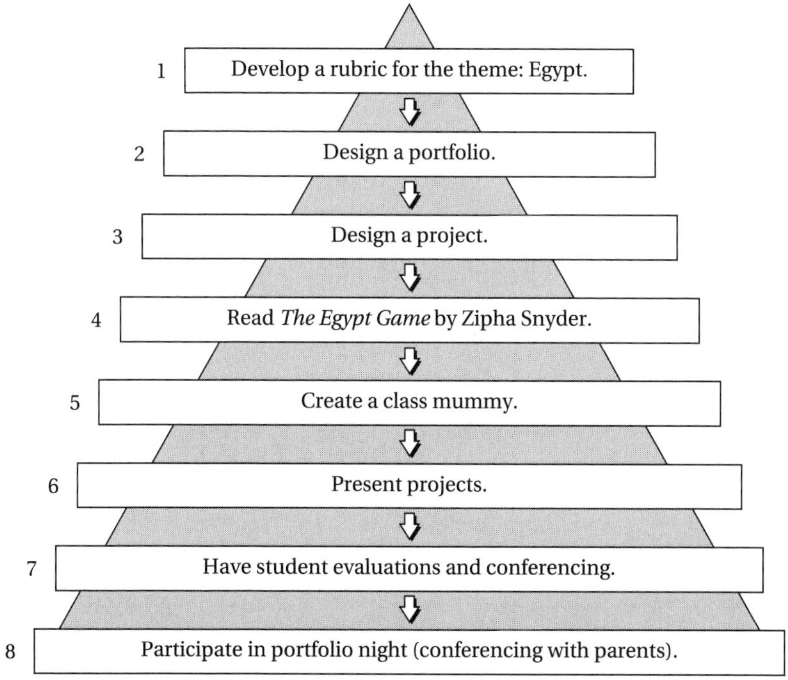

Student evaluation form for peer conferencing

Student's portfolio ______________________________

Student evaluator ______________________________

Date of conference ______________________________

Theme's title ______________________________

Please check if material is present and of good quality.

Portfolio items

______ Cover
______ Word search
______ Mummification paper
______ King Tut paper
______ Hieroglyphics
______ Mummy on black paper
______ Travel brochure
______ Mummy invitation
______ Final short story
______ Illustration
______ Project summary and/or grade sheet
______ Flowchart

What positive comments can you say about this portfolio?

1. ______________________________
____

2. ______________________________
____

Continue to strive to ______________________________
____

Portfolio night: This is important because ______________________________
____

I am proud of my work!

Student ______________________ Teacher ______________________

Conferencing for All

Evaluation methods: process decision program chart

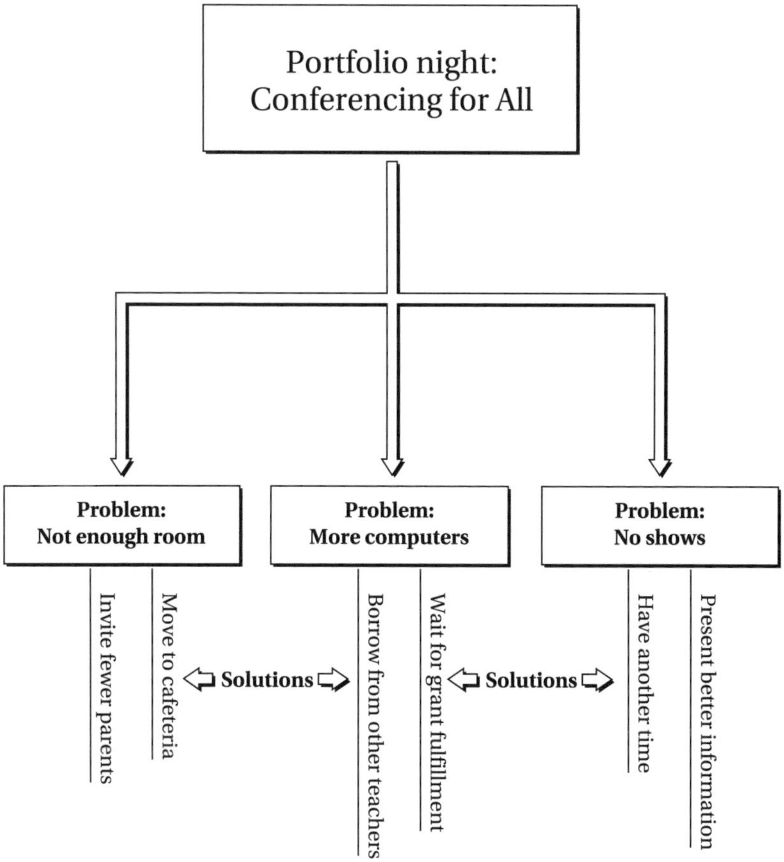

Traditional bell curves

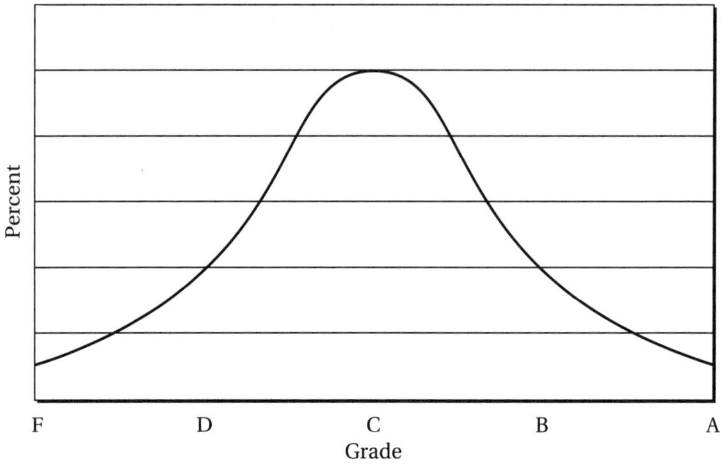

Pinellas County school

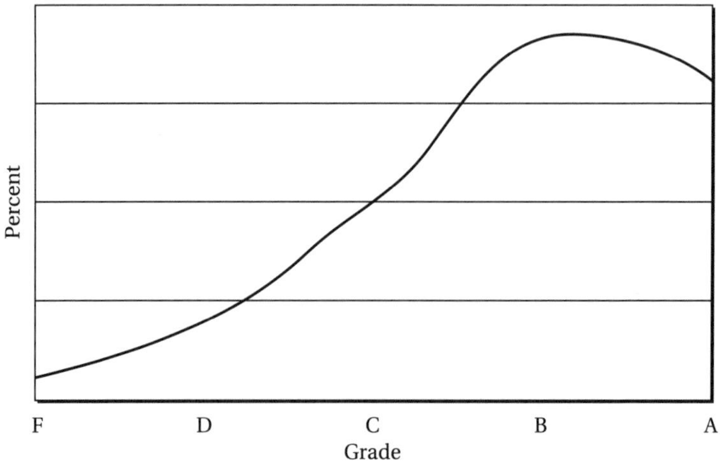

Grade comparisons

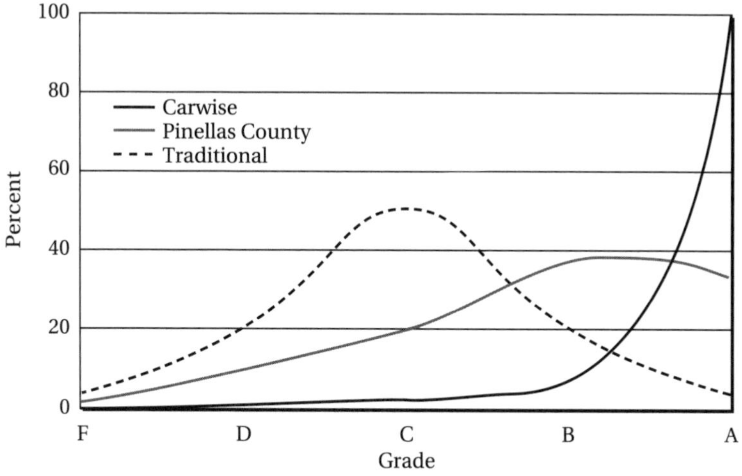

Carwise Middle School

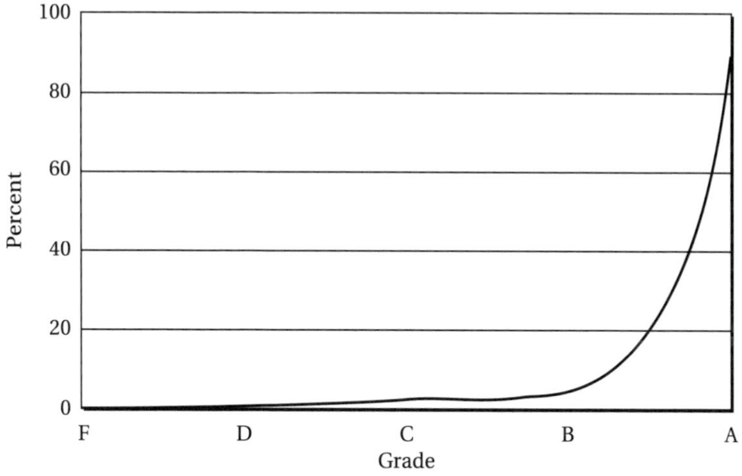

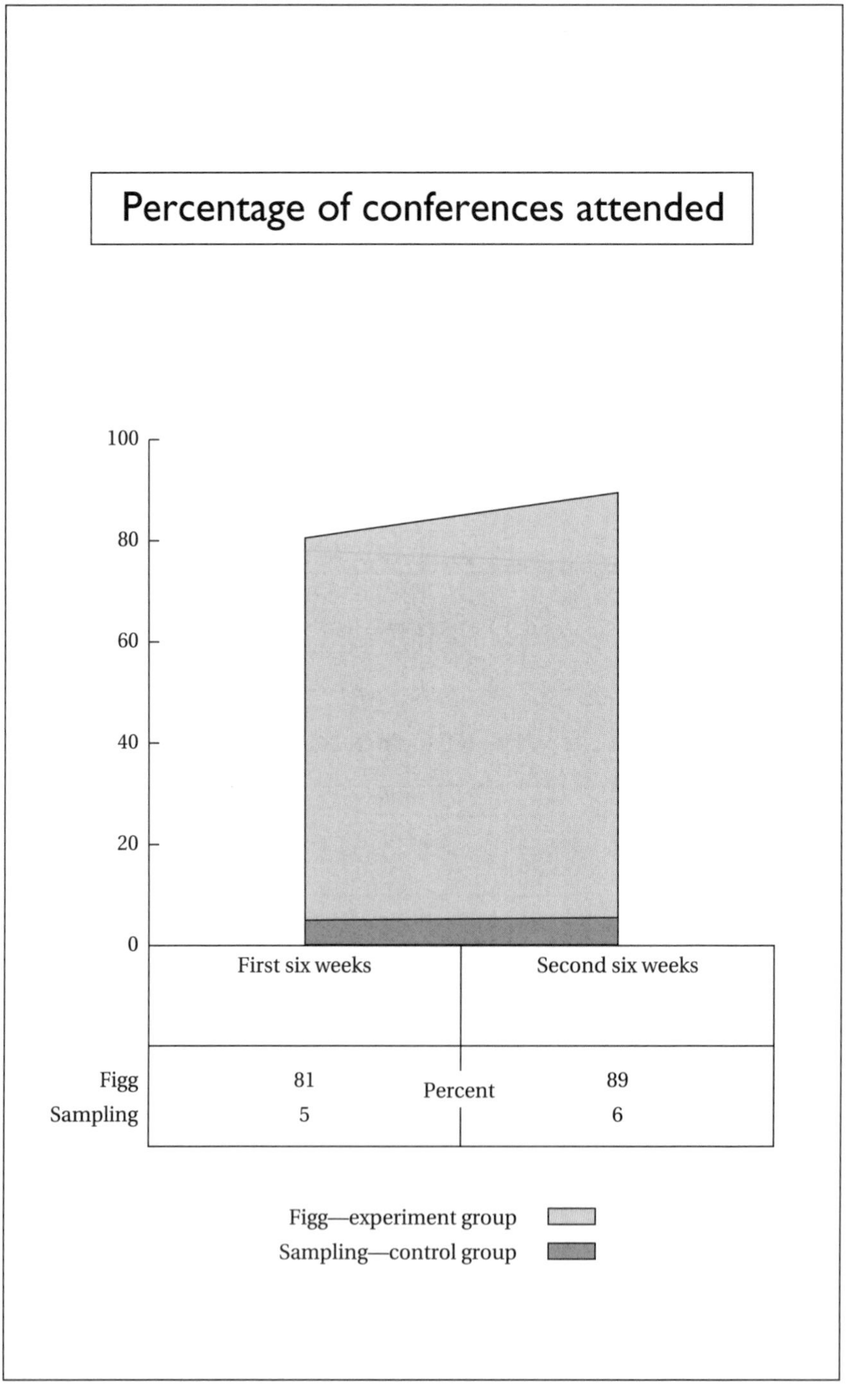
Percentage of conferences attended
100
80
60
40
20
0
First six weeks
Second six weeks
Figg
Sampling
81
5
Percent
89
6
Figg—experiment group
Sampling—control group

Portfolio assessment: Reflections of a self-directed learner

3. Three important things I've learned are:

2. Two applications that help me to achieve the above:

1. One action I will continue to improve:

Parent response:

I am proud of:

I will help you by:

Benchmarking Carwise's total grades to reading

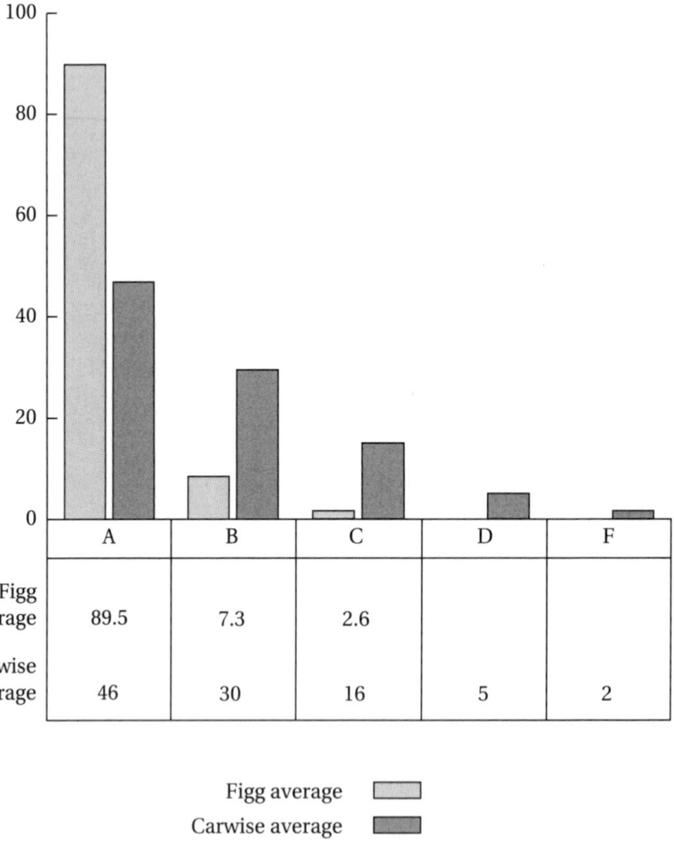

	A	B	C	D	F
Figg average	89.5	7.3	2.6		
Carwise average	46	30	16	5	2

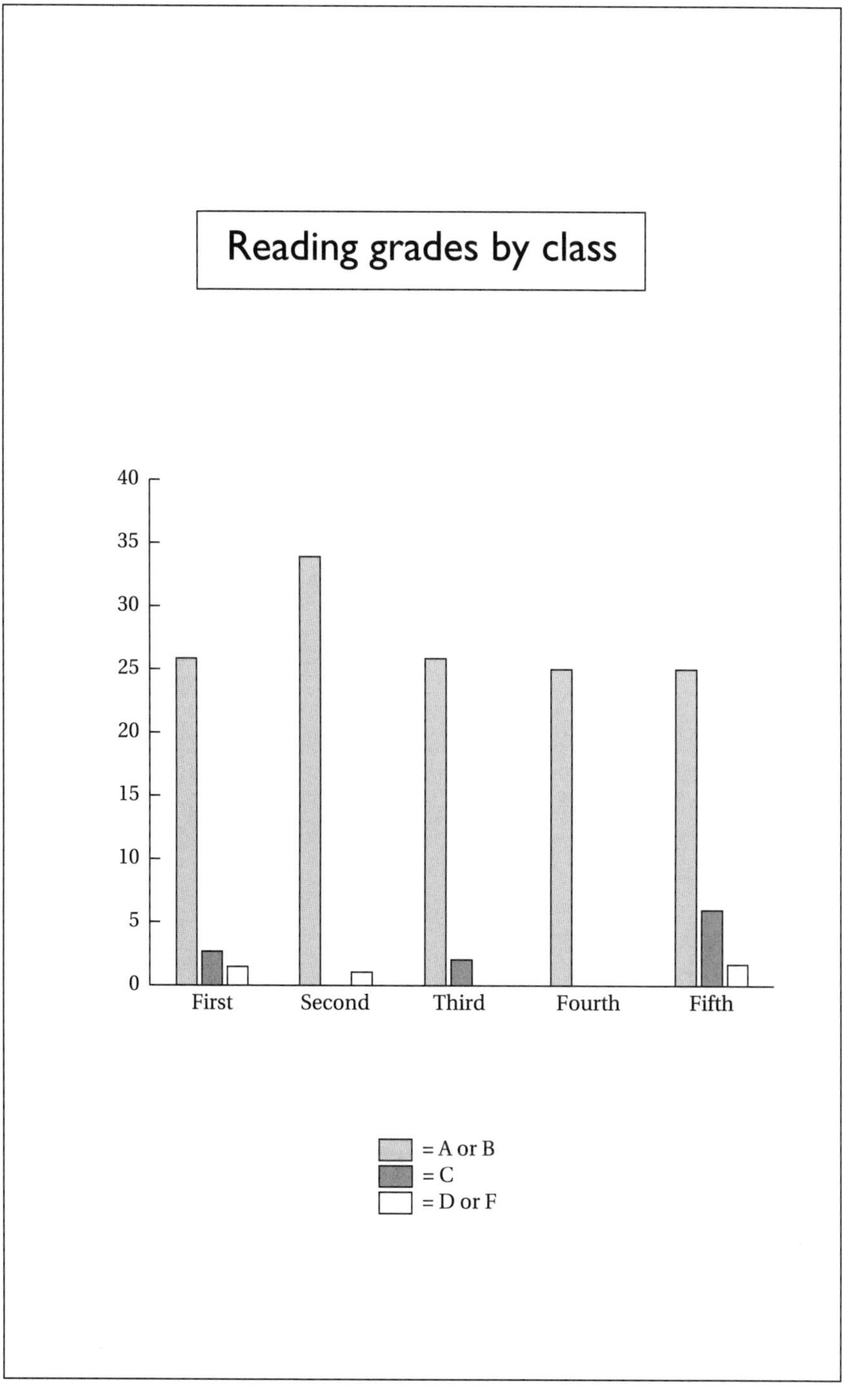
Reading grades by class
40
35
30
25
20
15
10
5
0
First
Second
Third
Fourth
Fifth
= A or B
= C
= D or F

Appendix B

COMPARISON OF PROBLEM-SOLVING STRUCTURES

This appendix is an expansion of the one contained in *The Pursuit of Quality Through Personal Change*. I wanted to make it more comprehensive and current than the original so that the expanded version is more valuable than the first.

The purpose of this appendix is to demonstrate the conceptual similarities and differences among various methods. This way you will have the benefit of a variety of approaches, not just one.

For methods with more or less than seven steps, the text has been placed beside the most similar step in the consensus model. In no case was any step reported out of its normal sequence.

Integrative	Alcoa	Eitington	FPL	Goal/QPC	Ingle
1. Find the reason for improvement.	Define the problems and opportunities. Select the problem or opportunity.	Define the problem.	Find the reason for improvement.	Decide which problem comes first. Create a problem statement.	Collect and select the problems.
2. Understand the current situation.		Generate data about the problem.	Prioritize and select opportunities.	Complete a picture of all possible causes.	Clearly define one problem.
3. Analyze the problem.	Analyze the causes and effects.		Analyze root causes.	Agree on basic causes.	Collect and analyze data.
4. Generate potential solutions.	Generate potential actions.	Generate ideas for problem resolution.	Select countermeasures.	Develop an effective and implementable solution.	Generate solutions.
5. Evaluate potential solutions.	Evaluate and select solutions.	Choose among alternative solutions.	Select solution.		Implement a plan of action.
6. Take action.	Implement solutions.	Implement the solution or decision.	Conduct trial implementation. Track effectiveness.	Implement the solution.	Do a trial run. Evaluate.
7. Appraise.	Test effectiveness.		Document and standardize.	Establish needed monitoring procedures and charts.	Inspect. Follow up.

Juran-Gryna	Kelly	Kepner-Tregoe	Miller	PQ Systems	QualTeam
1. Obtain proof of need.	Identify the. problem.	Create a deviation statement.	Define the problem.	Define the system.	Define the problem.
2. Identify the vital few.		Specify.	Brainstorm possible causes.	Assess the current situation.	Identify suspected causes.
3. Organize for breakthrough.	Analyze.	Develop possible causes.	Analyze the data.	Analyze the causes.	Verify most likely causes.
4. Analyze.	Evaluate alternatives.	Test for probable causes.	Brainstorm possible solutions.	Try out improvement theory.	Identify possible solutions.
5. Define the effect of proposed change. Overcome resistance to change.	Test and implement.	Verify.	Reach consensus.	Study the results.	Develop an action plan.
6. Take action.			Implement an action plan.	Standardize improvement.	
7. Control at new level.	Standardize.			Plan continuous improvement.	Evaluate the action plan.

Rosander	Scholtes	SPT	Snee	Technicomp	ISO 9001 (1994)*
1. Identify the problem.	Identify the reason for improvement.	Select a problem.	Flowchart the work processes.	Identify the problem.	Handling of customer complaints
2. Analyze the problem.	Analyze the situation.		Identify the uncontrollable factors.	Isolate and contain the problem.	
3. Collect the data.	Collect the data.	Analyze the data.	Prioritize the effects of uncontrollable factors.	Analyze the problem.	Investigation of cause of noncon-formance.
4. Analyze the data.	Analyze the data.	Select counter-measures.	Identify work process changes.	Select countermeasures.	
5. Plan.	Set goals.	Correct or reduce the problem.	Select the best alternative.		Determination of corrective action
6. Take action.	Take action.	Evaluate the results.	Make changes.		
7. Appraise.	Evaluate.	Determine the next steps.	Monitor the new work process. Standardize and hold the gains.	Monitor the process. Document the results.	. . . Ensure that corrective action is taken and . . . effective.

Source: ANSI/ASQC Q9001-1994 *Quality Systems—Model for Quality Assurance in Design, Development, Production, Installation, and Servicing* (Milwaukee, Wis. ASQC, 1994), 4.14.2.

Appendix C

TOOL PAGES

The objective of this appendix is to provide a concise description of each tool and to provide step-by-step instructions for its use. The description of each tool follows the guidelines suggested for a storyboard page; that is, by using words, numbers, and pictures.

This appendix has been made as comprehensive as possible. It is recognized that there may be other applications. By constructing this appendix in alphabetical order, it should be easy for you to add your favorite problem-solving tools as they are discovered.

AFFINITY DIAGRAM

The affinity diagram is used to demonstrate the relationship among various items, activities, or people. This is sometimes done by placing the name of one item or person on a notecard, then arranging all the cards on a board. Once the relationships are agreed to, the picture created can be permanently drawn.

INSTRUCTIONS FOR THE AFFINITY DIAGRAM

1. Use notecards to identify key persons, activities, or actions.
2. Use a table or bulletin board to place the notecards in the position that best shows their similarities or differences.
3. If you are working with a group, the affinity diagram can be used as a tool for a discussion of these relationships as they are, or as they need to be.
4. Make sure that the diagram and discussions focus on the task at hand, rather than on personal relationships.
5. You may wish to construct a diagram for both the current and desired situations.
6. You may wish to make a drawing from the notecards when the diagram is complete, especially if you are going to use it later.

APPLICATION OF THE AFFINITY DIAGRAM

A living affinity diagram was created by asking members of a work group to stand in the room in a way that showed how close or distant their work relationships were. The result was called the *fertile crescent,* because that was the shape of the cluster formed. It would be possible to photograph this form of affinity diagram for further discussion.

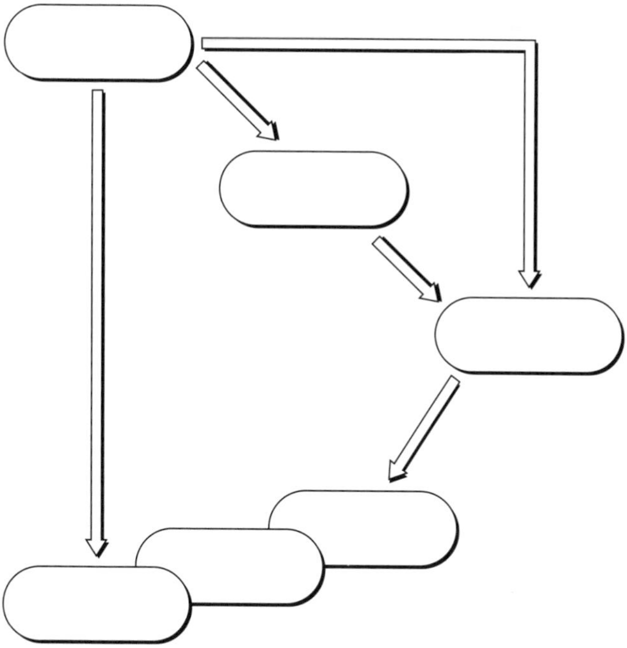

BAR CHART

The bar chart is used to indicate quantities or amounts. The example shows usage of a telephone line. Looking at this bar chart, you can see that this particular line begins getting heavy use at about 9:00 A.M., drops off at noon, and gets busy again in the afternoon.

When you begin to collect data, you do not know what form it will take. When you have sufficient data to truly represent a situation, a chart can then be used to help visualize the data.

This same data could be collected by day of the week, by week of month, or at shorter or longer intervals. This way you could see if other variations were more important than the hour-to-hour changes.

INSTRUCTIONS FOR THE BAR CHART

1. Begin to collect data. A check sheet is frequently a good place to start.
2. When sufficient data have been collected to cover the scope of the chart, construct the chart.
3. You may wish to run your data for a long period of time, to get an idea of the range or variation of each bar.
4. Be sure to label the chart, showing frequency of data collection and the name of each axis. You may also wish to include the name of the data collector and the dates or times when the data were collected. Notice that the quantity is typically on the vertical axis, and the things compared (in this case, hours of the day) are on the horizontal axis.
5. It can be useful to keep your original data attached to the back of the bar chart. Sometimes data need to be rearranged. As long as you have your original data, you can summarize it differently as needed.

APPLICATION OF THE BAR CHART

The example of telephone use has wide application in a special way. It is not unusual for incoming telephone traffic to a customer service department to vary widely, from almost nothing in certain hours to an average for several hours, and to more than double the average at other times. Incoming calls can also peak for short bursts of activity in five-minute to half-hour or even multihour segments.

Managing by the average in a case like this can get one into a lot of trouble. If you fence off a department called customer service and staff it for the average call level, you are sure to disturb a lot of customers when the call load is high. But you frequently can't afford to staff for the peak level at all times. The situation is complicated by the fact that employees go on vacation, and may not be replaced while off duty. The data, presented in bar chart form, can form the foundation for a discussion of customer service needs, reasons for the calls, and methods of addressing telephone inquiries.

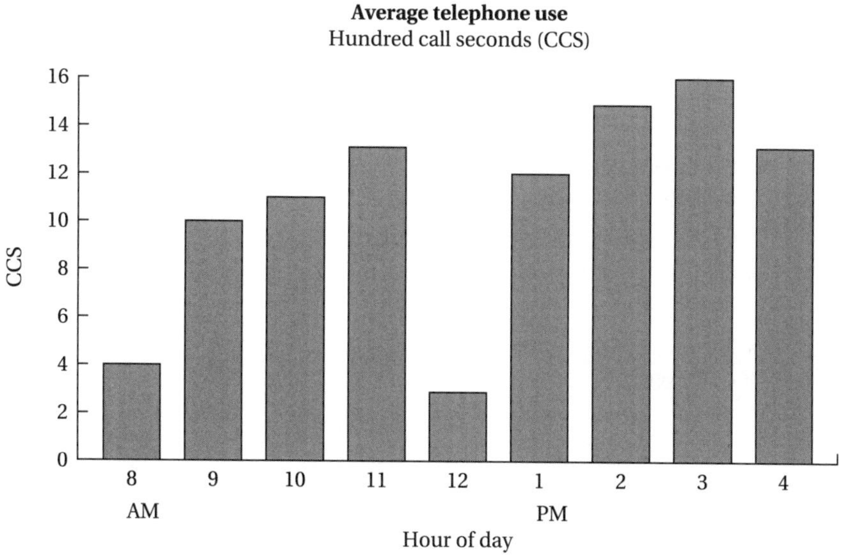

BRAINSTORMING

Brainstorming is the term generally used to describe wide-open, creative thinking in groups. When the same kind of thinking is done individually, it is sometimes called *mind mapping*. The purpose of brainstorming is to generate ideas in a short time.

INSTRUCTIONS FOR BRAINSTORMING

There are two forms of brainstorming—oral and written. In the oral form, individuals call out ideas as they come, while being considerate of their colleagues. In the written form, notecards are typically used, so that one idea can be written on each card. Later on, the cards can be reorganized or compared to provide better insight into the subject. This is called the Crawford Slip Method.

Regardless of the type of brainstorming being done, there are a few key rules that apply.

Do

- Relax. This will free your mind to explore ideas.
- Suspend all judgment. Avoid criticism of ideas.
- Build on ideas. Frequently one idea suggests another.

Do not

- Analyze. Analysis is done by a different part of your brain, and switching slows down the process.
- Criticize the ideas of others. This can cause hurt feelings, resulting in temporary or permanent damage to the brainstorming process, if not the relationship.

APPLICATION OF BRAINSTORMING

The senior executives for an industrial corporation were brought together by an outside facilitator to consider the future direction of the corporation. In a one-hour session, enough ideas were generated to keep them busy for more than five years, at which time there were still good ideas left over.

Small candies were given as rewards for ideas. One executive was embarrassed to take his goodies, but he took them, and then came up with even more ideas. As simple as it may seem, the goodies work.

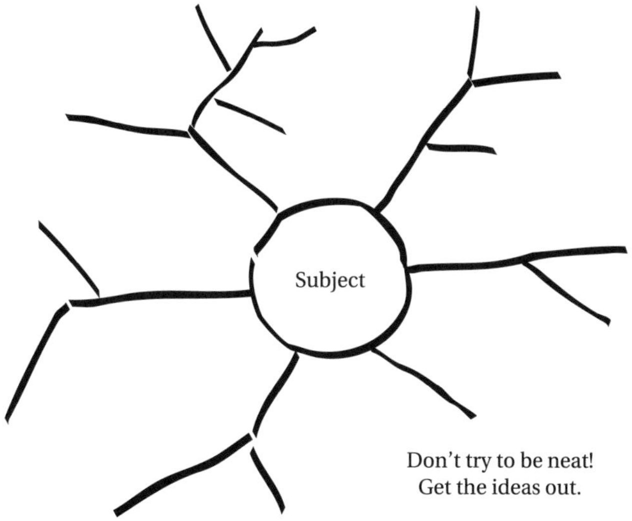

CHARTS AND GRAPHS

Charts and graphs help speed the understanding of critical information by making key points visual. In order to make good charts and graphs, you must first have good data.

GUIDELINES FOR GOOD DATA

Be consistent in your data collection method. If you are sampling, sample the same way each time. If you change the way you collect data due to new understandings, then make every effort to standardize the reporting so that old data and new data are as comparable as possible. Also do the following:

- State the source, date(s), time(s), method, and person who recorded the information.
- Remember, the purpose is to communicate, so make the chart or graph as clear as possible.
- Keep the data where you can find it. Perhaps staple it to the back of the chart or graph.
- Always label axes, and use legends when labels are too big to fit where needed.
- Avoid scale breaks. Where absolutely necessary, show the scale break clearly.
- Confine your chart and graph to the presentation of one idea at a time. Keep it simple.

REALITY CHECK FOR CHARTS AND GRAPHS

When you have completed your chart or graph, use the cloud pattern, or some other graphic tool, to highlight the key area. Then, beneath the chart or graph, make your point in one brief sentence.

Check the graph against the sentence you just wrote. If the graph does not clearly show the same thing that the sentence says, try again with a different graph.

CHECKLIST

The checklist is simply a listing of items, with a place to indicate their completion. The checklist is probably the most broadly applied tool in existence, including the shopping list, a desktop list of agenda items, a calendar or pocket reminder, and a meeting agenda. The checklist helps assure that things get done.

INSTRUCTIONS FOR THE CHECKLIST

1. List each item to be done.
2. Organize and prioritize; do first things first.
3. Line through things that have been done.
4. Add new items as they occur.
5. If the list gets too long, consider your options.
   a. If all must be done, get help or increase the pace.
   b. If some things should not be done, remove them.

APPLICATION OF THE CHECKLIST

Calendar-type organizers, either the physical type or the corresponding software on a computer, are sprouting like weeds, and for good reason. Many successful people are working 60–80 hour weeks and need every free minute they can get. People recognize that a missed meeting could result in lost opportunity, and that having goals and objectives set in advance helps avoid confusion. Stephen R. Covey, in his Seven Habits of Highly Effective People program even develops an organizer around the seven habits.

If you are not already using an organizer, consider it. You may be pleasantly surprised.

CHECK SHEET

The check sheet is a simple, yet effective way of gathering factual information about problem areas. It is simply a place to keep a tally of number of occurrences by category. A category can be determined by use of a fishbone diagram, a flowchart, brainstorming, or any other technique that will generate possible categories of investigation.

After a sufficient number of checks is accumulated, it is possible to identify a normal distribution, a Pareto distribution, or possibly even a nonproblem. In cases where awareness of the problem is the primary issue, the check sheet may be the only measurement tool you need to show results. The check sheet is an easy way to gather information.

INSTRUCTIONS FOR THE CHECK SHEET

1. Identify the things you need to count.
2. Create a row for each item.
3. Leave a few extra rows for occurrences that the operator thinks are important.
4. Give the check sheet to the operator or the person who has the information or does the work.
5. Specify the time constraints and clarify any questionable areas of data collection.
6. Review the information gathered to determine if some trend is identified.
7. Check the other row(s) to determine if new categories should be included in future data gathering.

APPLICATION OF THE CHECK SHEET

The telephone switchboard is fertile ground for any improvement enthusiast. While many companies are keenly aware of the importance of the switchboard operation to their business, just as many others delegate this vital function to low levels or ignore it altogether.

In an industrial company, a check sheet was created to determine the primary source of unanswered telephone calls. The check sheet pointed to one particular manager, who was frequently on the shop floor. Once the manager knew that he was the greatest source of unanswered customer calls, he changed his technology and his behavior to eliminate the problem. Key to this result was approaching the manager in a nonjudgmental way.

In a similar company, the same kind of check sheet was used to determine which department did the poorest job of answering calls the first time. The department with the worst record was the executive office. No action was taken.

Check sheet for telephone calls
Week of January 15

Type of call	Occurrences	Total
General information	~~||||~~ ~~||||~~	10
Sales	~~||||~~	5
Purchasing	/	1
Order status	~~||||~~ ~~||||~~ ~~||||~~	15
Executives	/||	3

CLUSTER ANALYSIS

Cluster analysis is a statistical procedure used to organize a wide variety of groups into a smaller number of groups with common characteristics. Consult Andrew W. Spisak's article "Cluster Analysis as a Quality Management Tool" (*Quality Progress* 25, no. 12 [December 1992]: 33–38) for a concise and understandable description of the subject. References are included. While this tool is valuable, it is beyond the scope of a short summary.

CRITICAL PATH

In its simplest form, the critical path is the path of action that determines the pace of a project. In building a room for instance, electrical wiring must be done before air-conditioning equipment is installed, but the electrician must come back to complete the connections after the air-conditioning equipment has been placed. The specific sequence of electrical-air-electrical is then the critical path.

While engineering firms have computer software for project planning that enables them to shorten the total time to complete a project, many projects can be completed simply by use of a Gantt chart. Even on apparently simple projects, it is useful to consider the best sequence of activities in order to make the best use of time.

APPLICATIONS OF THE CRITICAL PATH

R. Buckminster Fuller's book *Critical Path* applies the concept on a broad philosophical level. Some of the work begun by Fuller is getting a second life, as his ideas mature in the minds of others. The recent chemistry of the *buckyball* and the toys based upon his vector equilibrium are two examples.

DATA VISUALIZATION

Recent enhancements in spreadsheet and presentation software have provided workers with the ability to look at data in at least three dimensions. Even simple data can now be viewed in a variety of graphic forms simply by pressing one key. It is also possible, even for a relatively inexperienced user, to present data in a time series sequence. This is sometimes called a slide show.

Because these improvements in software have the potential of revolutionizing your ability to communicate, they are mentioned here as a tool, or rather, as a class of tools. Thus, graphic tools enhance your ability to see the big picture.

DECISION MATRIX

The decision matrix is a simple graphic method by which opinions and information are quantified in order to arrive at a decision. The two places where you can expect to see this type of matrix are in the selection of a problem to work on, and in the selection of a solution. Beyond that, the decision matrix can be used any time you need to distill a variety of options down to the one. Thus, the decision matrix can help prioritize options.

INSTRUCTIONS FOR THE DECISION MATRIX

1. Determine the factors important in making the decision. There is no limit to the criteria you can use.
2. Decide on the scale to use. Be sure all your scales go in the same direction. (That is, a positive number is good.) If there is no absolute scale, rank order items as compared to each other.
3. Decide whether to add or multiply to get a total.
4. When the matrix is complete, do a reality check with yourself or your group. Does the numeric winner agree with your perceptions, or have you missed something?
5. Remember that you, not the matrix, are in charge.

Item	Factor	Factor	Factor	Total

FACILITATION

The term *facilitation* derives from the root word, *facile,* meaning *easy.* The art of facilitation is a very broad concept, based on the concept that something that is easy is more likely to get done than something that is difficult. Therefore, there is value to be gained from making things easy.

Recently, the concept has been applied to quality. For example, in Philip Crosby's concept of hassle-free systems, and in management, there has been a move toward the manager as a coach or teacher, rather than as a director or boss. This involves use of the question, "What can I do to help?" in order to create a positive basis for a working relationship.

The most common use of the term *facilitation* is with reference to the role of facilitator on a quality or work team. The job of the facilitator is to act as an expert on the team process, to observe team interactions, to make constructive comments, and to perform any other function that aids the working of the team. In small organizations, where there is insufficient staff to accomplish this function, it must be shared by team members, or it may be provided by the team leader.

APPLICATION OF FACILITATION

There is a story about the difference between heaven and hell. In hell, there is a room with a long dining table. The occupants are sitting, one across from the other. Each has a very long spoon, so long, in fact, that one cannot hold the handle and feed oneself. While valiantly struggling, nobody can manage to feed themselves. Consequently, all the residents of hell are thin and undernourished.

In heaven, there is the same room, the same long table, the same seating arrangements, and the same spoons. But each person is using his or her long spoon to feed the person across the table. Consequently, all the residents of heaven are well fed and happy.

Now, that's facilitation!

FISHBONE DIAGRAM

The fishbone diagram is also known as the Ishikawa diagram after its inventor, or as the cause-and-effect diagram. It is used to examine and graphically communicate the reasons, or root causes, for a problem or improvement opportunity, which, if corrected, will create a systematic problem solution or improvement. In other words, you will cure the illness, rather than just treating the symptoms. The fishbone diagram shows how a problem or opportunity was analyzed.

INSTRUCTIONS FOR THE FISHBONE DIAGRAM

This diagram has a specific form, which is international in its application. For that reason, the standard form should be used where possible. The four Ms are man, materials, methods, and machinery. These are the main bones of the diagram. In addition, many people feel that information is deserving of a bone of its own. In any case, use and communication of information are frequently part of the system's problems, and will appear whether information has its own bone or not. Although there is a standard, you may label the bones any way that helps you to understand the problem.

The example shown includes not only major bones, but also subheadings. These are frequently discovered in practical application.

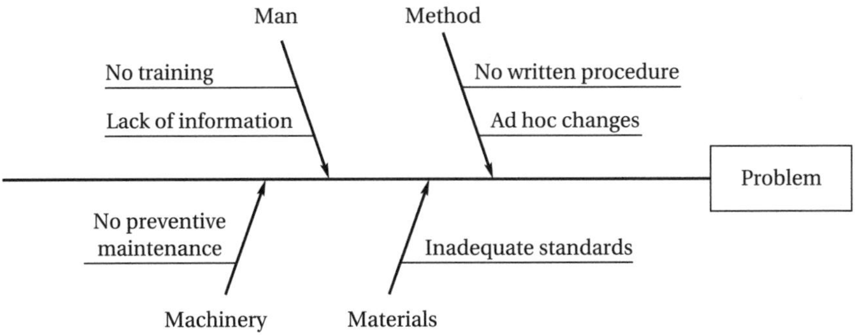

THE FIVE WHYS

The five whys are used to drive for root cause, by tracing the reasons backward from symptoms to disease. Sometimes the answers to the five whys can result in a tree diagram, because there may be more than one possible answer for each why.

INSTRUCTIONS FOR THE FIVE WHYS

1. State the apparent problem or opportunity.
2. Ask the reason for the problem; that is, ask Why?
3. As you move from the first why to the second and beyond, the answers will become more direct, more specific, and more personal. Ultimately, some individual did (or did not do) some thing that resulted in an unintended variation in the result. Thus, there was a reason why.
4. When a reason for the problem or variation is identified, which, when corrected will solve the problem, then you are finished. This is so whether you have used two whys or six. There is nothing magical about the number five.

APPLICATION OF THE FIVE WHYS

The five whys is an excellent tool for self-discovery, but you must be ready for the answers. It is possible to produce life-changing insights through the constructive use of this tool. For this reason, it is important when using this tool in groups to be nonjudgmental and to respect others.

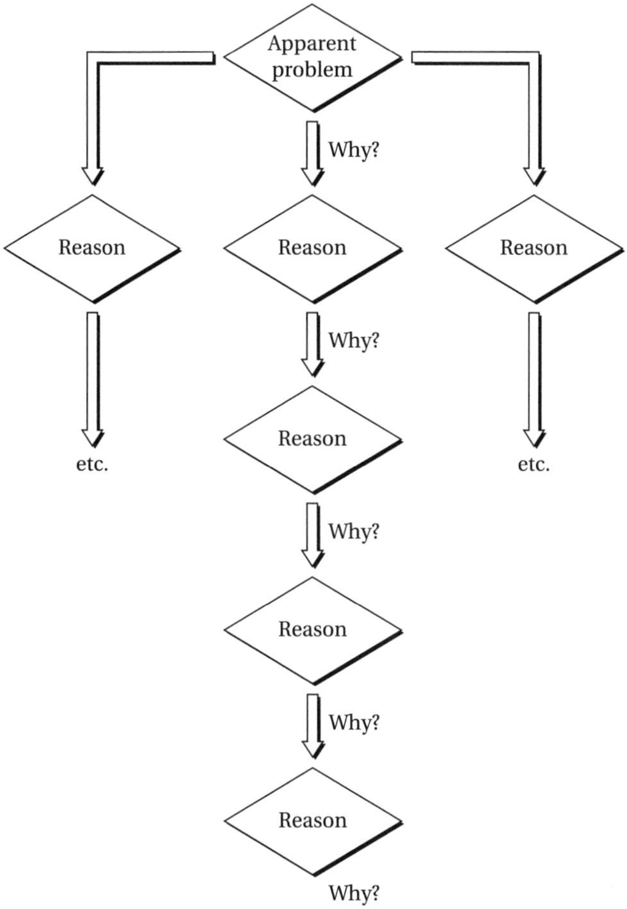

Apparent problem
Why?
Reason
Reason
Reason
Why?
Reason
etc.
etc.
Why?
Reason
Why?
Reason
Why?

FLOWCHART

A flowchart is simply a graphical description of the flow of activities in a system or organization. There are three basic universal symbols: the rectangle for an action; the diamond for a decision; and the arrow to indicate direction. All the other symbols are optional or trade specific. Here is a simple paradigm for flowcharting that combines the best of a variety of examples.

INSTRUCTIONS FOR THE FLOWCHART

If you are not sure what's going on, a flowchart is a good place to start. Not only does it help to understand who does what, but it is also an excellent tool to build a common view in a team.

Tips for using a flowchart include the following:

- Suspect each diamond as a source of variation.
- Ask the five whys for each box. Is it really needed?
- Check from bottom to top: Does each step have the necessary information to do the work?
- Ask a second time. People usually describe a system the first time in idealized form; the second time they will tell you what happens if.
- Consider doing two flowcharts—one as is and the other as you would like it to be. Then compare the two.
- When in doubt, follow one piece of paper, one person, or one thing.

APPLICATION OF THE FLOWCHART

Probably the most useful flowchart is one of the simplest. It is used as an example in this book. It is the flowchart that shows the executive decision-making process (Figure 4.6). Any weakness in this process can have a profound effect on a person or an organization. Although it requires some insight to do, the potential is staggering. Why not try it at your organization?

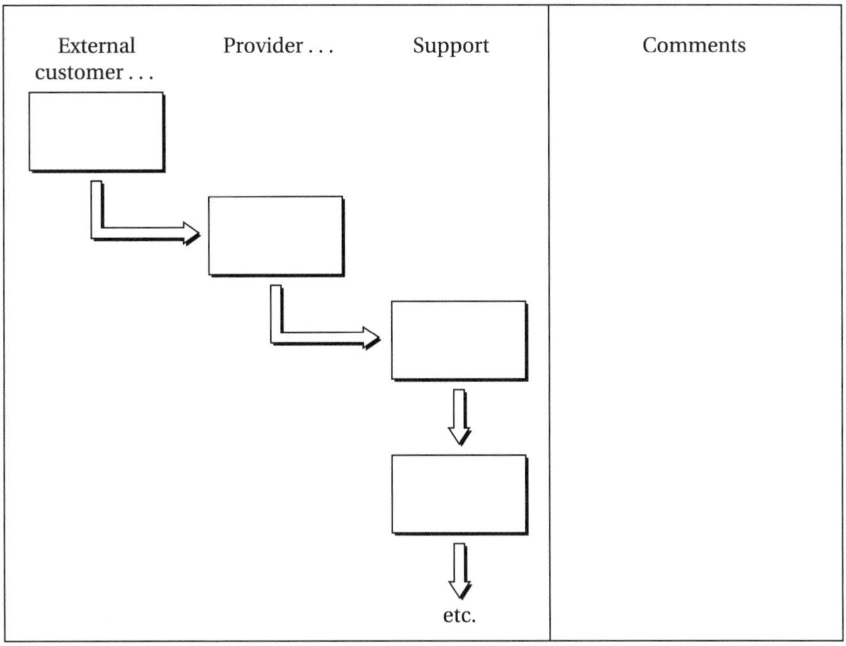
External customer . . .
Provider . . .
Support
etc.
Comments

FORCE FIELD ANALYSIS (BARRIERS AND AIDS)

The purpose of force field analysis, also known as barriers and aids, is to view the problem as a balance among restraining forces. The objective is to use this tool to develop a strategy that takes advantage of the forces in favor of change, while avoiding the pitfalls of the restraining forces. You must show the forces driving and restraining your issue.

INSTRUCTIONS FOR FORCE FIELD ANALYSIS

1. Brainstorm to identify driving forces (aids) and restraining forces (barriers).
2. Rank order the forces in order of relative strength, placing the strongest at the top.

Problem statement ______________________________

Driving forces (Aids)	Restraining forces (Barriers)
____________	____________
__________	__________
________	________
______	______
_____	_____
____	____
___	___
__	__

GANTT CHART

The Gantt chart is one of a family of charts used to control a project. This chart has a particular place in the problem-solving process, because it is the key to holding the project together. The psychological effect of having a schedule to keep is valuable to the team, and the Gantt chart is a convenient tool to monitor progress. The Gantt chart shows a project's status in a glance.

INSTRUCTIONS FOR THE GANTT CHART

Across the bottom of the chart is the time scale. You select the pace of the project. You will probably find that once you begin collecting data, you will continue at least until the completion of the project, if not beyond. Other steps are sequential. The steps used will depend upon which problem-solving method you choose, or which activities you wish to monitor.

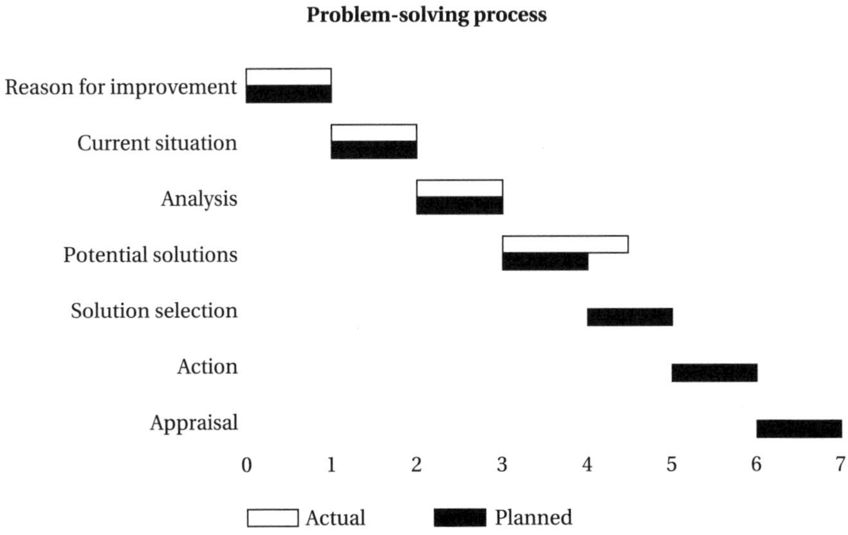

HISTOGRAM

A histogram shows frequency of occurrence, either of a class or a range within a class. An example of each is shown. While a bar chart indicates quantity, a histogram always indicates frequency of occurrence.

INSTRUCTIONS FOR THE HISTOGRAM

When you are measuring continuous data, like thickness of a pencil, you must divide the categories in even segments. For instance, the dimension .260 means .2600 to .26099999. You must have enough categories to demonstrate the distribution of counts. Only experience with the problem will tell you if your categories are too broad or too narrow. If they are too broad, you may miss something. If they are too narrow, you may work too hard to get your data.

APPLICATION OF THE HISTOGRAM

Perhaps the most famous histogram is the one created by Carl Friedrich Gauss (1777–1855) when he measured the distance to a star. His recognition that each measurement was slightly different led to the concept of frequency distribution around a central number. The result was the famous bell curve.

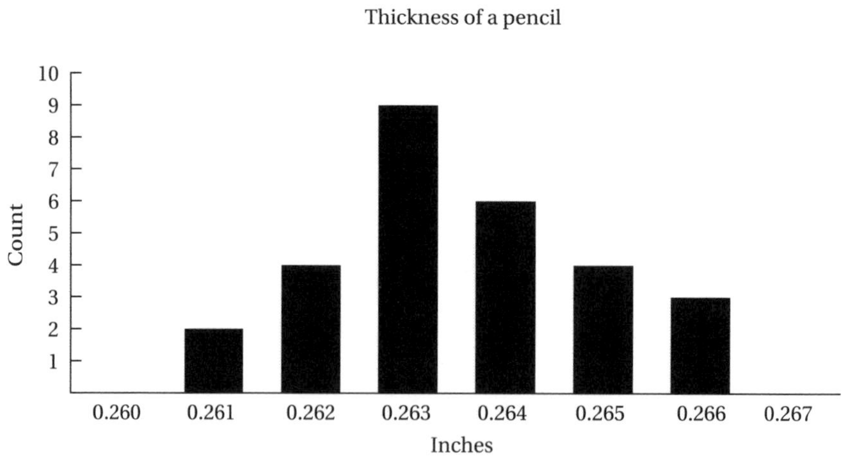

HUMOR

At the risk of dancing on the skinny branches, humor is a valuable tool for a variety of purposes.

1. It can help to break the tension (and there usually is some tension sooner or later).
2. It can make the work more interesting, helping with concentration.
3. It can allow an issue to be presented in a nonjudgmental way.

In order to use humor for these results, you must follow a few simple rules.

1. Make fun of yourself or a situation, not someone else.
2. Avoid teasing. It is an expression of anger.
3. Never use rude language.

APPLICATION OF HUMOR

Marianna Nunes, a speaker on humor in the workplace, believes that humor can have a positive effect on serious illness, in fact even causing remission of cancer and other serious diseases.

HYPERMEDIA

Hypermedia is the term used to describe the new technology that combines audio, visual, spreadsheet, and communications software into one bundle. Companies are beginning to organize around this concept, developing products with ever-broader capabilities. Hypermedia has the potential to significantly enhance your ability to pass along learning to others through animated, colorful, interesting storyboards.

The recent evolution of storyboarding could be described from a media standpoint as follows:

Plain spreadsheets:	Graphics had to be prepared separately.
Graphical spreadsheets:	Graphs are derived automatically from spreadsheets.
Graphics software:	Spreadsheets are input into programs with extensive graphic capabilities.
Integrated software:	Word processing, spreadsheet, and graphics are in one package.
Multimedia:	Sound is added to visual presentations through musical instrument digital interface (MIDI) connection.
CD technology:	Compact disc technology allows video, sound, and written data to all be stored on the same disc and to be integrated for presentation.

INTERVIEW, FOCUS GROUP, AND SURVEY

The interview can be used to gain information from customers regarding their needs, interests, or requirements. It can be useful to precede the interview with a focus group. A focus group is a meeting with a small group of selected individuals to explore an issue in depth. Frequently, the information gained in a focus group can assist in the development or improvement of questions for use in the interview.

On the large end of the scale is the survey, in which a large number of customers are asked the same questions. By asking specific, quantifiable questions, central tendency and variation can be established. The same survey can then be used occasionally to observe changes over time in the things being measured.

Approaching customers is sometimes difficult, because of the fear of creating an issue that has not already been raised. This fear must be addressed, by care in the design of the interview, focus group, or survey, and by assuring that those with a vital interest in the outcomes are included in the planning. The interview, focus group, and survey require additional study before use.

IS/IS-NOT MATRIX

The is/is-not matrix helps to break down information on a problem into areas of possible investigation, perhaps even pointing to root causes. The matrix is deceptively simple. In order to complete it, you will need to think creatively and expansively, and consider all the possibilities. Thus, the is/is-not matrix helps clarify a problem.

INSTRUCTIONS FOR THE IS/IS-NOT MATRIX

Use a Pareto chart, fishbone diagram, or any of your creative skills to identify suspected elements of the problem. If you are having difficulty identifying suspected causes, use who, what, when, where, and how as starter questions.

The objective here is to sort out the things that really do not affect the problem process. Typical examples include the following:

- Pet peeves associated with the problem, but not really connected
- Trends which, while true or valid, do not influence the outcome either way
- Other problems that are really separate

Keep in mind that most problems are not what they originally appear to be.

Suspected factor or cause	**This is a part of the problem**	**This is not part of the problem**

LEADERSHIP

Leadership has been an issue since the beginning of time. When problem solving with a team, there are some specific duties that the leader must perform.

- Provide the beginning definition of purpose.
- Maintain the schedule of events.
- Retain responsibility for keeping the team together.
- Provide an agenda.
- Negotiate or set meeting times.
- Report results.

In small companies, the leader may also have to perform duties, such as scribe, facilitator, or observer.

While volumes have been written about leadership, it appears that followers are relatively consistent in their requirements of leaders. They must be honest and fair and have an exceptional ability to communicate. Although each team will have individual requirements and needs as well, violation of these principles is a fatal leadership flaw.

MEETING SUMMARY

Among the most necessary tools for the team leader is the meeting summary. It usually will not need to be longer than one page, but it really helps keep things in focus and on track. The key elements of the meeting summary are shown.

> To: (List each member alphabetically.)
>
> From: (Name of team leader)
>
> Date: (Same date as meeting)
>
> Subject: Meeting summary
>
> Paragraph one: Brief summary of key points.
>
> Paragraph two: Outcomes (Who will do what and when)
>
> Date and time of next meeting.
>
> Thanks: (Please don't leave this on the word processor. Change it every time.)

MIND MAP

The term *mind mapping* is sometimes used to indicate brainstorming done on an individual basis. You can use the same form provided in the brainstorming section, or no form at all.

In order to do a mind map, simply find a quiet place, relax, and let the ideas flow. Write down everything that comes to mind, drawing connecting lines as you see fit. There really are no rules for mind mapping. Just capture the ideas.

APPLICATION OF THE MIND MAP

If you have a problem that is particularly confusing, this is an excellent tool. The mind map technique works just as well (and maybe even better) on personal issues as on organizational ones. The various twists and turns as you think about an issue can lead to key insights about the way you look at problems in general, and at the thoughts you carry with you as you begin to work on a problem.

MULTIVOTING

Multivoting is used to reduce a large number of possibilities to a small number of action items. It can be used any time you wish to focus a team on key issues. Multivoting is done by simply taking a series of votes.

INSTRUCTIONS FOR MULTIVOTING

1. List the ideas to be voted on.
2. Each person on the team casts one vote for each item he or she thinks is most deserving.
3. At each successive vote, limit the voting to only the top half of items selected from the previous vote. Each time you vote, you reduce the list by half. Frequently, you may find that the voting divides items naturally into keepers and others, in some proportion other than 50/50.
4. When you have finished, do a reality check of the participants. You should have achieved consensus through the use of the process. If the participants are still not in agreement, then discuss the points at issue and resolve them.

Multivoting for purchasing department team

Improvements	First vote	Second vote	Third vote
Order forms	5		
Line buys	1		
Fewer vendors	6 *	5	
SHOP practice	2		
Prompt payment	7 *	7 *	7
Answer phone	2		
Friendliness	6 *	5	
New computer	**9 ***	**9 ***	**10 ***
Programs	8 *	8 *	7
Inventory $	4		

NOMINAL GROUP TECHNIQUE

The purpose of the nominal group technique (NGT) is to assure that each person in the group has sufficient voice in the selection of an issue or action item. This will achieve buy in from the entire group. The NGT helps assure full participation from the group.

INSTRUCTIONS FOR THE NOMINAL GROUP TECHNIQUE

The simplest version I have seen goes as follows:

1. Write the options on an easel pad or chalkboard where everyone can see them.
2. Each person must rank the items in order of importance. (No ties, please.) This is done privately on a piece of paper or notecard.
3. Scoring is tallied, and items are treated in the order of the total score.

It is sometimes fun, as well as useful, to perform a reality check on the results of any voting scheme. Ask the group if the result is reasonable. Asking this question can sometimes point out a flaw in the method or the activity that would have forced a bad decision.

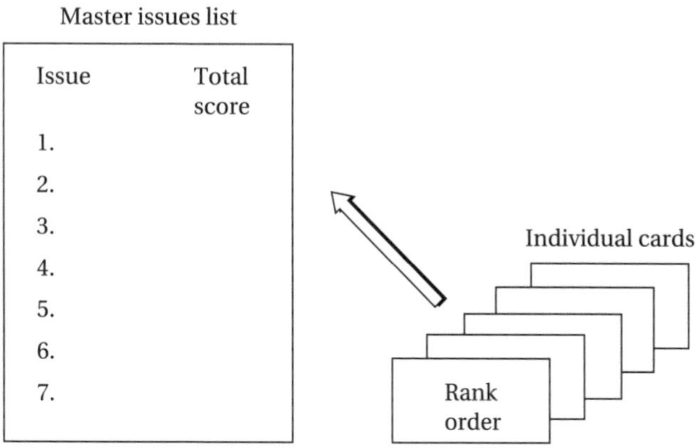

OBJECTIVE STATEMENT

The objective statement is used to focus an improvement activity on a specific, doable task that can be measured. It is similar in concept to a problem statement, except that the objective statement can be used for other reasons than to describe the problem. For instance the objective statement can be used to focus on a particular solution or to initiate a meeting. The fundamental components of an objective statement are a noun, verb, object, and the clause *as measured by*.

Noun	**Verb**	**Object**	**As measured by**
I or We	will	Thing you will act upon	Specific measurement tool or device
		For instance	
I	will increase	compliance	on form XXX reports.
We	will decrease	rejects	by seven pounds of scrap per day.
We	will eliminate	six warranty	claims per week.

OBSERVATION

Observation, as applied to continuous improvement teams, is usually targeted at the actions of individuals in team meetings. Beyond that, it is equally useful for taking notice of individual conversations or behavior styles. The purpose of observation is to improve the performance of a team by providing quantitative information regarding behavior.

The simplest way to apply this concept is to diagram the physical location of the participants, and draw arrows between them in the direction of conversation as it occurs. Once an arrow has been drawn, hash marks can be used to indicate the frequency of exchanges.

Another interesting observation is the order of response. It may be noticed that people respond to questions in a particular order, or in a pecking order.

A third observation may be time of speaking. Awareness of dominance in time, in order, or in frequency can be the first step in balancing a team to assure that all participants are heard. Many times people are unaware that they are dominating a conversation, but they are receptive to change. Use of these quantitative observations makes the reporting impersonal. Therefore, it can prevent an impression that the observer is being critical of an individual.

The role of observer is sometimes taught as a regular team function. The more balanced a team is to begin with, the less critical is the role of the observer.

Observation should never be formally undertaken without the consensus of the participants. They should be consulted regarding the activity itself and the type of observations to be made.

OPERATIONAL DEFINITION

The operational definition describes something by tangible measurements. For example, anxiety was once defined as a 1000-pound steel ball hanging over your head by a thin thread.

The word *operational* focuses on the fact that this definition is something on which you can actually apply or operate. To use the example, anxiety could be eliminated either by moving the person or removing the steel ball.

In terms of the definition, anxiety would not occur if the ball weighed either more or less than 1000 pounds. In the same way, the outcome of an improvement activity could be heavily weighted by the way the key indicators or activities are defined.

In order to check your definitions, ask three questions.

1. What am I measuring?
2. What is the scale?
3. How will I define success on this scale?

Clear definitions facilitate action.

PARETO CHART

I would be surprised to see any improvement activity documented without the use, at least somewhere, of the Pareto chart. The Pareto chart exemplifies the concept of identifying the vital few items or activities that most contribute to a problem or opportunity. The Pareto chart shows the importance of the vital few.

INSTRUCTIONS FOR CONSTRUCTING A PARETO CHART

1. Collect the data by category.
2. Organize the categories in decreasing order.
3. Use a bar chart to display the data.
4. Use a line graph to show the cumulative total
5. Observe the strength or weakness of the Pareto principle.

If you have a steep decline in bar height, then the Pareto principle is in action. If you have a moderate decline, there may still be some benefit to acting on the first few bars. If all bars are the same height, then you have not identified an overriding opportunity for improvement.

There are other reasons to act on an item besides its prominence on a Pareto chart. This tool should be used in concert with other reasoning to assure that you identify the best overall action to take.

APPLICATION OF THE PARETO PRINCIPLE

Vilfredo Pareto (1848–1923), an Italian economist, observed that 80 percent of the world's wealth was controlled by 20 percent of its population. Joseph Juran contributed to the broadening and popularization of Pareto's law, or the 80/20 rule, into "80 percent of the problems [or opportunities] come from 20 percent of the sources." Still probably the best example of the Pareto principle is the original work by Pareto himself on the demographics of wealth, which hasn't changed much since he did his original work.

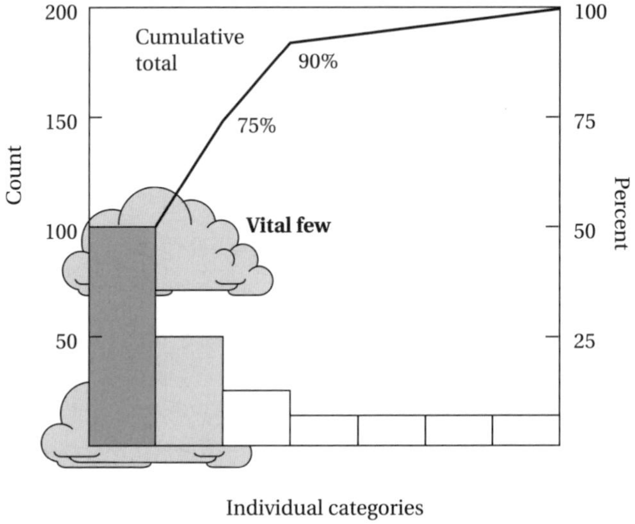
200
150
100
50
Count
Cumulative
total
90%
75%
Vital few
100
75
50
25
Percent
Individual categories

PIE CHART

A pie chart is useful for comparing the relative contribution of individual factors to the whole. A great deal of information can be displayed on a pie chart, so the value of each piece in communicating your message should be weighed. The pie chart is good for comparing elements of a problem. The example shows the basic information most frequently used.

INSTRUCTIONS FOR CONSTRUCTING A PIE CHART

1. Organize the data in descending order.
2. Determine the percent of the whole that each slice represents.
3. Present the percentages in clockwise order on the pie chart.
4. Be sure to label the segments of the chart.

If you have graphics software that works from a spreadsheet, such as Quattro or Lotus, press the button, and bingo, there's your graph.

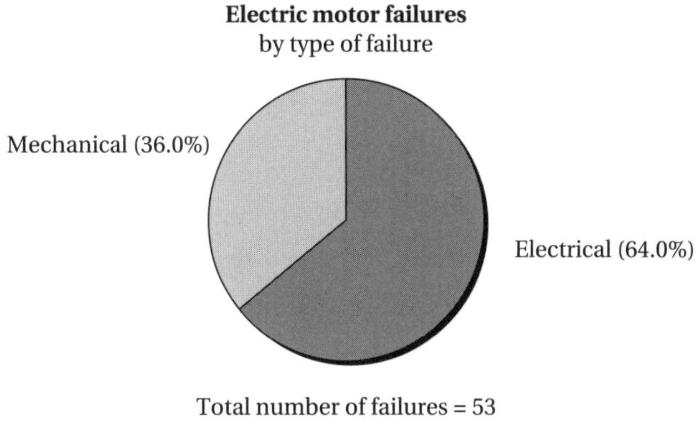

POLLING

Polling is used to assure that each individual in a group has expressed his or her opinion on an issue. There are at least three reasons for using polling.

1. The issue is particularly important, in terms of emotional intensity, time, or money.
2. Certain individuals in the group are dominant, often excluding others from the opportunity to speak.
3. Certain individuals in the group are quiet, and must be asked to speak.

It is handy to simply move in a single direction around the table or room, in order to avoid the appearance of priority. It is also important to assure that each person has been heard completely before going on to the next person. Cutting somebody off is a sure way to indicate that you are not interested in his or her ideas.

PROBLEM SELECTION MATRIX

Right at the beginning is the time to check on the need to do what you are about to do. The problem selection matrix is a useful tool for that purpose.

Among possible variables for decision making are: impact on the (outside) customer; effect on the key indicator (or key results area); feasibility (doability); timeliness; cost (savings); and general importance.

The problem selection matrix helps do first things first. You may either add or multiply across columns to achieve a total score.

SPECIAL CONSIDERATIONS FOR THE PROBLEM SELECTION MATRIX

Some variables are not easily quantified. This problem can be addressed in at least two ways. First, you can always rank order a variable that isn't quantified. In that way, there is never a tie, and each item is kept in context with the others. A second way is to weight the score of a nonquantifiable variable to give it less value than one that can be measured directly.

The important thing about the problem selection matrix is that you or your team are comfortable with the final decision about what to work on. The matrix is only a tool to help get you there.

Problems			**Total**

PROBLEM STATEMENT

The purpose of the problem statement is to get an improvement activity off to a good start by being as specific as possible, and by assuring that certain key factors have been considered. When you enter into the study of a problem, it is common to have incomplete information. The completion of a solid problem statement may very well represent half of the total time it takes to solve the problem. Once the problem is understood clearly, the solution may be simpler than suspected. The template shown can be used to construct a solid problem statement.

Who? What? When? Where?	
State the effect (not the cause).	
Identify the gap between the as-is and the optimal state.	
Measure.	
Be specific.	
Make a positive statement.	
Focus on the pain or hassle.	
Who is the customer?	

PROCEDURES

Frequently, problems occur at least partly because of the lack of a procedure, inadequate procedures, or differing procedures for the same task. The written procedure, then, is an important factor in holding the gains from an improvement activity. In addition, those who are expected to execute the procedure must be trained. The key elements of a procedure include the following:

- Procedure number and name
- Revision number and date
- Authority and signature
- Reason (Why is this procedure needed?)
- Scope (To whom and where does it apply?)
- Body (the actual steps of the procedure)
- Nonconformance (What should be done when things go wrong?)
- References to other procedures or standards

RADAR CHART

The radar chart is a good way to track many key indicators at once. It is not essential to the problem-solving process

INSTRUCTIONS FOR CONSTRUCTING A RADAR CHART

1. Decide which things should be measured and on what scale.
2. Spread a line for each measurement radially from the center point, thus representing individual scales.
3. The current situation is represented by marking the position on each indicator.
4. The pattern formed by connecting the dots is darkened, showing a radar pattern.
5. As changes occur, the radar chart can be updated, showing the situation as it was and as it is.

Percent of procedures written by department

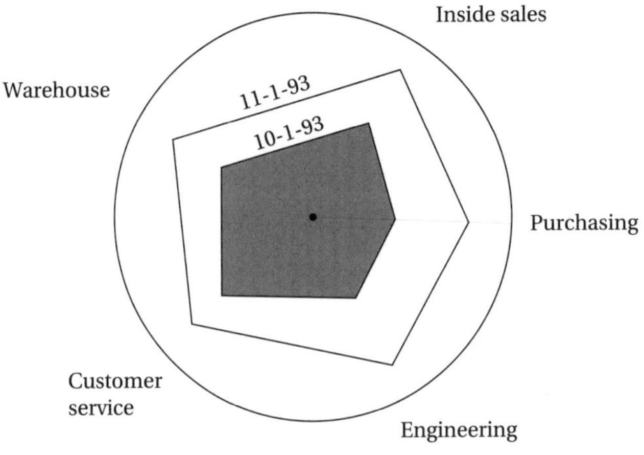

Outer circle = 100%

ROLE-PLAY

Role-play is the process of pretending you are someone else; it is acting. When considering the effect of business relationships on a problem, role-play can assist in gaining perspective. Role-play works best when conducted by a qualified professional.

INSTRUCTIONS FOR ROLE-PLAY

1. You must be in a facilitative environment. In other words, there must be some discussion about what you are going to do, and what you will not do.
2. When doing role-play, avoid casting your character in a bad light. It is not your objective to ridicule, but rather to understand the problem from that person's perspective.
3. Use an observer to give feedback on the role-play session.

VARIATION ON ROLE-PLAY

Actually do the person's job, cover his or her desk, or look over his or her shoulder for a period of time. You may be amazed at how different the actual work is from what it has appeared to be.

RUN CHART

A run chart is a line graph that indicates time on the horizontal scale and performance of a key indicator on the vertical scale. Other forms of graphs may be used, but the line graph is the most recognizable and common. The run chart is used to track the key indicator.

The run chart can evolve into a control chart, once customer requirements and process capabilities have been determined. If you do not know enough about statistics to develop a control chart, at least do a run chart and calculate the average. Observe the variation around the average and whether the average changes from time to time. Once you understand the movement of the average and the scale of the variation, you will be ready to try a control chart.

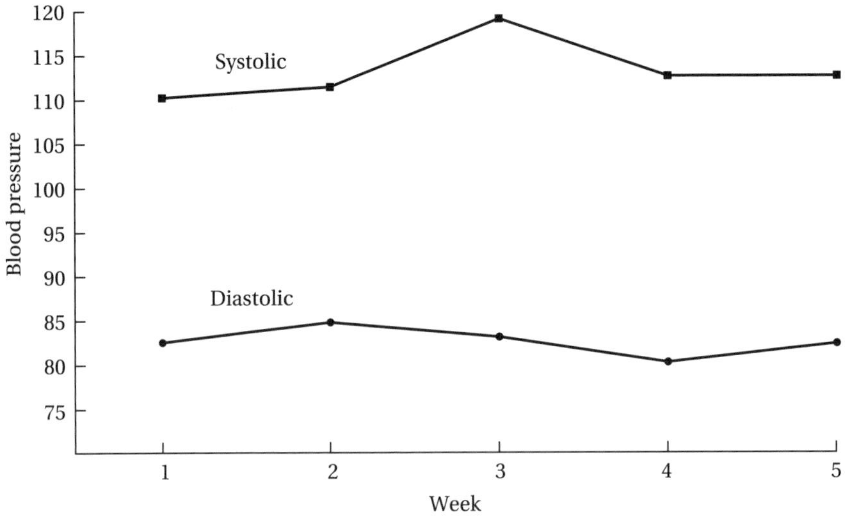

SCATTER DIAGRAM

The scatter diagram helps to visualize the relationship between two variables. With three-dimensional graphics now available, you can track three variables at once. A scatter diagram can be useful for identifying obvious relationships. For the less-obvious ones, you will need to use analysis of variance or correlation formulas, which are available in any good statistics text.

INSTRUCTIONS FOR THE SCATTER DIAGRAM

1. Determine the two variables whose interaction you want to track.
2. Measure one variable on the vertical axis, the other on the horizontal axis.
3. For each interval, measure both variables and plot a point that represents the intersection of the two.
4. If the points cluster around an imaginary line from lower left to upper right, you have a positive correlation. This does not prove that one variable influences the other, but indicates that they vary in the same direction. If the points cluster around an imaginary line from upper left to lower right, then you have a negative correlation. The two variables work in the opposite direction.

The scatter diagram is only one piece of the information puzzle that can help you understand a problem.

APPLICATION OF THE SCATTER DIAGRAM

It is normal for inventory levels to track sales levels. If you sell more, you usually must stock more in order to support the additional sales. In one industrial distributor, it was found that a disaster sequence could be identified, and it could be used to reduce the accumulation of excess inventory. Here's how it worked.

As shown in the diagram, inventory is rising as sales increase. At one point in the cycle (hook), sales decrease, but inventory increases as stock orders continue to arrive. If action is taken immediately to understand the change in sales and to delay or cancel orders for additional inventory, the balance may be restored. By this point, there are two likely alternatives: Either sales increase again, and inventory is restored to support sales; or the product is discontinued, and very little inventory remains to sell off.

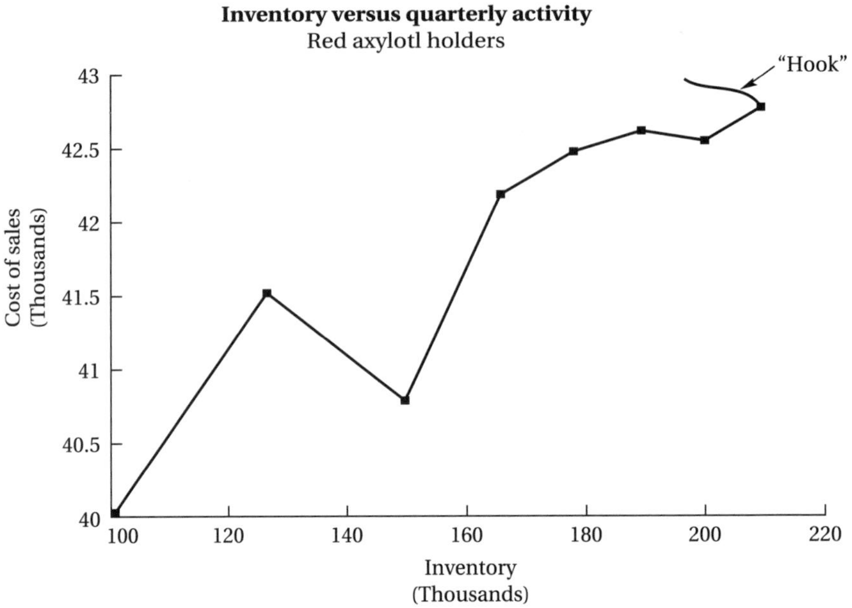
Inventory versus quarterly activity
Red axylotl holders
"Hook"
43
42.5
42
41.5
41
40.5
40
Cost of sales (Thousands)
100
120
140
160
180
200
220
Inventory (Thousands)

STATISTICS

By definition, statistics is simply the science of numerical facts. To that extent, you have probably been using statistics all your life.

But when it comes to the world of quality improvement, quality assurance, or quality control, statistics becomes an area of study. This book does not pretend to include the subject of statistics, but statistical knowledge can be a valuable part of your lifetime learning plan. It is important.

STORYBOARD

The storyboard is a tool that serves two functions: to assist the problem-solving process by providing a place to organize the useful tools, and to communicate the process and results to others.

The storyboard has a long history, beginning with cave drawings. With the advent of movies, and then television, the storyboard was used to plan stories and commercials. Walt Disney popularized its use in his Sunday evening television shows. The storyboard was then borrowed for use in industrial applications, and finally adopted by the quality community for use in continuous improvement projects.

There are many formats for the storyboard. The format is less important than the clarity with which it communicates. The three fundamental forms are notecards, the wall-mounted storyboard, and the storybook.

Card-based storyboard

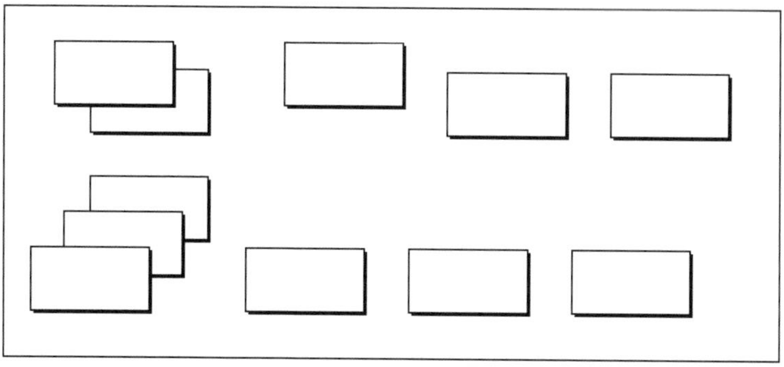

Wall-mounted storyboard

Storybook

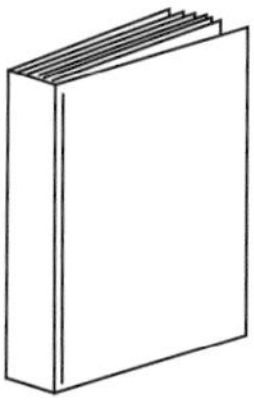

SOLUTION SELECTION MATRIX

The solution selection matrix is used to evaluate the wide variety of possible solutions your team has discovered through the creative process. As with any other matrix, you can add across the columns or multiply; you can weight one variable more than another; and you can rank order variables that aren't directly measurable. (See the matrix and problem selection matrix.)

Among the likely variables you may wish to consider are impact on the problem, ease of implementation, timeliness, and management support of each particular solution. Then, the solution selection matrix communicates your reasoning.

Solution	**Variable 1**	**Variable 2**	**Variable 3**	**Total**

STRUCTURED LIST

The purpose of the structured list is to assist users in clarifying the issues before prioritizing. It helps organize thinking by forcing forward thinking. The logic behind this tool is that the clearer the issues are in the first place, the better the prioritization will be.

The vision of results should be as sensory rich and vivid as possible, in order to facilitate the motivation process. The measurement should be something tangible that is easily quantified. The measurement should be connected to the problem as directly as possible.

Problem or opportunity	**Vision of results**	**Measurement**

SUGGESTION SYSTEM

A suggestion system is frequently one of the first ideas raised when the topic of improvement comes up. Where this falls short is that usually there already is, or has been, a suggestion system in place, and management has already shot its credibility by failure to respond on time; or worse, by failure to respond at all; or worse still, by punitive action against the suggestors.

Experience shows that suggestion systems can work well. In order to turn the situation around, a change in attitude must be seen and acknowledged by the potential system users. This can be accomplished many ways, and will probably be done differently in each organization.

By using teams, individuals have an increased connection between the problem and the solution. That is a strong reason to use teams for improvement activities. In other words, the suggestion does not have to go through multiple approvals, but can be implemented right in the workplace, maybe even immediately. Perhaps that is why there is more information about teams than about suggestion systems.

SURVEY

The survey is a great way to find out what's going on. Surveys frequently include scalable questions, asking the person to rate each question from one to five. A survey should also ask at least one open-ended question, such as "What needs to be improved?" Answers to questions like this can be extremely revealing, because they provide an opportunity to pick up important issues that the survey author did not consider.

The scope of the investigation should be seriously considered before asking anybody any questions. Preliminary work may indicate particular topics to be explored.

The survey may be used anywhere from the selection process at the beginning to the consideration of follow-up at the end. There are many good references on survey writing, and they should be consulted before attempting to design your own. The survey is a powerful tool, but requires study before design and implementation.

SWOT CHART

The SWOT chart is a good way to look at your present situation as it relates to your improvement activity. It simply consists of listing your strengths, weaknesses, opportunities, and threats. The SWOT chart helps generate ideas.

ADDITIONAL IDEAS FOR THE SWOT CHART

Once you have brainstormed to get all the ideas on the table, you may wish to consider each listed item, and check to see if it has an opposite. For instance, for a strength, will it imply a weakness that will operate against it? Will it create a weakness? Is one of the weaknesses that you have already listed working against this strength?

The SWOT chart is a good tool to generate ideas during your creative activities. Then you can apply your critical thinking to the SWOT chart to determine if there are particular areas on which to focus. Those areas could be indicated with a cloud diagram.

Strengths	**Weaknesses**
Opportunities	**Threats**

TREE DIAGRAM

The tree diagram, also known as a stem-and-leaf display, is used to assist in taking an idea into increased levels of detail. For instance, while considering root causes, the tree diagram could be used to record the answers to the question why. As each question may have more than one answer, the tree broadens.

A tree diagram may also be used to develop possible solutions, beginning with root causes. Then, possible solutions could be shown as branches for each root cause.

Sometimes a tree diagram is used to analyze the probability of achieving a certain result. By recording the estimated probability of each branch, it is possible to understand the relationship of one action to another, and better understand the relative value of individual actions.

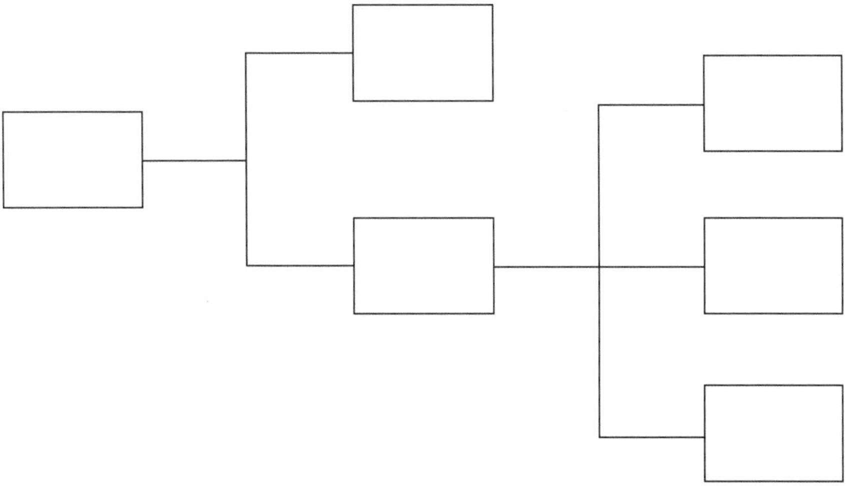

VISUALIZATION

Visualization, enhanced as it is with graphics-oriented spreadsheet programs, multimedia, hypermedia, and virtual reality, is a concept whose time has come. Frequently ignored in educational and organizational establishments, visualization is an important part of people's lives. The ability to imagine something when it is not in front of you forms the basis for goal setting, among other important activities.

One of the key points of this book is that people must support and extend their use of visual images, because they work. They are powerful additions to other problem-solving and communication skills, and they are interesting.

You are encouraged not only to use the examples shown here, but also to expand upon them, use them in combination, and invent new ones. All these activities require visualization.

WISHBONE DIAGRAM

The wishbone diagram visualizes the process of change, for both individuals and groups. Use of this diagram can help you manage the process of change within yourself, in dialog with other individuals, or in groups.

Once the present state has been identified, the work to move through the process can begin. Use the wishbone diagram as you would any other flowchart. If you have difficulties, work your way backward until you find the level where the difficulty lies, then overcome it and move forward.

You wouldn't expect to use the wishbone diagram in a storyboard, although it is possible. Rather use it privately to assist in understanding the situation and its requirements.

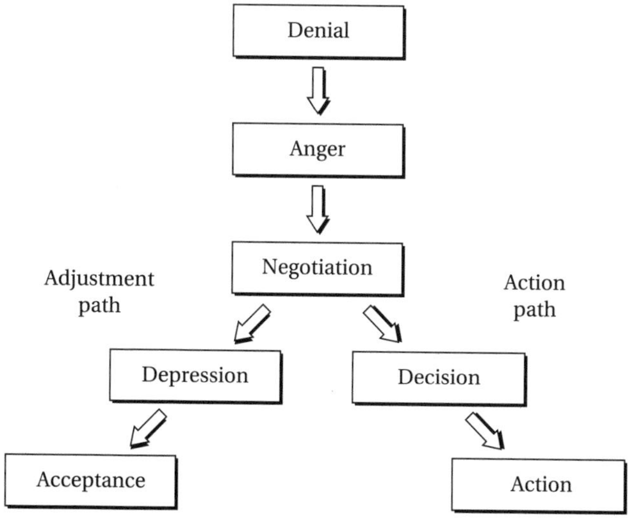

Note: Adapted from Noel M. Tichy and Mary Anne Devanna, *The Transformational Leader* (New York, John Wiley & Sons, 1990), p. 68.

ENDNOTES

CHAPTER 1

1. A variety of dictionaries were researched and used as background for this discussion.

2. Webster's *Third New International Dictionary,* s.v. "story." There are more current definitions, but this is the one that best fits the purposes of this text.

3. Southern Pacific Transportation Company and Qualtec, *Team Leader Course Participation Workbook* (San Francisco: Southern Pacific Transportation Company; Juno Beach, Fla.: Qualtec, 1991).

4. Ronald Schiller, *Distant Secrets* (New York: Birch Land Press, 1989), 208–210.

CHAPTER 2

1. W. Edwards Deming, *Out of the Crisis* (Cambridge, Mass.: MIT Center for Advanced Engineering Study, 1986), 52, 86.

2. Florida Power and Light, *Team Leader Training Course Participant Workbook* (Miami: Florida Power and Light, 1985), 46.

3. Ned Herrmann, *The Creative Brain* (Lake Lure, N.C.: Brain Books, 1990).

4. Peter R. Scholtes, *The Team Handbook* (Madison, Wis.: Joiner Associates, 1988), 6-4–6-8.

5. Thomas J. Werner and Robert F. Lynch, *Continuous Improvement: Teams and Tools* (Atlanta: QualTeam, 1992), 127–132.

6. Harry I. Forsha, *The Pursuit of Quality Through Personal Change* (Milwaukee: ASQC Quality Press, 1992), 132-135.

7. Thanks to Michael Savoie for this quote.

8. Scholtes, *The Team Handbook,* 3-12–3-15.

CHAPTER 3

1. Florida Power and Light.

2. Southern Pacific Transportation Company and Qualtec, *Team Leader Course Participation Workbook* (San Francisco: Southern Pacific Transportation Company; Juno Beach, Fla.: Qualtec, 1991).

3. Technicomp, *Problem Solving,* Technicomp, 1987, videocassette.

4. Marilyn R. Zuckerman and Lewis J. Hatala, *Incredibly American: Releasing the Heart of Quality* (Milwaukee: ASQC Quality Press, 1992).

5. Arthur B. Vangundy, *Creative Problem Solving* (New York: Quorum Books, 1987).

6. Harry I. Forsha, T*he Pursuit of Quality Through Personal Change* (Milwaukee: ASQC Quality Press, 1992).

7. Charles H. Kepner and Benjamin B. Tregoe, *The New Rational Manager* (Princeton, N.J.: Princeton Research Press, 1981), 32–56.

8. Julius E. Eitington, *The Winning Trainer,* 2d ed. (Houston: Gulf Publishing, 1989).

9. Kepner and Tregoe, *The New Rational Manager* (Princeton, N.J.: Princeton Research Press, 1981), 1–220.

CHAPTER 4

1. Stephen R. Covey, *The Seven Habits of Highly Effective People* (New York: Simon & Schuster, 1989).

2. Peter M. Senge, *The Fifth Discipline* (New York: Doubleday, 1990), 93–135.

CHAPTER 6

1. Peter M. Senge, *The Fifth Discipline* (New York: Doubleday, 1990).

CHAPTER 7

1. Masaaki Imai, *Basic and Advanced Kaizen Training Course Materials* (Austin, Tex.: Kaizen Institute of America, 1990).

SUGGESTED READINGS

ALCOA. *The Alcoa Eight-Step Quality Improvement Process.* Pittsburgh, Pa.: 1989.

Brassard, Michael., ed. *The Memory Jogger.* Methuen, Mass.: GOAL/QPC, 1988.

Brock, William E. *An American Imperative—Higher Expectations for Higher Education.* Racine, Wis.: The Johnson Foundation, 1993.

Burr, John T. "The Tools of Quality," Part I through VII. *Qualityy Progress* 23, nos. 6-12.

Cleary, Barbara A. "Company Cares About Customers' Calls." *Quality Progress* 26, no. 11 (November 1993): 69-73.

Eitington, Julius E. *The Winning Trainer.* 2d ed. Houston: Gulf Publishing, 1989.

Ingle, Sud. *In Search of Perfection.* Englewood Cliffs, N.J.: Prentice Hall, 1985.

Jones, Louis, and Ronald McBride. *An Introduction to Team-Approach Problem Solving.* Milwaukee: ASQC Quality Press, 1990.

Juran, J. M., and Frank M. Gryna. *Quality Planning and Analysis.* New York: McGraw-Hill, 1980.

Kelly, Michael, R. *Everyone's Problem-Solving Handbook.* White Plains, N.Y.: Quality Resources, 1992.

Kepner, Charles H., and Benjamin B. Tregoe. *The New Rational Manager.* Princeton, N.J.: Princeton Research Press, 1981.

Michalko, Michael. *Thinkertoys.* Berkeley, Calif.: Ten Speed Press, 1991.

Miller, Lawrence M., and Jennifer Howard. *Managing Quality Through Teams.* Atlanta: The Miller Consulting Group, 1992.

Nadler, Gerald, and Shozo Hibino. *Breakthrough Thinking.* Rocklin, Calif.: Prima Publishing and Communications.

PQ Systems. *Total Quality Transformation: Improvement Guide.* Cincinnati: PQ Systems, 1992.

Rosander, A. C. *The Quest for Quality in Services.* Milwaukee: ASQC Quality Press, 1989.

Scholtes, Peter R. *The Team Handbook.* Madison, Wisc.: Joiner Associates, 1988.

Snee, Ronald D. "Creating Robust Work Processes." *Quality Progress* 26, no. 2 (February 1993): 37-41.

Southern Pacific Transportation Company and Qualtec. *Team Leader Course Participation Workbook.* San Francisco: Southern Pacific Transportation Company; Juno Beach, Fla.: Qualtec, 1991.

The Staff of Goodmeasure, Inc. *Solving Quality and Productivity Problems: Goodmeasure's Guide to Corrective Action.* Milwaukee: ASQC Quality Press, 1988.

Technicomp. *Problem-Solving Series.* Cleveland: Technicomp, 1987. Videotape.

Vangundy, Arthur B. *Creative Problem Solving.* New York: Quorum Books.

von Oech, Roger. *Creative Whack Pack.* Stamford, Conn.: U.S. Games, 1990.

Werner, Thomas J., and Robert F. Lynch. *Continuous Improvement: Teams and Tools.* Atlanta: QualTeam, 1992.

INDEX